Cybersecurity Readiness

Sara Miller McCune founded SAGE Publishing in 1965 to support the dissemination of usable knowledge and educate a global community. SAGE publishes more than 1000 journals and over 600 new books each year, spanning a wide range of subject areas. Our growing selection of library products includes archives, data, case studies and video. SAGE remains majority owned by our founder and after her lifetime will become owned by a charitable trust that secures the company's continued independence.

Los Angeles | London | New Delhi | Singapore | Washington DC | Melbourne

Cybersecurity Readiness

A Holistic and
High-Performance Approach

Dave Chatterjee, Ph.D.

Associate Professor, MIS Department,
Terry College of Business, The University of Georgia

Visiting Professor, Pratt School of Engineering, Duke University

Los Angeles | London | New Delhi
Singapore | Washington DC | Melbourne

FOR INFORMATION:

SAGE Publications, Inc.
2455 Teller Road
Thousand Oaks, California 91320
Email: order@sagepub.com

SAGE Publications Ltd.
1 Oliver's Yard
55 City Road
London EC1Y 1SP
United Kingdom

SAGE Publications India Pvt. Ltd.
B 1/I 1 Mohan Cooperative Industrial Area
Mathura Road, New Delhi 110 044
India

SAGE Publications Asia-Pacific Pte. Ltd.
18 Cross Street #10-10/11/12
China Square Central
Singapore 048423

Library of Congress Cataloging-in-Publication Data

Names: Chatterjee, Dave, author.

Title: Cybersecurity readiness : a holistic and high-performance approach / Dave Chatterjee, Terry College of Business, The University of Georgia.

Description: Los Angeles : SAGE, [2021] | Includes bibliographical references and index.

Identifiers: LCCN 2021001020 | ISBN 9781071837337 (hardcover) | ISBN 9781071837344 (epub) | ISBN 9781071837351 (epub) | ISBN 9781071837368 (pdf)

Subjects: LCSH: Computer security. | Business enterprises—Security measures. | Electronic information resources—Access control. | Risk management. | Computer crimes—Prevention. | Readiness.

Classification: LCC QA76.9.A25 C4349 2021 | DDC 005.8—dc23
LC record available at https://lccn.loc.gov/2021001020

Acquisitions Editor: Andrew Boney
Editorial Assistant: Tamara Tanso
Development Editor: Sanford Robinson
Production Editor: Astha Jaiswal
Copy Editor: Integra
Typesetter: C&M Digitals (P) Ltd.
Proofreader: Larry Baker
Indexer: Integra
Cover Designer: Candice Harman
Marketing Manager: Brianna Griffith

21 22 23 24 25 10 9 8 7 6 5 4 3 2 1

To my father, Subroto Chatterjee

In my eyes, you are the practitioner's practitioner. You were the most charismatic, dynamic, and caring leader, loved and respected by your colleagues and subordinates. You supported me in every possible way, in all aspects of life, and encouraged me to be the very best I could be. Your selfless, honest, straightforward, bold, and courageous ways are and will always be a source of profound inspiration. I would like to honor you and your life with this book and hope today's and tomorrow's practitioners find value in the insights and recommendations.

To my mother, Kuljit Chatterjee

Your kind and noble ways never cease to amaze me.

To my grandparents, late Prof. Sushil Kumar and Smrity Chatterjee

Truly blessed to have experienced your love and nurturing during the formative years.

To my wife Bineeta, daughter Rhea, and son Victor

You are a source of great pride, joy, and inspiration.

Contents

Preface

I t often takes a major calamity such as the coronavirus pandemic to remind us of how vulnerable we are and the consequences of being underprepared. Seemingly secure and robust economies and companies have been brought to their knees by an invisible and unexpected enemy. Can we afford to be so reactive? Do we need major catastrophes to serve as wake-up calls on being proactive and thorough in our approach to preparedness? The consequences of cyberattacks can be equally devastating, especially if nuclear sites, power grids, water filtration plants, and other critical infrastructure resources are compromised.

This book is motivated by the need to encourage and aid organizations to take a proactive, deliberate, and conscientious stand on cybersecurity. While most organizations are not in the business of securing data and digital assets, protecting such assets is critical to survival and success in today's highly digitized and connected environment. With rapidly expanding attack surfaces and evolving attack vectors, organizations are in a perpetual state of breach and have to deal with this existential threat. Cybersecurity readiness is a critical and distinctive competency, and this book is intended to help organizations develop and enhance this capability. It is written with current and future practitioners in mind as individuals continue to be the strongest and weakest link of a cyber defense system. The overall goal of the book is to enhance cybersecurity awareness and preparedness among individuals and organizations.

To effectively prepare and respond to the ever-increasing and evolving cyberattacks, organizations must not only have a comprehensive plan but also execute that plan with great precision and consistency. This book draws upon high-reliability organization principles to identify characteristics and traits associated with a high-performance information security culture. It presents a set of seventeen cybersecurity readiness success factors uncovered from analyzing primary and secondary data gathered over several years.

I sincerely hope you will find the book useful. It is the latest outcome of a cybersecurity journey that has been quite enlightening. I have been studying this phenomenon for nearly a decade; I have authored and edited scholarly papers, consulted with companies, served on a cybersecurity SWAT team with chief information security officers (CISOs), conducted workshops and webinars, given expert radio and television interviews, and delivered numerous talks at academic and practitioner forums around the world. Information Security and Risk Management has been a core learning module in my graduate and undergraduate classes for several years.

Among the distinctive strengths of the book are its comprehensive scope and an easy-to-understand framework to help readers get their arms around cybersecurity readiness. It recognizes that the battle or war against current and future cyber threats must be fought holistically and comprehensively by adopting people-, process-, and technology-driven measures. The book presents a set of seventeen success factors associated with three high-performance information security culture traits—commitment, preparedness, and discipline. Further, numerous breach incidents, presented in the form of vignettes and cases, are used to highlight key challenges and issues and reinforce the recommendations. Included in the appendix section are cybersecurity readiness scorecard elements; list of physical, technical and administrative controls; information security monitoring control guide; an overview of cybersecurity and privacy laws and regulations; cybersecurity performance measures; and case studies.

Dave Chatterjee

Foreword

The evolution from the early days of information security to today's cybersecurity teams provides a varied and rich history of challenges, successes, and failures. As the systems used by society, businesses, and governments increase reliance on technology, we also see the opportunities for threat actors to take advantage of weaknesses in these systems or the people who regularly use or maintain these systems.

In the 1980s we got our first taste of cybersecurity challenges when the so-called Morris Worm was released by a student at MIT targeting vulnerabilities in Unix systems, and resulting in several days of disruption on the nascent Internet.

Further historical events led to more lessons. Active virus and malware (e.g. rootkits) development competed with antivirus makers and showed the limitations and challenges with signature-based detections. The Code Red (2001) and SQL Slammer (2003) worms reinforced the need for active patch management programs to apply system updates, as well as demonstrating the need for network defenses such as firewalls and intrusion prevention systems. 2015 saw the compromise of the Ukrainian power grid, later attributed to Russian actors, demonstrating both the weaknesses in SCADA and critical infrastructure systems, as well as providing a look into the future of cyberwarfare.

As the attacks and technologies have changed, so have the approaches. Cybersecurity practices have evolved from a set of philosophies to more active and proactive approaches. Concepts such as defense-in-depth, principle of least privilege, change management, and access control are necessary and required building blocks for good cybersecurity programs. The NIST Cybersecurity Framework and Center for Information Security provide roadmaps and approaches to help organizations prioritize and build strong cybersecurity programs. However, what is missing is an approach to building a cybersecurity culture within an organization, permeating all aspects of that organization. Dr. Chatterjee's book provides actionable recommendations to create and sustain a high-performance information security culture.

A key area of concern for organizations is the human element. Social engineering attacks, including phishing, have taught us that attackers can and will bypass the best defenses easily when targeting a human. Technology and tools alone cannot secure an organization; rather, security must be seen as a shared value and culture, and all members of the organization are accountable and have a role to play.

The human element is one of the reasons that advancements in technology and approaches to protect key assets and detect attacks continue to fall prey to debilitating attacks, loss of data, and in some cases, financial repercussions (fines or ransoms). Successful organizations have recognized what Dave Chatterjee will discuss in this book. A high performing cybersecurity culture requires commitment from leadership for a strategic and sustainable program; a prepared team with the right framework, processes, and tools in place; and the discipline to assess and adapt the program to meet the changing and evolving threat landscape.

Drawing from consulting experience, prior research, and expert interviews, Dave explores several key case studies on incidents and lessons learned, ultimately setting forth an easy-to-use framework that organizations can use to model a strong cybersecurity culture in their organization. As with other frameworks, it can and should be adapted to match an organization's objectives, but the core principles of commitment, preparedness, and discipline must permeate all aspects of the organization, not just the team directly responsible for cybersecurity defenses and response.

Each core principle leads to actionable strategies that can and should be implemented within an organization. Commitment requires active leadership involvement and support; preparedness requires assessing and implementing security protections across the organization, while improving the ability to detect attacks and issues as quickly as possible; and discipline requires active governance to ensure that cybersecurity efforts align with organizational goals, and the security operations are assessed for continuous improvement.

To get started, you will find useful resources that map common technical controls and approaches to the three core principles, scorecards to assess the maturity of your organization, and current security and privacy regulations that organizations should factor into the cybersecurity programs.

This book provides a much-needed organizational blueprint for organizations to build and mature not just a cybersecurity program but rather a cybersecurity culture that can adapt and change as risks and threat actors change and adapt.

Richard Biever
Chief Information Security Officer
Duke University
Durham, North Carolina, USA

Endorsements

Mauricio Angee, Chief Information Security Officer, GenesisCare USA, Fort Myers, Florida, USA

Information security has become an important and critical component of every organization. In his book, Professor Chatterjee explains the challenges that organizations experience to protect information assets. The book sheds light on different aspects of cybersecurity including a history and impact of the most recent security breaches, as well as the strategic and leadership components that help build strong cybersecurity programs. This book helps bridge the gap between academia and practice and provides important insights that may help professionals in every industry.

Vidhya Belapure, Chief Information Officer, Huber Engineered Materials & CP Kelco, Marietta, Georgia, USA

This book by Dave Chatterjee is by far the most comprehensive book on cybersecurity management. Cybersecurity is on top of the minds of board members, CEOs, and CIOs as they strive to protect their employees and intellectual property. This book is a must-read for CIOs and CISOs to build a robust cybersecurity program for their organizations.

Mike Benz, Partner and Fractional CIO, Fortium Partners, Minneapolis, Minnesota, USA

Professor Chatterjee's *Cybersecurity Readiness: A Holistic and High-Performance Approach* fills a critical unmet need for concise, timely, and actionable information for information technology and business leaders. So much of the literature available today is either too high level or too detailed to be usable by most practitioners. The book's novel Cybersecurity Readiness Scorecard is a tool that any business should be able to use to better manage their risk.

Shoukat Ali Bhamani, Chief Information and Digital Officer, Schaeffler, Fort Mill, South Carolina, USA

Business executives in today's world are aware of cybersecurity threats, but many of them are not comfortable with technical discussions. Dr. Chatterjee has made an excellent effort to help business executives understand cybersecurity risks and learn how to mitigate them at the management level. A systematic approach described in this book will help executives launch an effective cybersecurity strategy. I would highly recommend this book for all business and IT executives.

Professor Som Bhattacharya, Dean, College of Business and Management, University of Illinois at Springfield, Illinois, USA

It is time for a holistic (and high-performance) approach to cybersecurity. While cybersecurity remains, nay grows, a pandemic in its own right, it is increasingly more than simply an engineering problem, a network problem, an access problem, or a denial of service problem, awaiting technical solutions. It is all of the above and then some. It is an overarching and alarming business problem. From an accounting/auditing perspective, it represents a going concern issue; from a managerial standpoint, it may lead to reputation loss, capital market misgivings, internal audit harangues, external audit jitters, legal woes, privacy implications, customer flight, and penalties, and it questions the very survival of corporate and non-corporate entities. This book, in response, spans a wide range of issues such as privacy, national and transnational guidelines, opt-in vs. opt-out, ransomware, the use of crypto-currencies, the dark web, occasional sovereign nation sponsorships of miscreants and malware, and it presents a solution scorecard and other approaches that appeal to more than the technical or IT wings of an enterprise. These issues are more likely to be understood and acted upon by enterprise and enterprising managers. It is this holistic perspective, then, of a growing cyber pandemic, that sets this book apart and makes for its likely adoption by the government, the corporate sector and academia alike. Cybersecurity issues need to be addressed and managed holistically and this book tells us how.

Professor Indranil Bose, Indian Institute of Management Calcutta, Kolkata, India

In the age of pandemic, the importance of cybersecurity readiness cannot be overemphasized. While a number of authors have focused on the technical aspects of cybersecurity, this book uniquely blends technology with management of cybersecurity and does it in a lucid and comprehensive manner. The author's vast experience and regular interactions with people in the field is showcased in the engaging writing style involving practical examples and case studies. The book fulfills a gap that exists in the area and makes a timely and worthwhile contribution. The coverage of topics is extensive and depth of topics will fascinate even the specialized cybersecurity expert. This book is a must-have for academics and practitioners who want to learn about and manage the efforts toward creating cybersecurity awareness and preparedness in organizations.

Dr. Anne DeBeer, Former Senior Vice President & Chief Information Officer/Chief Financial Officer, Federal Reserve Bank of Atlanta, Georgia, USA

Dr. Dave Chatterjee is a renowned scholar and technology thought leader. His vast knowledge and insight into the world of cybersecurity is well known and widely sought after by industry, academic, and government leaders around the globe. Now he delivers a book that gives leaders a real-world, coherent understanding of what they face and the multiple dimensions necessary to prepare and respond. I highly recommend reading Dr. Chatterjee's book to learn and benefit from his years of experience and perceptions into this important subject.

Gretchen Hiley, Chief Information Security Officer, Senior Vice President, Global Information Security, Crawford & Company, Peachtree Corners, Georgia, USA

While there are many publications focused on the technical aspects of cybersecurity, very few provide such a well-formulated crosswalk between the technical and business sides of cyber risk. *Cybersecurity Readiness: A Holistic and High-Performance Approach* provides a clear roadmap for security practitioners to utilize as they build comprehensive information security programs, and it also guides business leaders and board members as they navigate through the journey of understanding and managing cyber risk as an enterprise risk.

Professor Ashish Kumar Jha, Trinity College Dublin, Ireland

With increasing importance of data as a source of competitive advantage, cybersecurity has moved beyond the confines of IT departments to an enterprise-wide endeavor. Professor Chatterjee takes a company culture–level perspective in his new book wherein he has dived deep into his years of experience as a cybersecurity expert and his role in advising firms and CIOs on this issue. This is an extremely relevant and timely piece of work that would advise many firms on the best organizational practices required to safeguard their data from cyberthreats. Professor Chatterjee leads his readers into the domain organizational aspects of cybersecurity and provides mechanisms to assess and plan a company's readiness for future vulnerabilities and not just respond to the threats from a technical viewpoint. The book would find favor with an entire generation of business leaders interested in creating a secure organization.

Professor Jimmie Lenz, Director, Master of Engineering in FinTech and Master of Engineering in Cybersecurity, Pratt School of Engineering, Duke University, Durham, North Carolina, USA

Very few issues in the modern world are as pervasive to individuals, corporations, and governments as that of cybersecurity. Dave brings to light aspects that have received too little attention, that is, the human factor, which provides a context that is central to this issue. The "success factors" he puts forward in the book provide any organization with the means to benchmark and monitor changes in programs of all sizes.

Mary Levins, President, Sierra Creek Consulting LLC, Dacula, Georgia, USA

This book is a valuable resource for cybersecurity readiness today. Many breaches in the past could have been prevented. This book reviews past leadership decisions and breach examples to provide an effective approach using lessons learned and best practices.

Professor Daniel O'Leary, Marshall School of Business, University of Southern California, Los Angeles, California, USA

Prof. Chatterjee's book is a very pragmatic and comprehensive guide to cybersecurity readiness. The governance framework is both powerful and easy to comprehend. Anchored on three high-performance security culture dimensions of commitment, preparedness, and discipline, the framework presents a set of seventeen cybersecurity success factors. Uncovered from analyzing primary and secondary data gathered over several years, these success factors encompass people-, process-, and technology-driven measures. Numerous breach incidents, presented in the form of vignettes and cases, are used to highlight vulnerabilities and lessons learned. The book also provides useful resources such as cybersecurity readiness scorecard elements; a list of physical, technical, and administrative controls; an information security monitoring control guide; an overview of cybersecurity and privacy laws and regulations; cybersecurity performance measures; and case studies.

Stoddard Mannikin, Chief Information Security Officer, Prominent U.S. Pediatric Healthcare Organization

Dr. Chatterjee's book fortifies the most essential truth when it comes to effective cybersecurity programs: "technology alone will not mitigate cybersecurity risks." He identifies key traits that need to be engrained in organizational culture to support the cybersecurity mission as well as seventeen success factors within that cultural framework that any student or practitioner should consider when evaluating their security posture.

Arun Kumar Narayan, Director, Audit & Asset Protection, Alshaya Group, Kuwait

Dr. Dave's book on cybersecurity management is an eye opener for all organizations in today's world. He has made tremendous efforts in presenting how to identify, defend, respond, and build resilience in case of cyber-attacks in a very simple way. This book is very easy to understand and very important for the senior leadership team of an organization to gain thorough knowledge on the subject of cybersecurity.

Joseph Pekala, President, ESP Holdings LLC, Richmond, Virginia, USA

Cyber threats, in their many and continuously evolving ways, remain more than ever an existential threat to virtually all companies, both large and small. In his new book *Cybersecurity Readiness: A Holistic and High-Performance Approach*, Dr. Chatterjee does an excellent job of breaking down these threats and providing a framework for creating a culture of engagement at all levels in an organization to effectively and proactively manage these threats. In my years leading enterprise IT organizations, I can personally attest to the effectiveness of the concepts outlined here and I wholeheartedly recommend this book. In fact, I believe that this should be required reading for anyone entering today's workforce, regardless of their role. Cybersecurity is not an IT issue, which Dr. Chatterjee makes clear, but rather something that requires everyone's knowledge and involvement. A must read!

Rob Purks, Senior Executive, Telecommunications Industry

Public and hybrid cloud adoption have made the boundaries of corporate IT infrastructure more nebulous, and the need for a well-defined and executed security strategy has never been greater. As companies increasingly pursue the financial benefits of cloudification by virtualizing and containerizing their application architectures, the architectural complexity and the number of potential vulnerabilities significantly increase. Dr. Chatterjee does a superb job of portraying both the business need and the technology approach to define a successful security strategy.

Azi Quinn, Agile Transformation Leader, Financial Services Industry

Our financial lives, our business lives, and even our personal lives are all online. Cybersecurity is a non-negotiable investment for almost every company in our global community. Just as we have to make sure people walking into a store are physically safe during their experience, we have to ensure their information is safe when they "walk into" the cyber version. Professor Chatterjee's book highlights the traits of a high-performing information security culture: commitment, preparedness, and discipline. His insight and accessible tactics make this book mandatory for any institution looking to mitigate financial and reputational risk.

Tushar Sachdev, Chief Technology Officer, KORE Wireless, Alpharetta, Georgia, USA

Commitment, preparedness, and discipline in cybersecurity are things Professor Chatterjee has been advocating for many years. The book is a comprehensive summary for executives who wish to understand how cybersecurity has moved from a "techie" topic to a serious boardroom agenda and is what organizations should be doing to not only defend but also respond and build resilience in case of a cyberattack. Professor Chatterjee's writing style is simple and offers an engaging, informative, and, most importantly, actionable read and is highly recommended as an executive leadership must-read and must-discuss book.

Zareer Siganporia, Chief Executive Officer, Trusted Tech Partners, Alpharetta, Georgia, USA

Information security is a part of everyone's responsibility; yet, too many people and organizations still do not completely understand and embrace this. People (and organization culture) continue to be the weakest link in most organization's security postures. Too often, information security teams focus on technical solutions and audit-driven processes, while not being able to drive the organization-wide awareness, buy-in, and culture change that is needed to holistically secure the enterprise.

Dr. Chatterjee's *Cybersecurity Readiness: A Holistic and High-Performance Approach* tackles this weakest link, the hardest part of information security. He uses high-performance culture traits, supporting success factors, and actionable guiding questions to integrate top-down and bottom-up human-centric approaches, to permeate information security awareness and ownership across the organization. His Cybersecurity Readiness Scorecard, built from these guiding questions, is an effective way to periodically assess and quantify an organization's cultural cybersecurity maturity.

This book is definitely a must-read for everyone in the knowledge economy. If your organization uses this approach to fortify its cybersecurity culture, it will ultimately save your jobs and your reputation, enhance your competitiveness, and avoid millions to billions of dollars in costs down the line! Cancel the rest of your meetings today and start reading!

Rohit Verma, Chief Executive Officer, Crawford & Company, Peachtree Corners, Georgia, USA

Professor Chatterjee's book is a must-read for any executive who views their organization's data as a strategic asset. It is one of the finest works I have read on giving a broad understanding of the dangerous cyber world we live in and why it is here to stay with us. His work provides an excellent framework for building and sustaining a high-performance security culture, with appropriate systems and processes, to achieve cyber risk resilience and operate business with confidence rather than fear.

Professor Hugh J. Watson, Management Information Systems Department, Terry College of Business, The University of Georgia, Athens, Georgia, USA

Organizations need to protect against cybersecurity attacks, not just respond to them, for it is too late then as most of the damage has already been done. Professor Chatterjee's book does an outstanding job of identifying the different kinds of cybersecurity attacks and describing the various managerial, organizational, and technological preventive measures. Dave's book is highly readable and actionable, with numerous examples drawn from recent accounts of cybersecurity attacks and data breaches.

Dr Edgar A. Whitley, London School of Economics and Political Science, United Kingdom

Data is an increasingly valuable resource for organisations. If it is not managed securely it runs the risk of becoming a toxic asset, yet how best to manage data securely is not always obvious. This invaluable book "Cybersecurity Readiness: A Holistic and High-Performance Approach" combines academic rigour with practitioner driven insights to provide clear guidance for organisations to enhance their cybersecurity readiness.

Acknowledgments

I am grateful to many who have directly and indirectly contributed towards the development of the book. It has been quite the journey—intellectually stimulating, emotionally demanding, physically challenging, and spiritually uplifting. While the first version of the book was crafted in the summer of 2019, cybersecurity research and teaching have been an ongoing endeavor for almost a decade. Over the years, I have presented the research findings at numerous practitioner and academic forums around the world and benefitted from valuable and thought-provoking feedback. I also had the opportunity to share my insights with the general public by conducting expert interviews in print media and on radio and TV.

Inspiration and motivation often come from the most unexpected quarters. On November 9, 2017, during a live interview session, Rich Casanova, the host of Pro Business Channel, very generously recognized my expertise and efforts to enhance cybersecurity awareness and education. I came away from that interview inspired and motivated to live up to Rich's kind words of praise. There is power in words and his surely did energize my cybersecurity journey.

It was truly an honor to be interviewed by hosts and media personalities such as Audrey Galex of AIB Network, Condace Pressley of 95.5 FM NewsTalk/WSB, and Rose Scott of WABE 90.1 FM (a National Public Radio affiliate). The reflective interactions shaped the evolution of ideas for the book.

I am grateful to Shandra Hill Smith, public relations professional and freelance writer, for creating opportunities to share my cybersecurity insights with the general public. In her quiet and professional way, Shandra was always looking for opportunities to get me in front of different audiences.

The following are representative of the invitations to present my work at numerous practitioner and academic forums around the world.

- London School of Economics and Political Sciences, London, United Kingdom (2020)

- The European Information Security Summit, London, United Kingdom (2020)

- Initiative for the Digital Economy at Exeter (INDEX), University of Exeter, London, United Kingdom (2020)

- Huber Engineered Materials (HEM) Executive Education Workshop, Terry College of Business, University of Georgia, Atlanta, Georgia, USA (2020)

- Mercer University, Macon, Georgia, USA (2020)

- Gowling, WLG, London, United Kingdom (2019)

- European Conference on Cyber Warfare and Security, Coimbra, Portugal (2019)

- Georgia GMIS Conference, Athens, Georgia, USA (2019 and 2017)

- Digital Business Transformation Summit, New York City, New York, USA (2019 and 2018)

- South Florida Chief Information Officer (CIO) Forum, Fort Lauderdale, Florida, USA (2018)

- Decision Sciences Institute Conference, Chicago, Illinois, USA (2018)

- Salesforce Tech Talk Forum, San Francisco, California, USA (2017)

- John Cabot University, Rome, Italy (2017)

- CDC University Business and Technology Forum, Atlanta, Georgia, USA (2017)

- European Conference on Cyber Warfare and Security, Dublin, Ireland (2017)

- European Conference on Information Systems, Genoa, Italy (2017)

- Indian Institute of Management, Kolkata, India (2017)

- Department of Computer Science, St. Xavier's College, Kolkata, India (2017)

- Society for Information Management (SIM) Atlanta Chapter Meeting, Atlanta, Georgia, USA (November 2017)

- Georgia-GMIS Conference, Savannah, Georgia, USA (October 9, 2017)

- Chief Information Officer (CIO) Forum and Executive IT Summit, Atlanta, Georgia (2014)

I am indebted to many for the talk invitations and warm hospitality. They include: Edgar Whitley, London School of Economics and Political Sciences; Rocio de la Cruz, Gowling WLG; Russell Lawson, European Information Security Summit; Wendy Gunther, Vrije Universiteit, Amsterdam; Lisa Newman, Mercer University; Indranil Bose, Indian Institute of Management; Ian Chakeres, Google; Cal Braunstein and Adam Braunstein, Robert Frances Group; Ian Roberts, Stefano Arnone, Silvia Pulino, and Joanne Bergamin, John Cabot University; and Rev. Dominic Savio and Shalabh Agarwal, St. Xavier's College.

One of the highlights of the speaking tour was an article penned by Mariia Bondar, then an undergraduate student at John Cabot University. Her succinct review of my talk (at that institution in 2017) made me realize that the cybersecurity recommendations were also resonating with the young minds.

This manuscript has greatly benefited from the content review and feedback offered by Richard Biever, Chief Information Security Officer, Duke University; Malcolm Harkins, Chief Security and Trust Officer, Cymatic; and Hugh Watson, Professor at The University of Georgia. The SAGE Publishing editorial team of Andrew Boney and Sanford Robinson have worked tirelessly to enhance the quality of this manuscript. I also wish to thank the production team led by Astha Jaiswal for their efforts. I am also immensely grateful to Larry Baker of SAGE Publishing and Katie Kish, Professional Development Program Associate, Unum Group, for proofreading the document.

I greatly appreciate the support of Connor Schlegel, Oracle; Amit Yoran, Tenable; John Ballard and Laurie Webb-Des Jardins, Circadence; and Amrita Mitra, Asigosec Technologies in obtaining permission to reproduce some of the figures in this book. My daughter Rhea was very kind to take time out of her busy schedule and help me with some of the graphics.

It is truly an honor to receive endorsements from accomplished practitioners and academics: Mauricio Angee, CISO, GenesisCare USA, Fort Myers, Florida; Vidhya Belapure, CIO, Huber Engineered Materials & CP Kelco, Marietta, Georgia; Mike Benz, Partner and Fractional CIO, Fortium Partners, Minneapolis, Minnesota; Prof. Somnath Bhattacharya, Dean & Professor of Accountancy, College of Business and Management, University of Illinois Springfield; Shoukat Ali Bhimani, Chief Information and Digital Officer, Schaeffler, Fort Mill, South Carolina; Prof. Indranil Bose, Indian Institute of Management Calcutta, Kolkata, India; Dr. Anne DeBeer, Former Senior Vice President & Chief Information Officer/Chief Financial Officer, Federal Reserve Bank of Atlanta, Georgia; Gretchen Hiley, Chief Information

Security Officer, Senior Vice President Global Information Security, Crawford & Company, Peachtree Corners, Georgia; Prof. Ashish Kumar Jha, Trinity College Dublin, Ireland; Dr. Jimmie Lenz, Director, Master of Engineering in FinTech and Master of Engineering in Cybersecurity, Pratt School of Engineering, Duke University, Durham, North Carolina; Mary Levins, President, Sierra Creek Consulting LLC, Dacula, Georgia; Stoddard Mannikin, Chief Information Security Officer, prominent U.S. pediatric healthcare organization; Arun Kumar Narayan, Director, Audit & Asset Protection, Alshaya Group, Kuwait; Joseph Pekala, President, ESP Holdings LLC, Richmond, Virginia; Rob Purks, Senior Executive, telecommunications industry; Azi Quinn, Agile Transformation Leader, financial services industry; Tushar Sachdev, Chief Technology Officer, KORE Wireless, Alpharetta, Georgia; Zareer Siganporia, Chief Executive Officer, Trusted Tech Partners, Alpharetta, Georgia; Rohit Verma, Chief Executive Officer, Crawford & Company, Peachtree Corners, Georgia; and Prof. Hugh J. Watson, Terry College of Business, University of Georgia, Athens, Georgia.

Finally, I would like to recognize my physio team—Kathy Lee Handley and Brooke Padilla—for their efforts to keep me mobile and pain-free. Challenging myself to achieve higher levels of fitness, successfully completing two half-marathons, and returning to competitive tennis, were essential diversions during the intense book authoring, editing, and publishing period.

About the Author

Dave Chatterjee, Ph.D., is Associate Professor in the Department of Management Information Systems at the University of Georgia's Terry College of Business and Visiting Professor at Duke University's Pratt School of Engineering. Dr. Chatterjee's interest and expertise lie in the various facets of information technology management, with current focus on cybersecurity and enterprise digitization. His work has been accepted and published in prestigious outlets such as the *Wall Street Journal*, *MIT Sloan Management Review*, *California Management Review*, *Business Horizons*, *MIS Quarterly*, and *Journal of Management Information Systems*. Dr. Chatterjee has significant experience teaching undergraduate, graduate, and executive education classes. He also serves as Senior Editor of the *Journal for Organizational Computing and Electronic Commerce*, a Taylor & Francis research journal, with full oversight over cybersecurity research. Dr. Chatterjee delivers talks around the world, moderates CXO panel discussions, conducts corporate training and workshops as well as webinars, and provides consulting and advisory services. He has appeared on radio and TV interviews and is often quoted by news media on major technology-related developments. He has served on the corporate and community leadership board of a prestigious cybersecurity network of CISOs and on a CISO SWAT team. For more details please visit https://dchatte.com.

Introduction
The Challenge of Cybersecurity

P rotecting organizational assets from cybersecurity attacks is a cost of doing business today. Such assets include customer and product information, business processes, company websites, social media accounts and content, business plans, trademarks, patents, proprietary hardware, and software.[1] In addition to profiteering and gaining competitive advantage, cyberattacks are also motivated by national, social, political, and ideological agendas.[2] As attacks continue to become more sophisticated and innovative, firms are being compelled to pay attention and to formulate and implement appropriate information security strategies. Although some organizations are thorough and deliberate in their approach, others seem willing to take chances and stumble and fumble in their actions and reactions to cyberattacks.[3]

Because there is no guaranteed immunity from such threats and attacks, senior leadership is often at crossroads when it comes to making cyber investments. During a top management meeting at a major healthcare organization, the chief executive officer (CEO) encouraged the leadership team to focus on the mission of providing quality care and not waste time, money, and effort to try and bulletproof the organization from potential attacks. Another senior leader argued that it was beneficial for the company to be attacked, as that is how they would learn about the organization's vulnerabilities.

With heavy fines being imposed on negligent organizations and the existence of laws, such as the Sarbanes-Oxley (SOX) Act of 2002, that could send executives to jail, turning a blind eye to cyber threats and preparedness is a high-risk strategy. It was a landmark moment and decision when, in 2019, British Airways was found in violation of the European Union's General Data Protection Regulation (GDPR) and fined a record amount of $228 million. The reputed airlines suffered a breach that exposed personal data of 500,000 customers.[4] Equifax, one of the largest credit-reporting agencies, met a similar fate and settled to pay a penalty of $700 million for a breach that compromised 148 million customer records.[5]

These massive breach incidents should get the leadership thinking

> whether they are content to live with the jeopardy of data
> protection fines running into the potential nine-figure bracket,
> or whether it's more prudent to invest a fraction of that total on
> better cybersecurity procedures and technologies.[6]

Cybersecurity governance challenges are numerous and daunting and there are no easy fixes. The book attempts to provide an easy-to-comprehend framework to help readers get their arms around cybersecurity readiness. It recognizes that the battle or war against current and future cyber threats must be fought holistically and comprehensively by adopting people-, process-, and technology-driven measures. Technology alone will not mitigate information security risks. There are several pieces to the complex puzzle of cybersecurity management and technology is only one of them. Committed leadership, robust governance procedures, and informed and motivated personnel are other success factors. The book presents a set of seventeen success factors associated with three high-performance information security culture traits: commitment, preparedness, and discipline.

Chapter 2 begins with a discussion of the global epidemic of cyber-attacks enabled by ever expanding attack surfaces and constantly evolving hacking methods and techniques. The consequences and impacts of data breaches are also presented. In Chapter 3, specific breach incidents are reviewed to understand the causes, adverse impacts, and organizational shortcomings. Each case review concludes with a set of summary takeaways and lessons learned. Chapter 4 draws upon the organizational culture and high-reliability organization literature to identify the three cornerstones of a high-performing security culture—commitment, preparedness, and discipline. How each of these cultural traits relates to cybersecurity readiness success factors and best practices is the focus of discussion in Chapters 5, 6, and 7. Key takeaways and actionable recommendations are presented in Chapter 8. Included in the appendix section are six useful resources: a) Information Security Monitoring Controls, b) Cybersecurity Performance Measures, c) Cybersecurity Readiness Scorecards, d) Cybersecurity and Privacy Laws and Regulations, e) Physical, Technical, and Administrative Controls: A Representative List, and f) Case Studies.

NOTES TO CHAPTER 1 ————————————————————

1. Griffin, T. (2019, December 23). How to Protect Your Company's Digital Assets. *Forbes*. https://www.forbes.com/sites/forbestechcouncil/2019/12/23/how-to-protect-your companys-digital-assets/#5f66e6a06c5f
2. Sutherland, L. (2016, March 31). Know Your Enemy: Understanding the Motivation behind Cyberattacks. *Security Intelligence*. https://securityintelligence.com/know-your enemy-understanding-the-motivation-behind-cyberattacks/
3. Abraham, C., Chatterjee, D., & Sims, R. (2019). Muddling through Cybersecurity: Insights from the U.S. Healthcare Industry. *Business Horizons*, 62(4), pp. 539–548.
4. Rogan, M. (2019, September 12). GDPR's Big Moment Has Just Arrived—With a $228 Million Data Breach Fine. *CPO Magazine*. https://www.cpomagazine.com/data-protection/gdprs-big-moment-has-just-arrived-with-a-228-million-data-breach-fine/
5. Electronic Privacy Information Center. *Equifax Data Breach*. Retrieved September 15, 2019 from https://epic.org/privacy/data-breach/equifax/
6. Rogan, M. (2019, September 12). GDPR's Big Moment Has Just Arrived—With a $228 Million Data Breach Fine. *CPO Magazine*. https://www.cpomagazine.com/data-protection/gdprs-big-moment-has-just-arrived-with-a-228-million-data-breach-fine/

CHAPTER 2

The Cyberattack Epidemic

Research and survey reports reveal a continual rise in the frequency and severity of cyberattacks. No country and no industry is being spared; small and large organizations are being targeted; both public and private infrastructures are under attack (Table 1). The United States has been experiencing, on average, 130 large-scale targeted breaches per year and the number is growing by 27% every year. In 2017, the average number of breaches per country was reported to be 24,089. It is predicted that "cybercrimes will cost the world $6 trillion annually by 2021, up from $3 trillion in 2015."[1] The forces fueling the cyberattack epidemic and the nature and extent of its impact are discussed in the following sections.

Table 1 Cybersecurity Statistics	
On average, every 39 seconds a computer (with internet access) is being hacked.[a]	2017 University of Maryland Study
Global spending on cybersecurity is projected to reach $133.7 billion by 2022.[b]	2018 Gartner Report
Security breaches have increased by 11% since 2018 and 67% since 2014.[c]	2019 Accenture and Poneman Institute Report
The average time to identify a breach is 206 days.[d]	2019 IBM Report
The average lifecycle of a breach is 314 days (from the breach to containment).	2019 IBM Report
The average total cost of a data breach is $3.92 million.	2019 IBM Report
The average size of a data breach is 25,575 records.	2019 IBM Report

(Continued)

Table 1   (Continued)

43% of cyberattacks target small businesses.[e]	2020 Fundera Report
60% of small businesses that are victims of a cyberattack go out of business within 6 months.	2020 Fundera Report
Cybercrime costs small and medium businesses more than $2.2 million a year.	2020 Fundera Report
There was a 424% increase in new small business cyber breaches in 2018.	2020 Fundera Report
47% of small businesses have no understanding of how to protect themselves against cyberattacks.	2020 Fundera Report

Sources:

a. https://www.securitymagazine.com/articles/87787-hackers-attack-every-39-seconds, accessed on April 7, 2020

b. https://www.gartner.com/en/newsroom/press-releases/2018-08-15-gartner-forecasts-worldwide-information-security-spending-to-exceed-124-billion-in-2019, accessed on April 7, 2020.

c. https://www.accenture.com/us-en/insights/security/cost-cybercrime-study, accessed on April 7, 2020.

d. https://www.ibm.com/security/data-breach, accessed on April 7, 2020.

e. https://www.fundera.com/resources/small-business-cyber-security-statistics, accessed on August 2, 2020.

2.1 Expanding Hardware and Software Attack Surfaces

The more networked the business environment, the greater the opportunities for hackers to break into one system and then find their way into many others.[2] The Target retail chain experienced an external intrusion when hackers stole a HVAC vendor's access credentials to gain access to the retail giant's network and systems. Once they were inside Target's network, the perpetrators were able to infect 40,000 of the 60,000 point-of-sale payment card readers with malware.[3]

Increasing dependency on cloud-based services is also adding to organizations' vulnerability points. Capital One, for example, experienced a major breach of customer records when a perpetrator was able to gain access to an Amazon Web Services server (that stored Capital One data) by exploiting a misconfigured web application firewall.[4]

The growing use of Internet of Things (IoT) devices is also increasing the attack surface. Although these smart devices offer many benefits and capabilities, they are known to have weaker security protections and are not easily patchable or updatable.[5] Hackers were able to steal customer data of a casino by exploiting a security vulnerability in the smart sensor used to remotely monitor the casino's aquarium.[6] In the healthcare industry, there is a heavy use of IoT devices for a variety of purposes such as tracking hospital bed occupancy, remotely monitoring patients, providing device malfunction alerts, and timely administration of medication.[7] A recent research report finds that a majority (82%) of healthcare organizations experienced IoT-focused attacks within a one-year period. The breach consequences ranged from stolen health records to disruption of service, compromised end-user safety, and reputational damage.[8]

Today's mobile devices, such as smart phones, are another attractive target for cybercriminals. With organizations allowing employees to use their personal device for work, breaking into such devices will net not only personally identifiable information (PII) but also confidential business data. Such devices are extremely vulnerable and provide a pathway for malware to reach an organization's cloud or on-premise networks. According to a recent cybersecurity report that polled IT professionals, 59% did not use a mobile threat defense solution to protect employee devices. No wonder hackers are able to successfully compromise these devices in different ways, such as launching phishing and man-in-the-middle (MITM) attacks and installing rogue applications. Lost or stolen devices that have not been appropriately configured for security and remote wipe-outs are prime sources of data breach.[9]

Thus, with increasing digitization and transformation of business processes and models, a highly mobile work environment, greater dependency on cloud-based services, infusion of wearable and IoT devices, and a high level of interorganizational connectivity, hardware and software attack surfaces are growing exponentially. The coronavirus pandemic that began early in 2020 is further fueling the explosion of attack surfaces by compelling remote work. In their rush to embrace extreme digitization, many organizations are sacrificing their cybersecurity postures and temporarily allowing employees to access critical systems and data via insecure devices and networks. Use of social media platforms for confidential and crisis communications and storing work data in low-security storage locations are further exacerbating the security vulnerability problem.[10]

2.2 The Human Vulnerability Factor

A widely reported 2019 survey found that 99% of cyberattacks are focused on exploiting human vulnerabilities by targeting people instead of computer systems and infrastructure.[11] Cybercriminals are continuously refining their social engineering techniques to lead unsuspecting people to commit acts such as downloading and installing malicious email attachments, clicking on fraudulent website links, and unknowingly handing over personal information and login credentials. Some of the most significant data breaches were carried out after stealing login credentials from human actors.

The Yahoo breach that compromised three billion user accounts and cost the company $117.5 million in settlement fines was caused by a spear-phishing attack. One of the Yahoo employees unsuspectingly clicked on an email sent by a Latvian hacker, and this led to the installation of a malicious code. This malware allowed the perpetrators to set up a backdoor opening to a Yahoo server and steal user information.[12]

Similar to Yahoo, eBay suffered a data breach when three of its corporate employees fell for a spear-phishing campaign. Using the access credentials of those employees, attackers were able to break into the company servers and steal personally identifiable information (PII) such as names, emails, physical addresses, phone numbers, and birth dates.[13]

A record-breaking fine of 183M pounds was imposed on British Airways when it was found negligent in protecting customer data. This breach was triggered when humans—British Airways customers—were tricked into completing travel reservations on a rogue site that resembled a legitimate British Airways portal.[14]

The following vignette provides a telling account of how susceptible humans are to innovative social engineering techniques.

Hacking into ParentCo's Systems

Mike was an ex-hacker who had started his own company that performed legal hacking. Legal hacking is where companies pay someone to attempt to break into their computer systems. Mike sat down with Dave, the CEO of a large corporation called ParentCo, and told him that ParentCo was very much at risk of having its data compromised. He explained to Dave how much money it could potentially cost ParentCo. "One global company suffered a large breach and spent over 100 million on investigating the incident," Mike told him. "Subsequently they suffered a multibillion-dollar loss in market capitalization because investors lost confidence in them."

Dave didn't think that Mike would be able to break into ParentCo's systems because they had the latest updates on their servers, the best firewalls in place, and layers of security that made it hard for hackers to break through. Since Mike would only charge him if he successfully broke into the system, Dave signed a contract allowing Mike to attempt to break into ParentCo's computer system.

The next day, Mike came to Dave with several sheets of paper. They contained employee social security numbers, customer and employee bank account numbers, and additionally, sensitive corporate information. Dave was floored. "How did you do this?" he asked Mike.

Mike proceeded to explain that earlier the same day, dressed in blue coveralls, he had walked up to the secretary (who had seen him twice before), flashed an ID card and said, "Hello, I'm Mike with AT&T, and we are upgrading the lines coming to your building. I'm afraid we cut something that we weren't supposed to, and I need access to the server room in order to make sure that you guys don't lose connectivity." Mike showed Dave the card. It was the ID card from the building that Mike worked at; it had his picture but didn't say anything about AT&T.

Knowing that everyone would be upset if the lines got shut down, the secretary led him to the server room, typed in the security code in the door lock, and opened the door. "Let me know if there is anything you need. We definitely don't need our telephones to cut off," she said, as she turned to walk to her desk, leaving Mike alone in the server room.

After a few minutes, Mike had walked back out to the secretary, "Looks like we may be ok, but I need to check one more thing. I need your username and password to check that the MAC addresses and TCP protocols haven't been affected."

"Sure thing," said the secretary, and she jotted her information down for him on a sticky note. Thirty minutes later, Mike was in Dave's office with a stack of documents containing sensitive information, printed out using one of the ParentCo's printers. Mike was able to effectively hack ParentCo's computers using a non-technical method of intrusion in less than an hour. On top of that, Dave's company didn't even use AT&T as a provider.

"So, we've got a problem," said Dave as he signed a check over to Mike. "How do we fix it?"

2.3 Growing Attack Vectors

The term *attack vectors* refers to methods used by hackers to break into systems and networks and steal sensitive data. These techniques are constantly evolving, and it is a challenge for organizations to keep up with the hacking community and secure their infrastructure from new forms of attacks. Before discussing the delivery channels, let's first review the different types of malware.

2.3.1 Malware Types

Malicious code, or malware, is used by cybercriminals to steal information and identities, disrupt operations, execute fraudulent transactions, and more. Some common forms of malware are viruses, worms, Trojans, ransomware, spyware, and adware.[15]

Viruses usually appear as executable files (.exe) and are capable of corrupting and deleting files, altering the way a computer operates, and shutting down devices and networks. True to their biological namesakes, viruses infect clean files and can spread uncontrollably.

Computer worms can self-replicate and inflict the same types of damage as viruses. However, unlike viruses, worms are standalone software, and do not require the help of a human or a host program to propagate. Worms exploit a vulnerability to enter the targeted system and then uses file-transport or information-transport features to travel and spread. Often different social engineering techniques (i.e., methods of exploiting perceived trust to elicit sensitive information such as login credentials) are used to trick users to execute computer worm files.

Similar to the large wooden horse left outside the gates of the besieged ancient city of Troy—once the Trojans had hauled the apparent gift inside, enemy soldiers emerged and won the battle for control of the city—the **Trojan** malicious code is often sent as a seemingly legitimate email attachment or as part of a free program download. When the unsuspecting victim clicks on the attachment or downloads the free software, the malware gets transferred to the user's device. If detected, the victim will see a message as depicted in Figure 1. If it stays undetected, the transmitted code can self-execute as timed and cause damage. Some Trojan viruses create a "backdoor" access to the victim's computer, thereby enabling the attacker to access and download confidential files, modify or delete data, and cause other forms of damage. Others have triggered Distributed Denial of Service (DDoS) attacks that flood the network devices with traffic and disrupt operations. Then there is the Trojan banker code that is designed to steal financial account information from user

Figure 1 Trojan Virus Detection Message

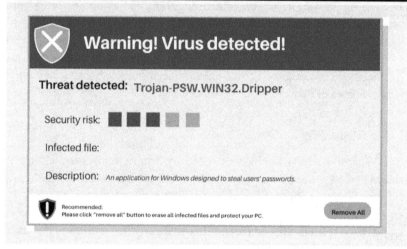

Source: Adapted from Bell, P. (2015). "What Is a Trojan Virus?" April 13, 2015, https://techreviewfeed.com/what-is-a-trojan-virus/.

devices. A new variant of Ursnif, a Trojan malware, is spreading via Word documents with the intent of stealing financial and personal information.[16]

Ransomware is another very popular and devastating form of attack where the malware freezes the victim's machines and networks and the criminals demand a ransom, typically in cryptocurrency such as bitcoins, for victims to regain access to their data. The malicious program encrypts all the data and puts up a screen demanding money to return access to the victim. The ransom amount increases over time until the end of a count-down, when the files are destroyed. There is no guarantee that paying the demanded amount will ensure a full recovery of encrypted files and imme-diate restoration of interrupted services.

This malicious code is typically spread through phishing emails when victims unknowingly visit rogue sites.[17] In addition to email attachments, this malware also spreads through "infected software apps, infected exter-nal storage devices, and compromised websites."[18] Ransomware attacks are often carried out via a Trojan that delivers a malicious payload disguised as a legitimate file.

Figure 2 presents the message that flashed on the screens of more than 200,000 computers that were infected by the WannaCry ransomware. It was a global hacking attack (Figure 3) that affected devices in 150 coun-tries in 2017. Victims included organizations from the healthcare industry,

Figure 2 WannaCry Ransomware Attack

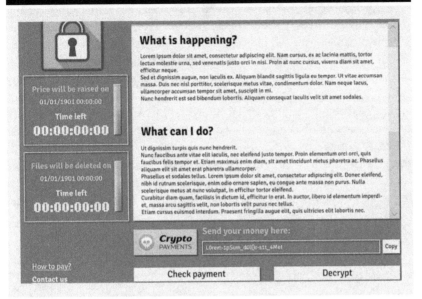

Figure 3 Global Impact of WannaCry Ransomware

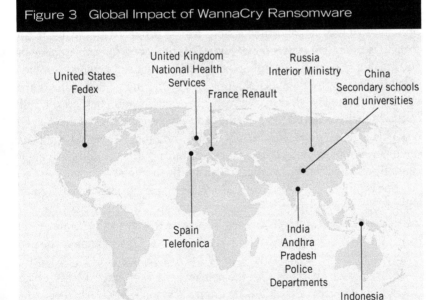

shipping and logistics service providers, government agencies, automotive manufacturers, and telecommunication and gas companies.

The **spyware** malware is designed to spy on the victim's computer and online activities. This type of malicious software, installed without user consent, is capable of recording every keystroke and surfing history and sharing the same with hackers and other interested third parties. **Keyloggers** is a type of spyware that focuses on capturing every keystroke and thereby gaining access to login credentials and other confidential information. They are also capable of taking screenshots of sites visited by a user during a browsing session. When the focus of the software is to covertly gather user purchasing interests, preferences, and behavior, and sharing the same with marketing and advertising firms, the spyware is known as **adware**. Other forms of spyware are capable of hijacking a browser and pointing it to a rogue website or get your device to automatically place calls and send texts.

2.3.2 Malware Distribution Methods and Channels

The different types of malware payload can be distributed using different methods and techniques such as phishing, man-in-the-middle (MITM), drive-by-download, SQL injection, cross-site scripting (XSS), and denial-of-service (DoS) attacks.

Phishing attacks are probably the most common type of attack vector that targets the weakest link in the cybersecurity defense system—the humans. The hackers are able to dupe victims to open an email attachment or a link to a website, and such actions lead to installation of malware (or malicious code) that allows the criminals to gain access to login credentials and break into servers containing sensitive data. Figure 4 depicts a spoofed email that is sent to members of a university community. If any one of the users were to follow through with the instructions and click on the link to renew their password, they would land on a bogus website that would resemble a genuine password renewal site. Once the user would complete the renewal process and hit the submit command, they would have inadvertently shared their login credentials with the hackers.

Spear phishing is a type of social engineering campaign where the email appears to originate from a legitimate source within an organization. For instance, when an employee receives an email that seems to be coming from their peer or supervisor, they are likely to open it. Government-sponsored hackers are known to carry out such attacks. As depicted in Figure 5, once one of the targeted users falls for the phishing attack, a remote access Trojan (RAT) malware gets installed on the target computer. The RAT allows the hackers to gain administrative control and engage in a range of activities from accessing confidential data to activating a system's webcam and recording

Figure 4   Example of a Phishing Attack

Source: https://www.imperva.com/learn/application-security/phishing-attack-scam/

Figure 5   Generic Model of a Spear Phishing Attack

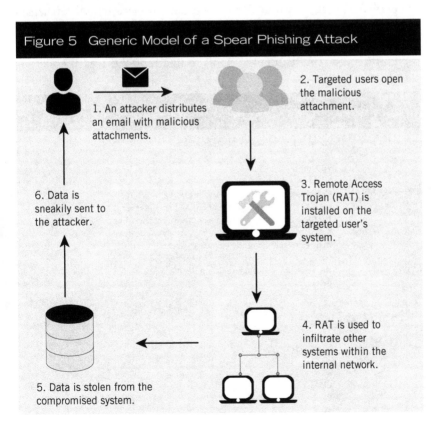

1. An attacker distributes an email with malicious attachments.

2. Targeted users open the malicious attachment.

3. Remote Access Trojan (RAT) is installed on the targeted user's system.

4. RAT is used to infiltrate other systems within the internal network.

5. Data is stolen from the compromised system.

6. Data is sneakily sent to the attacker.

video, monitoring user behavior (using spyware), formatting drives, deleting and altering files, and distributing the virus to other devices on the network.

Whale phishing is another version of targeted phishing attack designed to manipulate high-profile employees such as chief executive officers (CEOs) and chief financial officers (CFOs) to permit high-value wire transfers. Figure 6 depicts an attacker requesting prompt payment. The recipient might overlook the fact that the email is not coming from the same organizational domain; the attacker has registered a similar domain name that ends with a double "s."

AI-enabled voice cloning is emerging as a new form of phishing attack. The CEO of a UK-based energy firm fell for this scam when he followed the orders of his boss, the chief executive of the German parent company, and transferred $243,000 to a Hungarian vendor. The CEO was on a call with his boss and did not realize that it was actually a fraudster, imitating his boss's German accent, who ordered the fund transfer.[19] This is a very disturbing development, as the technology exists to capture audio recordings and convincingly clone the voice to broadcast fake messages and orders.[20]

Man-in-the-Middle (MITM) is an interception technique whereby the perpetrator (as shown in Figure 7) is able to place himself or herself between the victim and the entity with which the victim is trying to communicate. Taking advantage of an unsecured or a poorly secured Wi-Fi router, the cybercriminal deploys tools to intercept and read the victim's

---

Figure 6   Example of a Whale Phishing Attack

Amelia Hall <ahall@vanpartnerss.com>

Hi Molly,

Greetings from Paris! Hope you are doing well. I just met with Trickium Inc., one of our major vendors at the business intelligence conference. They have a pending payment of $250,000 and are unhappy about the delay in disbursement. Could you please wire transfer the amount to so I can write them a personal check within the next day or two. The account details are appended below.

Thanks so much for your prompt attention to this matter.

Sincerely,

Amelia Hall
CEO
VanPartnerss Inc.

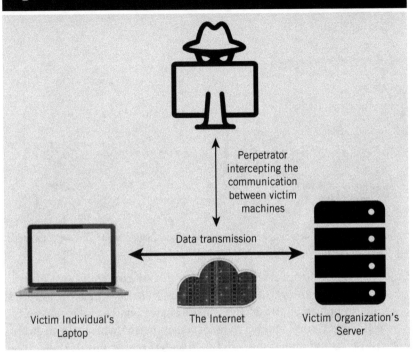

Figure 7   Man-in-the-Middle Attack

Perpetrator intercepting the communication between victim machines

Data transmission

Victim Individual's Laptop

The Internet

Victim Organization's Server

transmitted data. By eavesdropping on the communication, the perpetrator is able to steal login credentials and other sensitive information and is able to carry out different types of fraudulent activities.

Wi-Fi eavesdropping is one of many forms of MITM attack. The TK Maxx security breach was caused by hackers cracking WEP (Wired Equivalent Privacy), a weak Wi-Fi encryption protocol, and intercepting the transmission of data between the cash registers, the price scanning devices, and computer servers at one of the company's stores in Minnesota. The intruders stole 45 million customer records, and that included PII, bank, and credit card data.[21]

Internet Protocol (IP) spoofing is another type where the attacker tricks the victim into thinking that they are communicating with the intended website. Actually, it is a rogue website that is capturing and relaying (to the perpetrator) all the information shared by the victim. By modifying the IP address to impersonate another computer system, the attacker is able to direct traffic from the victim's machine to their site.[22]

Another popular way of infecting a victim's machine is through a **drive-by-download**. As depicted in Figure 8, the malware starts downloading

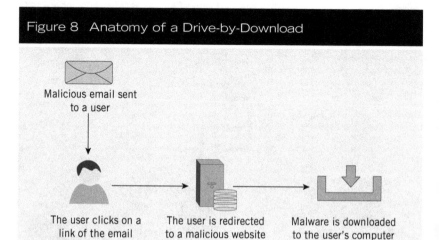

Malicious email sent
to a user

The user clicks on a
link of the email

The user is redirected
to a malicious website

Malware is downloaded
to the user's computer

Source: https://www.thesecuritybuddy.com/malware-prevention/what-is-drive-by-download-and-how-to-prevent-it/. Reproduced by permission.

onto the victim's device as soon as the user visits the malicious site. The victim may not even know that it is a hacker-controlled site. Links to such sites are sent through email attachments, text messages, and social media posts.

SQL injection is another type of attack vector whereby a malicious code is used to manipulate backend databases to access sensitive data. More specifically, as shown in Figure 9, it is a code injection technique in which malicious SQL statements are inserted into an entry field for execution. The SQL server does not recognize the malicious input and reads it as programming code. Poorly designed web applications, with vulnerabilities in the application's database management system, are candidates for such attacks.

SQL injection attacks allow attackers to become administrators of the database server and thereby be in a position to steal identity information, void transactions, change balances, delete data, and publish all the data.[23]

Another form of malware injection is **cross-site scripting (XSS),** where malicious code is injected into reputable websites. The attacker uses a web application to send malicious code, generally in the form of a browser side script.[24] As shown in Figure 10, the victim's device gets infected with the malicious code as soon they interact with the compromised website. This malware injection method is able to circumvent the Same Origin Policy; that is, scripts originating in one website cannot interact with scripts from another site. It is designed to take advantage of the inability of browsers to differentiate between valid and attacker-controlled markup. The XSS technique "exploits the vulnerability of a website the victim visits and gets the website to deliver the malicious script for the attacker."[25]

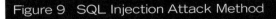
Figure 9 SQL Injection Attack Method

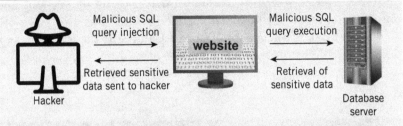

Hacker | Malicious SQL query injection → | website | Malicious SQL query execution → | Database server

Retrieved sensitive data sent to hacker ← | Retrieval of sensitive data ←

Figure 10 Cross-Site Scripting

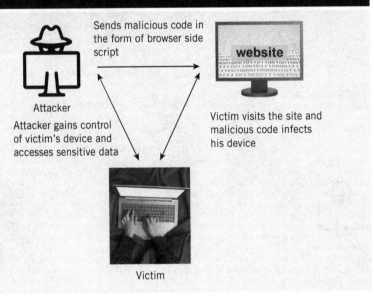

Attacker

Sends malicious code in the form of browser side script →

website

Attacker gains control of victim's device and accesses sensitive data

Victim visits the site and malicious code infects his device

Victim

A very popular form of attack used to interrupt business operations is the **Denial-of-Service (DoS)** attack. It is designed to deny legitimate users' access to computing and related services by flooding the host/targeted server with fake requests from numerous compromised devices (also known as zombies) on the Internet. The flood of incoming messages, connection requests, or malformed data packets forces the target server to slow down or crash and thereby deny service to legitimate users. Exploited machines include computers and IoT devices and since these resources could be located anywhere, a DoS attack is often referred to as a

Distributed-Denial-of-Service (DDoS) attack. Figure 11 presents a high-level depiction of the anatomy of such an attack. As shown in Figure 12, this type of attack resembles a traffic jam clogging up the highway and preventing regular traffic from reaching their destination.

Adversarial Artificial Intelligence (AI) attacks are emerging as a major attack vector as hackers get proficient in using machine-learning tools to automatically detect and exploit vulnerabilities.[26] Very little time or

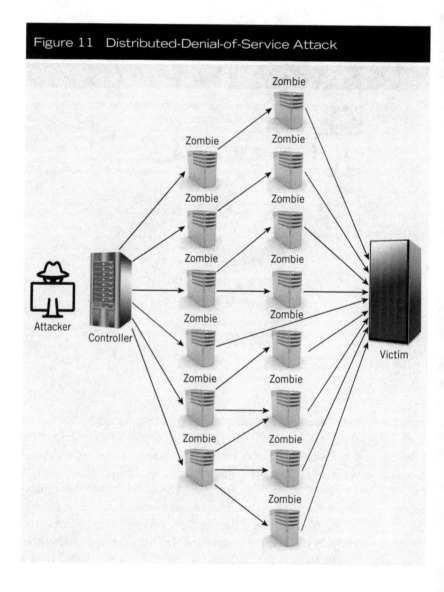

Figure 11   Distributed-Denial-of-Service Attack

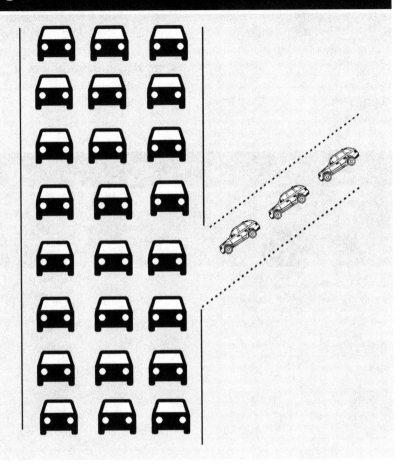

Figure 12   Denial-of-Service Attack

energy is needed to launch such attacks; an attacker is able to set in motion repeated attacks by writing a few lines of code. Sybil is a common form of AI-enabled attack where the web browser's auto-complete function is manipulated to "suggest the word "fraud" at the end of an auto-completed sentence with the target company name in it."[27] Digital home assistants can be taken over and instructed to order a product. Smart home appliances can be compromised to alter various settings such as power and temperature. Home and office security devices can be instructed to unlock doors.[28] Adversarial AI attack opportunities are endless with the growing proliferation of smart devices connected via the Internet.

2.4 Nature and Extent of Impact

A review of some of the biggest data breaches of the twenty-first century reveals wide-ranging impact, from compromising the information privacy and security of individuals to financial losses for organizations, disruption of public and private sector operations, reputation damage, loss of customer loyalty, and more. Table 2 showcases a representative list of the staggering number of individual records exposed and settlement fines awarded to victims.

Table 2 Impact of Organizational Data Breaches			
Name of Company	Incident Date	No. of Records Exposed/Stolen	Estimated Financial Cost (Class Action Lawsuit Settlement/Fines/Penalties)
Adobe	October 2013	38 million	1.2 million plus
Adult Friend Finder	May 2015	412.2 million	Data not available
Anthem	February 2015	78.8 million	115 million
Ashley Madison	July 2015	32 million	12.8 million
British Airways	September 2018	500,000	230 million
Capital One	July 2019	100 million	100–150 million (estimate)
eBay	May 2014	145 million	5 million (sued amount)
Equifax	September 2017	143 million	700 million
Facebook	September 2019	50 million	5 billion
Heartland Payment Systems	May 2015	134 million	140 million
Home Depot	September 2014	56 million	19.5 million
JP Morgan Chase	October 2014	76 million	Data not available
Marriott	November 2018	500 million	12.5 billion (sued amount)
RSA Security	March 2011	40 million	66 million

(Continued)

Table 2   (Continued)

Name of Company	Incident Date	No. of Records Exposed/Stolen	Estimated Financial Cost (Class Action Lawsuit Settlement/Fines/ Penalties)
Sony's PlayStation Network	April 2011	77 million	15 million
Stanford University Hospital	December 2017	Nearly 10,000	4.1 million
Target	December 2013	110 million	28.5 million
TJX Companies	December 2006	94 million	>200 million
U.S. Office of Personnel Management	June 2015	22 million	Data not available
Yahoo	July 2012	3 billion	117 million

Source: Data are in the public domain.

Considering that all the settlement fines stem from lawsuits filed by (or on behalf of) victim consumers, it is to be expected that accused organizations also deal with the wrath and ire of unhappy customers. The lawsuits are primarily anchored on two key accusations: a) the defendant organization did not make every reasonable effort to protect customer data and b) the defendant organization was not prompt and forthcoming in communicating with the victims about the breach. Appendix 4 provides a summary overview of the various cybersecurity laws and regulations and the expected compliance requirements.

A global survey of 10,000 individuals (conducted by Gemalto Paints) revealed that "70% would stop doing business with a company that had experienced a data breach."[29] The telecom company TalkTalk claimed that a data breach in 2015 caused a major uproar on social media and resulted in 101,000 customers choosing to end their business relationship with them. Another study, conducted by Radware, found 43% of the sampled companies admitting having experienced negative customer feedback and reputation loss after a breach incident. A Marsh and Microsoft Global Cyber Risk Perception survey conducted in 2018 provided further validation: 59% of the survey respondents rated reputation loss after a cyberattack as their biggest concern.[30] The following measurable losses were reported by a 2017 Annual Cybersecurity Report:

- "More than half of businesses surveyed that had their data breached were subjected to public scrutiny as a result.

- 29% of businesses that were breached lost revenue; 38% of those lost more than 20% of their revenues.

- 23% of businesses lost business opportunities after a cyberattack; 42% of those lost more than 20% of their potential new business.

- 22% of businesses that suffered a cyberattack lost customers; 40% of those lost more than 20% of their customers."[31]

Sixty percent of small- and medium-sized businesses (SMBs) are known to go out of business within six months of being hacked.[32]

Equally concerning and devastating are attacks on state and government agencies and critical infrastructures and public service resources. The WannaCry attack launched in 2017 crippled more than 230,000 computing systems in 150 countries and caused financial losses estimated at approximately $4 billion. Britain's National Health Services was one of the major national infrastructure organizations hit by this attack. Its services were significantly hampered and disrupted; for instance, "20,000 appointments got cancelled as hospitals and clients were forced offline."[33]

In March of 2018, the City of Atlanta suffered one of the largest and most expensive ransomware attacks, costing upward of $17 million. During the early morning hours of March 22, 2018, the city and its agencies' systems and networks were brought to a screeching halt by the attack. The extortionists were able to successfully cripple several critical systems, thereby forcing many of the agencies to operate manually. Law enforcement was forced to write incident reports by hand and lost access to in-vehicle video footage. Utilities departments and municipal courts could no longer accept payments and fines online. In-person payment of water bills, renewals of business licenses, and payment of parking tickets and traffic fines became the new order of business. The wireless network at Hartsfield–Jackson Atlanta International Airport, one of the nation's largest and busiest airports, was turned off for a couple of weeks for precautionary reasons.[34]

The Ukrainian power grid was compromised in 2015 and 2016, causing power disruption for several hours. Although the inconvenience wasn't major, the real concern lay in the ability of the attackers to successfully break into the computer-controlled operational environment. More specifically, "the hackers overwrote the firmware on the remote-terminal units that controlled the substation breakers"[35] and thereby disabled the remote power restoration capability. The perpetrators were also able to overwrite critical operating system files, causing them to crash and become inoperable. According to security analysts and experts, "someone, or various individuals, may be using the country as a testbed for refining attacks on critical infrastructure that could be used across the world."[36] This successful attempt at compromising the power transmission and distribution centers is a telling indication of how vulnerable critical infrastructure resources are to cyberattacks.

Financial institutions are also very vulnerable to different forms of attacks. Bangladesh Bank was a victim of a major cyber heist in which the criminals successfully diverted $81 million to bank accounts in Philippines, Sri Lanka, and other Asian countries. The hackers were able to steal the SWIFT (Society for Worldwide Interbank Financial Telecommunication) platform access credentials of bank employees and execute fund transfers. They installed malware on the bank's systems and network to hide traces of the fraudulent transactions.[37]

Even water supply systems are very susceptible to attacks. According to one research report, "the US Department of Homeland Security (DHS) responded to 25 cybersecurity incidents in the Water sector. Between 2014 and 2015, the reported number of Water Sector incidents actually increased by 78.6% (from 14 to 25 incidents)."[38] Though these statistics are not very recent, they are still a cause for alarm and concern. If hackers were to break into the computer systems and network that control the chlorination of a wastewater plant, they could potentially cause the mass outbreak of diseases such as cholera and dysentery.[39]

The possibility of state or privately sponsored attacks on nuclear facilities is also disturbing news. There is evidence of hacking of nuclear power plants in Iran, South Korea, and Germany.[40] According to a media report, the U.S. government has accused Russia of carrying out a "series of cyberattacks on U.S. and European nuclear power plants and water and electric systems from 2015 through 2017." The report goes on to suggest that Russian hackers had been infiltrating the business systems of the Wolf Creek nuclear plant in Burlington, Kansas.[41]

Financial institutions and markets could also collapse if the hackers were able to break into one or more of the computing systems enabling operations of a central bank, a custodial bank, or a clearing house. Especially in countries where individual deposits are not insured by the government as in the United States (by the Federal Deposit Insurance

Corporation), wiping out account balance data could cause severe hardship to individuals.[42]

Thus, the actual and potential impact of cyberattacks is quite immense. Individuals, organizations, and countries are exposed to all kinds of risks—from financial and revenue loss to brand reputation damage, loss of intellectual property, interruption of operations, regulatory sanctions, and survival. According to the business tycoon and investor Warren Buffett, cyberattacks are a bigger threat to humanity than nuclear weapons.[43] The following chapter delves into some of the breach incidents to highlight key facts, figures, insights, and takeaways.

NOTES TO CHAPTER 2 ⎯⎯⎯⎯⎯⎯⎯⎯

1. Morgan, S. (2017, October 16). Cybercrime Damages $6 Trillion by 2021. *Cybersecurity Ventures.* https://cybersecurityventures.com/hackerpocalypse-cybercrime-report-2016/
2. Ahmed, M. (2019, April 15). The Increasing Attack Surface in 2019. *Krontech.* https://krontech.com/the-increasing-attack-surface-in-2019/
3. Krebs, B. (2014, January 14). A First Look at the Target Intrusion Malware. *Krebs on Security.* http://krebsonsecurity.com/2014/01/a-first-look-at-the-target-intrusion-malware/
4. Brandom, R. (2019, July 31). The Capital One Breach Is More Complicated Than It Looks. *The Verge.* https://www.theverge.com/2019/7/31/20748886/capitalone-breach-hack-thompson-security-data
5. Abraham, C., Chatterjee, D., & Sims, R. (2019). Muddling through Cybersecurity: Insights from the U.S. Healthcare Industry. *Business Horizons*, 62(4), pp. 539–548.
6. Maker.io (2019, February 20). *"5 Leading IoT Security Breaches and What We Can Learn from Them,"* Digi-Key, Maker.Io. https://www.digikey.com/en/maker/blogs/2019/5-leading-iot-security-breaches-and-what-we-can-learn-from-them.
7. Matthews, K. (2020, June 26). 6 Exciting IoT Use Cases in Healthcare. *IoT for All.* https://www.iotforall.com/exciting-iot-use-cases-in-healthcare/
8. Davis, J. (2019, August 30). 82% IoT Devices of Health Providers, Vendors Targeted by Cyberattacks. *Health IT Security.* https://healthitsecurity.com/news/82-iot-devices-of-health-providers-vendors-targeted-by-cyberattacks
9. Jablonski, F. (2019, April 23). Top 5 Types of Mobile Device Breaches. *Progress.* https://blog.ipswitch.com/top-5-types-of-mobile-device-breaches
10. Boehm, J., Kaplan, J., Sorel, M., Sportsman, N., & Steen, T. (2020, March) Cybersecurity Tactics for the Coronavirus Pandemic. *McKinsey & Company.*
11. Proofpoint. (2019). *The Human Factor 2019* [White paper]. https://www.proofpoint.com/us/resources/threat-reports/human-factor
12. Williams, M. (2017, October 4). Inside the Russian Hack of Yahoo: How They Did It. *CSO.* https://www.csoonline.com/article/3180762/inside-the-russian-hack-ofyahoo-how-they-did-it.html

13. Finkle, J. and Seetharaman, D. (2014, May 27). Cyber Thieves Took Data on 145 Million eBay Customers by Hacking 3 Corporate Employees. *Business Insider*. https://www.businessinsider.com/cyber-thieves-took-data-on-145-million-ebaycustomers-by-hacking-3-corporate-employees-2014-5

14. British Broadcasting Corporation. (2018, September 7). British Airways Breach: How Did Hackers Get In? https://www.bbc.com/news/technology-45446529

15. LIFARS. (2020, March 4). Motivations behind Cyber-Attacks. https://lifars.com/2020/03/motivations-behind-cyber-attacks/

16. Palmer, D. (2019, August 8). *Phishing: Watch Out for This New Version of Trojan Malware That Spreads through Malicious Word Documents*. ZDNet. https://www.zdnet.com/article/phishing-watch-out-for-this-new-version-of-trojanmalware-that-spreads-through-malicious-word-documents/

17. Cybersecurity and Infrastructure. *Ransomware Guidance and Resources*. Cybersecurity & Infrastructure Security Agency. Retrieved December 7, 2020, from https://www.us-cert.gov/Ransomware

18. Rouse, M. (2019). *Ransomware*. Search Security. Retrieved September 27, 2019, https://searchsecurity.techtarget.com/definition/ransomware

19. Damiani, J. (2019, September 3). A Voice Deepfake Was Used to Scam a CEO out of $243,000. *Forbes*. https://www.forbes.com/sites/jessedamiani/2019/09/03/a-voice-deepfake-was-used-to-scam-a-ceo-out-of-243000/?sh=3bd0178f2241

20. Kan, M. (2020, February 26). Is AI-Enabled Voice Cloning the Next Big Security Scam? *PC Mag*. Retrieved July 6, 2020, from https://www.pcmag.com/news/is-ai-enabled-voice-cloning-the-next-big-security-scam

21. Espiner, T. (2007, May 8). Wi-Fi Hack Caused TK Maxx Security Breach. *ZDNet*. Retrieved July 17, 2020, from https://www.zdnet.com/article/wi-fi-hack-caused-tk-maxx-security-breach/

22. Chivers, K. (2020, December 7). What Is a Man-in-the-Middle Attack? *Norton*. Retrieved March 26, 2020, from https://us.norton.com/internetsecurity-wifi-what-is-a-man-in-the-middle-attack.html

23. Zorabedian, J. (2016, November 22). SQL Injection Attacks and How to Prevent Them [INFOGRAPHIC]. *Veracode*. Retrieved September 26, 2019 from https://www.veracode.com/blog/intro-appsec/sql-injection-attacks-and-how-prevent-them-infographic

24. Dobran, B. (2019, February 21). 17 Types of Cyber Attacks to Secure Your Company from in 2019. *PhoenixNAP*. Retrieved September 26, 2019 from https://phoenixnap.com/blog/cyber-security-attack-types

25. Rouse, M. (2018, February). Cross-site Scripting (XSS). *TechTarget*. Retrieved September 28, 2019 from https://searchsecurity.techtarget.com/definition/cross-site-scripting

26. Wiens, C. (2020, January 16). 5 Cybersecurity Threats That Will Dominate 2020. *Security Boulevard*. Retrieved July 12, 2020 from https://securityboulevard.com/2020/01/5-cybersecurity-threats-that-will-dominate-2020/

27. Sattler, J. (2019, November 7). 5 Adversarial AI Attacks That Show Machines Have More to Fear from People Than the Other Way Around. *F-Secure*. Retrieved July 12, 2020 from https://blog.f-secure.com/5-adversarial-ai-attacks-that-show-machines/

28. Dickson, B. (2020, April 27). Adversarial AI: Blocking the Hidden Backdoor in Neural Networks. *Tech Talks*. Retrieved July 12, 2020, from https://bdtechtalks.com/2020/04/27/deep-learningmode-connectivity-adversarial-attacks/

29. Hebblethwaite, C. (2017, November 28). Majority of Consumers Would Stop Doing Business with Companies Following a Data Breach. *MarketingTech*. Retrieved December 7, 2020, from https://marketingtechnews.net/news/2017/nov/28/majority-consumers-say-they-would-stop-doing-business-companies-following-data-breach/

30. WebTitan (2019, January 25). *New Research Reveals Extent of Reputation Loss after a Cyberattack*. Retrieved September 29, 2019, from https://www.spam-titan.com/web-filtering/new-research-reveals-extent-of-reputation-loss-after-a-cyberattack/#:~:text=The%20study%20revealed%2043%25%20of,has%20experienced%20a%20data%20breach.

31. Lesonsky, R. What Does Your Business Stand to Lose in a Cyber Attack? *AllBusiness*. Retrieved September 29, 2019 from https://www.allbusiness.com/business-stand-lose-cyber-attack-112648-1.html

32. Galvin, G. (2018, May 7). 60 Percent of Small Businesses Fold within 6 Months of a Cyber Attack. Here's How to Protect Yourself. *Inc.* Retrieved August 28, 2020 from https://www.inc.com/joe-galvin/60-percent-of-small-businesses-fold-within-6-months-of-a-cyberattack-heres-how-to-protect-yourself.html

33. Cooper, C. (2018, May 15). WannaCry: Lessons Learned 1 Year Later. *Symantec*. Retrieved September 29, 2019 from https://www.symantec.com/blogs/feature-stories/wannacry-lessons-learned-1-year-later

34. Deere, S. (2018, August 1). CONFIDENTIAL REPORT: Atlanta's Cyber Attack Could Cost Taxpayers $17 Million. *Atlanta Journal-Constitution*. Retrieved September 13, 2019 from https://www.ajc.com/news/confidential-report-atlanta-cyber-attack-could-hit-million/GAljmndAF3EQdVWlMcXS0K/

35. Zetter, K. (2017, January 10). The Ukranian Power Grid Was Hacked Again. *Vice*. Retrieved September 29, 2019 from www.vice.com/en_us/article/bmvkn4/ukrainian-power-station-hackingdecember-2016-report

36. Ibid.

37. Zetter, K. (2016, May 17). That Insane, $81M Bangladesh Bank Heist? Here's What We Know. *Wired*, Retrieved July 9 2020 from https://www.wired.com/2016/05/insane-81m-bangladesh-bank-heist-heres-know/

38. Clark, R.M., Panguluri, S., Nelson, T.D., & Wyman, R.P. Water Utilities from Cyber Threats. Accepted manuscript prepared for the *U.S. Department of Energy Office of Nuclear Energy* Under DOE Idaho Operations Office Contract DE-AC07-05ID14517.

39. Sobczak, B. (2019, March 28). Hackers Force Water Utilities to Sink or Swim. *E&E News*. Retrieved September 29, 2019 from https://www.eenews.net/stories/1060131769

40. Assante, M. (2016, December 7). Outpacing Cyber Threats: Priorities for Cybersecurity at Nuclear Facilities. *NTI*. Retrieved September 29, 2019 from https://www.nti.org/analysis/reports/outpacing-cyber-threats-priorities-cybersecurity-nuclear-facilities/

41. Stoutland, P. (2018, March 19). Cyberattacks on Nuclear Power Plants: How Worried Should We Be? *NTI*. Retrieved September 29, 2019 from https://www.nti.org/analysis/atomic-pulse/cyberattacks-nuclear-power-plants-how-worried-should-we-be/

42. Pisani, B. (2018, September 13). A Cyberattack Could Trigger the Next Financial Crisis, New Report Says. *CNBC*. Retrieved September 29, 2019. https://www.cnbc.com/2018/09/13/a-cyberattack-could-trigger-the-next-financial-crisis.html#:~:text=A%20cyberattack%20could%20trigger%20the%20next%20

financial%20crisis%2C%20new%20report%20says&text=Interconnectivity%20and%20the%20concentration%20of,rest%20of%20the%20financial%20system.

43. Oyedele, A. (2017, May 6). BUFFETT: This is 'the Number One Problem with Mankind. *Business Insider*. Retrieved September 29, 2017 from https://www.businessinsider.com/warren-buffett-cybersecurity-berkshire-hathaway-meeting-2017-5

3

Breach Incidents and Lessons Learned

This chapter reviews some of the major data breaches (i.e., over a million exposed records) across different industries. The examination sheds light on the attack causes, vulnerabilities, organization responses, and consequences. Each case discussion concludes with a reflection on key takeaways and lessons learned.

3.1 The Capital One Breach That Exposed 100 Million Applicants and Customer Information

A former employee of Amazon Web Services, Paige Thompson, hacked into the Capital One directory on an Amazon server. According to a court report, the perpetrator was able to gain access by exploiting a misconfigured web application firewall. She was able to access and download a ton of information on 100 million credit card applicants and customers—from names, addresses, credit scores, credit limits and balances, to U.S. social security numbers, Canadian social insurance numbers, and bank account numbers. Customer applicant data from as early as 2005 was exposed.[1]

In addition to publishing the stolen data on GitHub, a leading software development platform, the hacker flaunted her exploits on social media platforms such as Slack. Paige, a software development engineer, made little effort to conceal her identity—she used the same screen name, "erratic," on Slack, Twitter, and Meetup. After she had published the content, a friend replied, "sketchy shit . . . don't go to jail plz." Paige responded, "I wanna get it off my server, that's why I'm archiving all of it, lol. It's all encrypted. I just don't want it around, though." The casual nature of her conversation is quite alarming, especially from a highly skilled software professional who once worked for a top employer.[2]

The breach happened in stages between March and April of 2019; Capital One became aware of the hacking incident on July 17, 2019. Downplaying the potential impact, the company claimed, "No credit card account numbers or log-in credentials were compromised and less than one percent of Social Security numbers were compromised. Based on our analysis to date, we believe it is unlikely that the information was used for fraud or disseminated by this individual."[3]

The company's stock took a slight beating, going down by 5% in pre-market trading on Tuesday, July 30, 2019. Capital One is likely to incur between $100 and $150 million on post-hacking related expenses such as customer notifications, credit monitoring, technology upgrade, and legal expenses.

Chairman and CEO Richard Fairbank expressed his sincere regret about the incident and promised to do everything within his power to make it right for all stakeholders. He reassured the public about being fully committed to safeguarding information and staying invested in cybersecurity. The company reported that it had fixed the problem that caused the breach and was cooperating with federal law enforcement to thoroughly investigate the incident.[4]

Although the complete technical details of the breach are not available, experts are of the opinion that Capital One did not properly configure the Amazon server. A savvy developer sniffed out the security loopholes and nonchalantly shared the sensitive data with the entire world. Considering she didn't try to make any money off the downloaded data and shared it publicly, one is at a loss to understand her motivation.

Why did she carry out the breach? Did she not realize that she was committing a crime? The other pressing questions relate to the preparedness and commitment of Capital One and Amazon. Since server misconfiguration has become a common problem, what controls were in place from the standpoint of both the companies, to prevent such a breach? Did they not carry out regular security drills to prepare for such incidents? While Capital One is obviously liable to its victim customers and credit card applicants, should Amazon also shoulder some responsibility? Should there be provisions in the service level agreements (SLAs) to establish shared responsibility and empower the client organization (under certain conditions) to claim damages in the event of such data security breaches?

Lessons Learned

This case should serve as a caution for all organizations that outsource the storage of sensitive data and management of related digital assets to third-party service providers. During the vendor selection process, the client company must thoroughly review the confidentiality, integrity, and access-related controls offered by the vendor. For instance, the client should inquire about the vendor's encryption technology standard, access control methods, security alert notification process, monitoring and detection mechanisms, and incident response capabilities. Interconnection Security Arrangement (ISA) details—that is, how their respective networks and systems will connect and transfer data—and data ownership issues should also be the subject of discussion. The customer must be satisfied in the vendor's ability to meet the regulatory compliance requirements.

A golden rule is to ensure that the level of security and protection is at least on par with the client organization's standards and expectations. Even after the onboarding process is complete, vendor's security management practices should be closely monitored. When crafting the service level agreement (SLA), the performance criteria relating to measures such as system response time, service availability, and data protection must be agreed upon and clearly documented. Penalties associated with noncompliance and underperformance must also be explicitly included in the SLA.

Desirably, the SLA provisions should incentivize a high level of commitment on the part of the service provider. It would be ideal if the vendor would agree to shared responsibility and partnership in protecting customer data. Robust oversight mechanisms and procedures must be in place to ensure the outsourcing arrangement is working well. Such processes would include regular monitoring and testing of the security controls to protect the data. Since service providers understand best the security configuration of their servers, they should guide and help the client in setting up the servers appropriately. Ideally, if available, sophisticated artificial intelligence tools should be used to configure the servers and do regular security checks.

3.2 British Airways Ordered to Pay a Record Fine of $230 Million

British Airways (BA), the flagship airline of the United Kingdom, suffered a major data breach in the summer of 2018. According to the Information

Commissioner's Office (ICO), a hacking group called Magecart exploited a JavaScript vulnerability on BA's payment-processing website and app. They were able to divert passenger data to a similar sounding rogue site called baways.com. About a half million passengers' personal data were compromised, and that included names, addresses, contact information, and payment card details including the three-digit security code ("card verification value," or CVV). Though BA claimed that the stolen data were not used for fraudulent purposes, one of the victims, David Champion, reported otherwise. Champion's credit card company notified him about an apparent fraudulent activity—there was an attempt to use his stolen credit card to shop at Harrods in London while he was in Malaysia.

According to security expert Andrew Dwyer, the vulnerability in Modernizr, a JavaScript library, is well known, and he was surprised that British Airways had not updated the script since 2012. He was also of the opinion that effective monitoring would have revealed the weakness and BA could have averted the major breach. Even more disconcerting is that BA hadn't fixed the problem even after a year of the attack.[5]

On July 9, 2019, authorities levied British Airways with a record-breaking 183-million-pound fine for violating the General Data Protection Regulations (GDPR). Although the company did follow the GDPR guidelines and report the breach within 72 hours of discovery, it was found negligent, guilty of poor security arrangements and not having provided adequate protection of customer data. A spokesperson from the ICO summarized the situation in simple but powerful words: "When you are entrusted with personal data, you must look after it."[6]

Lessons Learned

Organizations should make every effort to protect confidential customer data. They should have a comprehensive security plan and execute it with great consistency and efficiency. They should pay close attention to the relevant cybersecurity and privacy laws and regulations (See Appendix 4) and ensure compliance. Such a robust plan would include periodic identification of sensitive data and review of protection measures. There should be a monitoring system in place, and the reports should be carefully reviewed and acted on. If a decision is made not to follow through with a certain recommendation, the rationale needs to be documented. Training and awareness programs should include customers whereby they are alerted to the different attack methods and advised on appropriate precautionary measures. Disaster recovery plans and protocols should be well vetted and rehearsed; this will allow the incident response teams to act swiftly and decisively as soon as a breach has been identified or reported. Senior leadership should actively engage in the development and deployment of information security programs and closely monitor their effectiveness. If the due diligence is thorough, the company is likely to fare a lot better in the court of law and public opinion.

3.3 Target Retail Chain Experiences an External Intrusion That Compromised Millions of Customer's Data

In November 2013, the Target retail chain experienced an external intrusion when hackers stole Fazio Mechanical's (a HVAC vendor) access credentials to Target's systems. According to experts, the reconnaissance by attackers must have revealed a list of Target vendors and how they interact with the retail chain's systems. There is also a publicly available case study (on the Microsoft website) that describes Target's technical architecture and infrastructure and how the company uses the Microsoft virtualization software and the Microsoft System Center Configuration to deploy security patches and system updates. Armed with such knowledge, the hackers sent an email with a malware attachment to the refrigeration company Fazio Mechanical. This malicious code was designed to steal passwords such as access credentials to Target's online vendor portal.[7]

Upon gaining access to the company's network and systems, the perpetrators were able to infect 40,000 of the 60,000 point-of-sale payment card readers with malware (in the form of an executable file). The malicious code was designed to go undetected by virus scanners. The software was able to capture and forward customer information as soon as credit cards were swiped through a POS reader. Over 11 GB of data, comprising of contact and credit/debit card information of millions of Target customers, were stolen.[8]

The breach that began before Thanksgiving went undetected for several weeks before the Department of Justice brought it to Target's attention. Equally concerning was the fact that Target did not pay heed to the alert sent out by FireEye, a monitoring company.[9]

The retail giant agreed to pay $18.5 million as part of a multistate settlement with 47 states and the District of Columbia. The penalty amount would cover free credit monitoring services for all affected customers and up to $10,000 for any victim that could provide evidence of losses suffered due to the breach.[10]

Lessons Learned

This incident speaks to the importance of paying heed to intelligence and taking prompt action. Organizations should have sophisticated intelligence gathering and security monitoring systems in place and also structures and procedures that ensure quick decision making along with logging of the findings and the decisions made. Access control mechanisms should be strengthened and regularly reviewed and tested by experts. To Target's credit, they have taken steps to strengthen their security—from creating a customized security framework to establishing sophisticated monitoring capabilities.[11] As discussed previously, information security credentials of vendors must be checked before entering into a contractual relationship. Relevant security certifications must be furnished by the vendor on a regular basis.

3.4 Adult Friend Finder Site Breach Exposes Millions of Customer Records

In May 2015, Adult Friend Finder, an adult entertainment company, suffered the first of two consecutive breaches that happened within a year apart. Its website was compromised, and the hacker exposed the subscribers on a darknet forum. The information leaked was just not the usual names, addresses, date of birth, contact information, and credit card details. Very personal details such as sexual preferences, willingness to have extramarital relationships, and membership on other adult websites were also revealed. Thus, the victims were vulnerable not only to fraudulent credit card transactions but also to internet shaming, blackmail, and extortion.

Yet another cause of concern was that the company did not purge old and expired accounts, and these accounts dated back 20 years. The company kept information on users even after they had deleted their accounts. A particular victim complained that his information was included in the leaked documents even though he had deleted his account after trying the service.

The investigation reports also revealed that the perpetrator, an administrator on the hacker forum HELL, was acting out of revenge because the adult entertainment company owed money to his friend. He exploited a local file inclusion (LFI) vulnerability to access all the sites of the Adult Friend Finder's network. In addition to publishing the data files, he also demanded a ransom of $100,000.[12] Supposedly, the company did not have in place strong password controls. User passwords were either stored in plain text, that is, without protection, or the very weak SHA1 hashing algorithms were used.[13] Weak passwords were one of the identified reasons for the Ashley Madison (dating website) breach. An investigation revealed that at least 15 million passwords were protected with MD5, a low-grade algorithm, compared to the more robust Bcrypt encryption method.[14]

Lessons Learned

Consistent with the Generally Accepted Privacy Principles (GAPP), organizations should follow the minimization principle when it comes to collecting and storing customer information. They should not only limit the collection of personally identifiable information (PII) but also purge it as soon as the purpose has been served. Often, the technology used to collect data (such as web access logs and sensory data) gathers more than what is necessary. Under such situations, the collecting organization must provide full disclosure to the client and destroy the unnecessary information as soon as possible.

Yet another important GAPP principle is that organizations must take every step to secure the collected information from unauthorized access. The different vulnerability points must be identified and appropriate safety measures put in place. For instance, strong password controls should be in place, such as the following: a) accept only strong passwords, b) require users to change passwords every couple of months, and c) use multifactor authentication (MFA). Sophisticated and highly robust algorithms should be used to protect passwords and other customer information.

Adhering to the aforementioned principles is also a step in the right direction toward compliance with the relevant privacy and data protection laws (see Appendix 4).

3.5 Three Billion Yahoo User Accounts Compromised

Three billion user accounts were compromised when Russian hackers were able to break into Yahoo systems and steal subscriber information. Names, email addresses, and passwords of every single account holder of Yahoo and its associates—Tumblr, Fantasy, and Flickr—were stolen.[15]

Although the breach took place during the 2013–2014 period, Yahoo didn't disclose the breach till 2016 and was fined $35 million by the Securities and Exchange Commission for the notification delay. The company has also been directed by the court to create a $117.5 million settlement fund to compensate the victims. Yahoo also took a hit on its acquisition price—Verizon lowered its purchase price for the company by $350 million after learning of the breach.[16]

According to court documents and FBI reports, a spear-phishing email was sent to Yahoo employees, and it took just one click (by an unsuspecting recipient) to install the malware. This malicious code allowed Aleksey Belan, one of the Latvian hackers hired by Russian agents, to install a backdoor on a Yahoo server and steal the company's user database. Now he had access to names, phone numbers, password challenge questions and answers, password recovery emails, and the unique cryptographic value for each user account. Using recovery email addresses and cryptographic values, the hacking team was able to generate access cookies that allowed them access to user email accounts.[17]

Thus, a single click was all that it took to trigger the world's largest data breach. The plaintiffs accused Yahoo of negligence. For instance, an outdated hashing algorithm, MD5, was used to scramble many of the user passwords; according to experts, Yahoo should have consistently used the industry standard Bcrypt algorithm to encrypt the passwords. The plaintiffs also alleged that Yahoo consciously and deliberately did not promptly notify the affected customers.[18]

Lessons Learned

It is imperative that organizations be honest, candid, and transparent in their communications with all stakeholders. Especially during breach incidents, victims should be promptly notified of the attack and potential consequences. In their defense, many companies have argued that they did not wish to rush the communication without being sure of the facts. While that is understandable, a brief communication of the potential breach and the steps the organization is taking to get to the bottom of it would be a more desirable practice. Stakeholders would also be most appreciative of periodic briefings and updates.

Continuous training and awareness programs are essential to mitigate risks from different types of attacks, including phishing. In addition, there needs to be constant monitoring and testing to detect suspicious activities and files. Using strong algorithms to encrypt passwords and all other forms of personally identifiable information (PII) is another best practice.

3.6 Equifax Data Breach Exposes Millions of Customers' Data

In March 2017, Equifax's systems were breached and PII of 147 million customers was stolen. One of the major credit reporting agencies in the United States, Equifax collects financial information on U.S. citizens and residents to generate credit scores and reports. Headquartered in Atlanta, Georgia, Equifax also serves customers globally by providing data analytics services.

According to the breach investigation report, the hackers exploited a vulnerability on the customer complaint web portal and were able to gain access to several servers. The patch for this vulnerability was released on March 7 by Apache Software Foundation, and Equifax was advised to apply the patch on March 9. The company failed to follow through with the recommendation. Equifax also ignored the advice of Mandiant, a secure consulting firm, which had detected several unpatched and misconfigured systems. Their scanning systems failed to flag several vulnerable systems that needed a security update. Furthermore, the usernames and passwords were not encrypted (they were found to be stored in plain text) and the networks not adequately segmented. The attack went undetected for several months, partly because Equifax had failed to renew the public-key certificates on tools that are capable of decrypting and analyzing network traffic and also detect data exfiltration."[19]

Testifying before the U.S. Congress, Richard F. Smith, then CEO of Equifax, pinned the blame for the fiasco on one particular individual who worked in the technology department. According to Smith, the employee had "failed to heed security warnings and did not ensure the implementation of software fixes that would have prevented the breach."[20]

Equifax's post-breach actions have also come under significant scrutiny and criticism. The domain name (equifaxsecurity.com) for the dedicated site to engage with affected customers seemed to closely resemble lookalike domain names used for phishing scams. Expecting customers to trust such an URL was unwise. Equifax had the wrong domain name (securityequifax2017.com) listed in their official social media announcements. Several experts were also of the opinion that the real Equifax site (for affected customers) was insecure. Offering free enrollment in an Equifax ID monitoring and protection service was also criticized; victims were unlikely to sign-up with a company that had betrayed their trust.

Interestingly, the stolen data were not leaked or sold on dark websites. According to the U.S. Justice Department report, it was a state-sponsored cyber espionage attack. "The attorney general said the attack on Equifax was just the latest in a long string of cyber espionage attacks that sought trade secrets and sensitive data from a broad range of industries."[21]

Equifax reached a record-breaking settlement of $425 million to resolve consumer claims.[22] They also spent $1.4 billion to upgrade and transform their technology and security infrastructure. Several senior executives were relieved of their positions and in June 2019, Moody's downgraded the company's financial rating.

Lessons Learned

Organizations should pay heed to information security intelligence and take prompt and decisive action on that basis. If the decision is not to act on the insights gained, the rationale must be documented in a report. Regular technology review and upgrades, robust security monitoring and detection processes, and rehearsing disaster recovery plans are essential to cybersecurity readiness. Top management must be on top of security initiatives and issues and provide close oversight. Actions speak louder than words; organizations must exhibit genuine intent and effort to protect sensitive data and be transparent and fair in their dealings with breach victims.

3.7 Adobe Breach Exposes 38 Million Customer Records

Adobe, the creator of innovative multimedia software products such as Adobe Acrobat, Photoshop, and Illustrator, was the victim of a major breach in 2013, when cybercriminals were able to access a backup server and gain access to 152 million usernames and passwords as well as the credit card details and contact information of 38 million customers. They also stole the source code for some of the company products—Adobe's ColdFusion, Acrobat, and Reader. In addition to making money from selling customer information on the dark web, the hackers could also sell the source code to current and future competitors. They could also manipulate the code to carry out future attacks on Adobe's customers.[23] The company had to deal with several breach consequences, from salvaging reputation to class action lawsuits, fines and penalties, intellectual property theft, paying for credit monitoring services of the victims, and remedial security measures.[24] Although the total settlement costs are unknown, the reported amount is in excess of a million dollars.

The root cause of the breach was the poor encryption system deployed by the company; supposedly the same encryption key was used for all passwords.[25] As the company transitioned from a desktop-based licensing environment to a cloud-based software-as-a-service (SaaS) environment, it failed to recognize that the encryption method that worked for an on-premise desktop architecture was not ideal for the cloud.[26] For instance, in an on-premise desktop environment, each computer could be secured with a unique encryption key that didn't need to be changed very often. However, this is a poor practice in the cloud because if the attackers are able to break into one server, they can access the other connected machines.

While centralizing its operations, the company was negligent in leaving "copies of their customer records on multiple internal network locations that were no longer as protected as Adobe's globally centralized storefront."[27]

Lessons Learned

First and foremost, this breach is a chilling reminder that no company, including the tech-savvy software companies, can take security lightly. They should be constantly on their guard and practice the best possible cybersecurity hygiene. Fortunately, Adobe learned from its mistakes and took several positive steps to improve its security posture after the breach. The chief security officer (CSO) role was created and the security organization was suitably restructured to integrate the widely dispersed personnel teams. The overall goal of the security function was formalized and communicated, and roles and responsibilities were clearly articulated. The newly appointed CSO made it his mission to "improve security privately, but to communicate publicly." Adobe is also using the services of Okta, a security solutions provider, to secure access and strengthen authorization mechanisms.[28] It has essentially taken a defense-in-depth and a proactive approach to strengthen every aspect of its security operations. It would be reasonable to assume that Adobe would be leveraging automated device and data discovery services to locate all critical data and digital assets. Constant monitoring and intelligence gathering will help the organization stay abreast of potential attack scenarios and regular security audits and penetration tests will help detect vulnerabilities and enable Adobe to take prompt remedial action.

3.8 Anthem Breach
Affects 78.8 Million People

Anthem Inc., one of the largest U.S. healthcare insurance providers, was breached on February 18, 2014, when an employee of one of its subsidiaries became a victim of an email phishing attack. Opening the email led to downloading of malicious files, and the hackers were able to gain remote access to the user's computer. From that computer, the attackers were able to move laterally and penetrate dozens of other systems including the company's data warehouse. Approximately 78.8 million unique customer records were compromised and personally identifiable information (PII)—names, birthdays, social security numbers, street addresses, email addresses, and employment information—was stolen.[29]

According to investigation reports, the large-scale attack was caused by a foreign nation-state. Anthem became aware of the breach on January 27, 2015, and made a public announcement in early February 2015. It is quite concerning that the company was unaware of the attack for a year. Equally concerning was the delay in notifying all the victims. In March 2015, Joseph Swedish, Anthem president and CEO, received a letter from the U.S. Health Committee, asking him to notify all 78.8 million potentially impacted customers. The letter, written by the chairman of the Health Committee and ranking member, stated that "while we appreciate your efforts to keep our Committee informed of your efforts to respond to the attack after you became aware of it, we are troubled by Anthem's delay in notifying these 78.8 million Americans." On the positive side, the investigation also concluded the insurer had taken reasonable measures to protect sensitive data and was quick and effective in its breach response.[30]

The financial consequences of the attack included $2.5 million for hiring expert consultants, $31 million to notify the victims, $112 million for credit monitoring and protection services, and $115 million toward additional security measures.[31]

Anthem took several important steps to boost security, such as implementing two-factor authentication on all remote access devices and tools, investing in a privileged account management solution, and adding enhanced logging capabilities to its security event and incident management solutions. The company also implemented superior monitoring solutions, replaced existing Network Admin IDs with new IDs, reset the passwords for all privileged account holders, and suspended remote access pending implementation of two-factor authentication.[32]

Lessons Learned

Humans continue to be a significant vulnerability and are a popular target for hackers. Every effort needs to be made to mitigate the human risk factor. Continuous and customized training, frequent testing and assessment, rewards and incentive schemes, and fostering an employee-friendly culture are essential elements of a comprehensive approach to enhancing and sustaining employee skill sets and motivation. Sophisticated AI-enabled tools should be in place to continuously monitor all network access points and proactively detect and repel attacks. The monitoring system must be supported with a highly vigilant and responsive security team that will promptly review and act on the threat intelligence. Conducting penetration testing and security audits on a regular basis are also effective means of staying abreast of potential vulnerabilities. Finally, the incident response protocol needs to be well rehearsed and must include transparent and prompt communication with all stakeholders.

As highlighted in Table 3, the review of breach incidents reveals several shortcomings ranging from gross negligence to lack of transparency, inadequate preparation, and poor communication. To effectively address these weaknesses, the organization must adopt a multipronged and holistic approach that encompasses people, process, and technology-related defense and control measures. Organizational values and beliefs as reflected in its culture are likely to influence the shaping, adoption, and sustenance of the security measures. The next chapter focuses on identifying the key dimensions and traits of a high-performance approach to information security.

Table 3 Summary of Breach Incidents and Lessons Learned

Organization	Exploited Vulnerabilities	Weaknesses	Areas for Improvement
Capital One	Misconfigured web application firewall.	Late detection of breach. Inability to properly configure the security settings of the third-party data server.	Enhance expertise in securing third-party servers. Preferably, develop or find an AI driven automated solution. Be extremely deliberate and thorough in selecting a cloud-based party service provider for storage and other computing services. Suitably craft SLA provisions to establish a certain level of shared responsibility and accountability for protecting sensitive data. Vendor should also be required to provide regular security test reports. Regularly review vendor performance in protecting customer data.
British Airways	Customers were the victim of a phishing attack.	The vulnerability in Modernizr, a JavaScript library, is well known and British Airways had not updated the script since 2012. Lack of robust monitoring capabilities. Delay in fixing the vulnerability. British Airways hadn't fixed the problem even a year after the attack.	Implement sophisticated monitoring and reporting capabilities and promptly act on the alerts and intelligence. Customers must participate in security training and awareness programs to mitigate the risk of them falling for a phishing attack.

Organization	Exploited Vulnerabilities	Weaknesses	Areas for Improvement
	A Javascript vulnerability on BA's payment processing website and app.		Incident response and recovery drills must be thoughtfully planned and tested.
			Senior leadership should provide strong oversight and if feasible, actively engage in security planning, implementation, and performance-monitoring activities.
Target	External vendor fell for a phishing attack. The hackers stole Fazio Mechanical's (a HVAC vendor) access credentials to Target's systems.	The breach went undetected for several weeks. Target did not pay heed to the alert sent by a monitoring company.	The intelligence gathering and threat-detection procedure must include mechanisms for prompt review and response.
			This incident speaks to the importance of paying heed to intelligence and taking prompt action.
			The vendor must furnish requisite security credentials and certifications to earn client business.
			Oversight mechanisms should include periodic review and testing of vendor's security processes.
			Network access protection must be strengthened with multiple layers of controls and regular penetration testing.

(Continued)

Organization	Exploited Vulnerabilities	Weaknesses	Areas for Improvement
Adult Friend Finder	Exploited a local file inclusion (LFI) vulnerability.	Weak password controls. User passwords were either stored in plaintext or the very weak SHA1 hashing algorithms were used. The company did not purge old and expired accounts.	A clear and consistent data-purge policy must be in place and followed. Robust access-control measures must be adopted such as strong password controls and multifactor authentication. Sensitive customer data must be secured with the most powerful encryption mechanism. Only the bare minimum personally identifiable information (PII) should be collected and stored.
Yahoo	An employee fell victim to a spear-phishing email.	Use of an outdated hashing algorithm MD5 to scramble many of the user passwords. Yahoo did not promptly notify the affected customers.	Continuous employee training and awareness programs. Constant monitoring and testing to detect suspicious activities and files. Use of strong algorithms to encrypt passwords and all other forms of PII. Need to develop and adhere to a sound communication plan and protocol. Such a plan should be part of business continuity plan and disaster recovery plan. The communication plan should be rehearsed and tested by conducting tabletop exercises.

Organization	Exploited Vulnerabilities	Weaknesses	Areas for Improvement
Equifax	Exploited a vulnerability on the customer complaint web portal. Several unpatched and misconfigured systems.	Ignored advice to apply the software patches released to address security loopholes. Ignored the advice of a secure firm that had detected several unpatched and misconfigured systems. The scanning systems failed to flag several vulnerable systems that needed a security update. The usernames and passwords were not encrypted (they were found to be stored in plaintext). The networks were not adequately segmented. Failed to renew the public-key certificates on tools that are capable of decrypting and analyzing network traffic and also detecting data exfiltration.	Organizations must be vigilant and promptly act on the information security intelligence. There must be a procedure for logging all intelligence alerts and also documenting the response along with the rationale. Software updates should be automated. Senior leadership must stay informed on security initiatives and issues and provide close oversight.

(Continued)

45

Organization	Exploited Vulnerabilities	Weaknesses	Areas for Improvement
Adobe	Poor encryption system deployed by the company; same encryption key was used for all passwords.	Negligent in leaving copies of customer records on multiple internal network locations.	Adopt a defense-in-depth and a proactive approach to strengthen every aspect of its security operations. Maintain an updated inventory of hardware and software assets. Constant monitoring and intelligence gathering. Regular security audits and penetration tests.
Anthem	An employee became a victim of an email phishing attack.	The company was unaware of the breach for a year. The company delayed in notifying all the victims.	Continuous and customized information security awareness training. Fostering an employee-friendly culture. Sophisticated AI-enabled threat monitoring and detection systems. Highly vigilant and responsive security team that will promptly review and act on the threat intelligence. Use of strong algorithms to encrypt passwords and all other forms of PII. Need to develop and adhere to a sound communication plan and protocol. Such a plan should be part of business continuity plan and disaster recovery plan. The communication plan should be rehearsed and tested by conducting tabletop exercises.

NOTES TO CHAPTER 3 ———————

1. Russell, B. (2019, July 31). *It Can Be Hard to Tell Legitimate Research from Criminal Enterprise*. The Verge. Retrieved December 8, 2020, from https://www.theverge.com/2019/7/31/20748886/capital-one-breach-hack-thompson-security-data
2. Brandom, R. (2019, July 31). *The Capital One Breach Is More Complicated Than It Looks*. The Verge. https://www.theverge.com/2019/7/31/20748886/capital-one-breach-hack-thompson-security-data
3. CapitalOne. (2019, September 23). *Information on the Capital One Cyber Incident*. Retrieved December 8, 2020 from https://www.capitalone.com/facts2019/
4. Ibid
5. Stokel-Walker, C. (2019, July 8). *A Simple Fix Could Have Saved British Airways from Its £183m Fine*. Wired. Retrieved July 8, 2019 from https://www.wired.co.uk/article/british-airways-data-breach-gdpr fine#:~:text=A%20simple%20fix%20could%20have%20saved%20British%20Airways%20from%20its%20%C2%A3183m%20fine&text=British%20Airways%20may%20finally%20be,cent%20of%20its%20global%20turnover
6. Ibid.
7. Krebs, B. (2014, January 14). *A First Look at the Target Intrusion Malware*. Krebs on Security. Retrieved December 8, 2020 from https://krebsonsecurity.com/2014/01/a-first-look-at-the-target-intrusion-malware/
8. Radichel, T. (2014, August 5). *Case Study: Critical Controls That Could Have Prevented Target Breach*. SANS Institute. Retrieved August 26, 2019 from https://www.sans.org/reading-room/whitepapers/casestudies/case-study-critical-controls-prevented-target-breach-35412
9. Ibid.
10. McCoy, K. (2017, May 23). *Target to Pay $18.5M for 2013 Data Breach That Affected 41 Million Consumers*. USA Today. Retrieved December 8, 2020 from story/money/2017/05/23/target-pay-185m-2013-data-breach-affected-consumers/102063932/
11. CompTIA. (2018, April 16). *Building a Culture of Cybersecurity: A Guide for Corporate Executives and Board Members*. https://www.comptia.org/content/white papers/building-a-culture-of-cybersecurity-a-guide-for-corporate-executives-and-board-members
12. Trend Micro. (2015, May 22). *Data Breach of Adult Dating Site Exposes Victims to a Different Kind of Threat*. Retrieved May 22, 2015 from https://www.trendmicro.com/vinfo/es/security/news/cybercrime-and-digital-threats/data-breach-of-adult-dating-site-exposes-victims-to-a-different-kind-of-threat
13. Dickey, M. R. (2016, November 13). FriendFinder Networks Hack Reportedly Exposed over 412 Million Accounts.Techcrunch. Retrieved December 8, 2020, from https://techcrunch.com/2016/11/13/friendfinder-hack-412-million-accounts-breached/
14. Panda Security. (2018, October 6). *A Dating Site and Corporate Cyber-Security Lessons to Be Learned*. Retrieved July 8, 2020 from https://www.pandasecurity.com/en/mediacenter/security/lessons-ashley-madison-data-breach/
15. Larson, S. (2017, October 3). Every Single Yahoo Account Was Hacked—3 Billion in All. *CNN*. Retrieved October 4, 2017 from https://money.cnn.com/2017/10/03/technology/business/yahoo-breach-3-billion-accounts/index.html#:~:text=An%20epic%20and%20historic%20data,company%20initially%20reported%20in%202016.
16. Zetlin, M. (2018, October 25). *Remember the 2013 Yahoo Data Breach? The Company May Owe You $375*. Inc. Retrieved August 28, 2019 from

https://www.inc.com/minda-zetlin/yahoo-data-breach-50-million-lawsuit-settlement-account-holders-375.html

17. Williams, M. (2017, October 4). Inside the Russian Hack of Yahoo: How They Did It. CSO. Retrieved August 28, 2019 from https://www.csoonline.com/article/3180762/inside-the-russian-hack-ofyahoo-how-they-did-it.html

18. Constantin, L. (2016, September 23). Here's What You Should Know, and Do, about the Yahoo Breach. CSO. Retrieved August 28, 2019 from https://www.csoonline.com/article/3123403/hereswhat-you-should-know-and-do-about-the-yahoo-breach.html

19. Fruhlinger, J. (2020, February 12). Equifax Data Breach FAQ: What Happened, Who Was Affected, What Was the Impact?" CSO. Retrieved March 5, 2020 from https://www.csoonline.com/article/3444488/equifax-data-breach-faq-what-happened-who-was-affectedwhat-was-the-impact.html

20. Bernard, T.S. and Cowley, S. (2017, October 13). Equifax Breach Caused by Lone Employee's Error, Former C.E.O. Says. *The New York Times*.

21. Krebs, B. (2020, February 10). *U.S. Charged 4 Chinese Military Officers in 2017 Equifax Hack*. Krebs on Security. Retrieved April 5, 2020 from https://krebsonsecurity.com/2020/02/u-s-charges-4-chinese-military-officers-in-2017-equifax-hack/

22. Federal Trade Commission. (2020, April 5). *Recent FTC Cases Resulting in Refunds*. Retrieved April 5, 2020 from https://www.ftc.gov/enforcement/cases-proceedings/refunds/equifax-databreach-settlement

23. Higgins, K.J. (2013, October 7). Hacking the Adobe Probe. *Dark Reading*. Retrieved July 11, 2020 from https://www.darkreading.com/attacks-breaches/hacking-the-adobe-breach/d/did/1140620

24. Marciano, C. (2013, November 1). *Adobe Data Breach Insurance Case Study*. Data Breach Insurance. Retrieved July 11, 2020 from https://databreachinsurancequote.com/data-breach-insurance-2/adobe-data-breach-insurance-case-study/

25. Pauli, D. (2015, August 17). Adobe Pays US$1.2M Plus Settlements to End 2013 Breach Class Action. *The Register*. https://www.theregister.com/2015/08/17/adobe_settles_claims_for_data_breach/

26. Bell, T. (2018, April 12). Adobe's CSO Talks Security, the 2013 Breach, and How He Sets Priorities. *CSO*. https://www.csoonline.com/article/3268035/adobe-scso-talks-security-the-2013-breach-and-how-he-sets-priorities.html

27. Krebs, B. (2016, November 17). *Adobe Fined $1M in Multistate Suit over 2013 Breach; No Jail for Spamhaus*. Krebs on Security. Retrieved July 11, 2020 from https://krebsonsecurity.com/2016/11/adobe-fined-1m-in-multistate-suit-over-2013-breach-no-jail-for-spamhaus-attacker/

28. Bell, T. (2018, April 12). Adobe's CSO talks security, the 2013 breach, and how he sets priorities. *CSO*. https://www.csoonline.com/article/3268035/adobe-s-cso-talks-security-the-2013-breach-and-how-he-sets-priorities.html

29. McGee, M. K. (2017, January 10). *A New In-Depth Analysis of Anthem Breach*. Bank Info Security. Retrieved July 16, 2020 from https://www.bankinfosecurity.com/new-in-depth-analysisanthem-breach-a-9627

30. Snell, E. (2017, January 9). *Anthem Data Breach Reportedly Caused by Foreign Nation Attack*. Health IT Security. Retrieved July 16, 2020 from https://healthitsecurity.com/news/anthem-data-breach-reportedly-caused-by-foreign-nation-attack#:~:text=January%2009%2C%202017%20%2D%20The%20large,the%20California%20Department%20of%20Insurance

31. McGee, M. K. (2017, January 10). *A New In-Depth Analysis of Anthem Breach*. Bank Info Security. Retrieved July 16, 2020 from https://www.bankinfosecurity.com/new-in-depth-analysisanthem-breach-a-9627

32. Ibid.

Foundations of the High-Performance Information Security Culture Framework

Information security challenges are not going away. They have become part of the digital business reality, and organizations need to develop a mature and effective approach to mitigating such hazards. To effectively prepare and respond to these ever-increasing and evolving cyberattacks, organizations must not only have a comprehensive plan but also execute that plan with great precision and consistency. There is little room for errors or mistakes. Such errors can be catastrophic, especially for organizations and operations such as air traffic control systems, nuclear power plants, emergency room services in hospitals, assembly of aircraft, water purification plants, and nuclear naval operations.

What are the key elements and characteristics of a relatively error-free and high-performance approach to cybersecurity governance? To answer this question, it is essential to delve into the role of culture in influencing organizational performance. For cybersecurity governance to be effective, organizational members must be willing to comply with the policy guidelines and the various control mechanisms. Research finds that positive compliance behaviors are dependent on cultural factors such as subjective norms, organizational values, and expectations.[1] "The company culture must emphasize and value cybersecurity" for organizations to sustain an effective and long-term defense campaign.[2]

4.1 Organizational Culture and Firm Performance

Organizational culture, in its various forms and manifestations, has been found to play a significant role in positively impacting firm trajectories and performance.[3] It has been likened to a foundation or anchor that binds together organizational members around a common vision, values, purpose, and beliefs.[4] It has also been defined "as a mechanism by which an organization and its members learn to both manage external challenges and achieve internal integration."[5] Leadership and management styles, strategic emphasis, structural alignment, and performance measurement systems emanate from the cultural orientation of an organization. Studies have found organizations with unique and inimitable cultures able to sustain competitive advantage over a long period of time.[6] In the words of Lou Gerstner, former CEO of IBM, "culture isn't just one aspect of the game—it is the game. . . . In short, businesses with high-performance cultures are winners."[7] Culture, defined as "shared values, is featured at the core of the McKinsey 7-S framework for creating an intelligent organization.[8]

Numerous empirical and case studies have found organizational culture to have a significant positive impact on performance. Both strength and content of organizational culture are found to be important predictors of strong performance.[9] One particular study found the Developmental Culture type, characterized by flexibility and external orientation, to be the strongest predictor of performance, where product quality and innovation were the performance measures.[10] The five cultural attributes— managing change, achieving goals, coordinating teamwork, building a strong shared culture, and focusing on customer satisfaction—were found to positively impact the performance of Air National Guards, a large public-sector organization.[11]

A comparative study found several cultural traits and characteristic associated with high-performing hospitals. Strong top-down command and control leadership style with a high level of commitment, clear and unequivocal lines of upward accountability, sophisticated information systems to support performance evaluation, heavy emphasis on employee training and development, and the ability to build strong external partnerships were some of the attributes of the culture in the high-performing hospitals.[12] In another empirical study involving insurance companies, a strong and adaptive organizational culture was found to positively impact asset and premium growth.[13]

4.2 Organizational Culture and Cybersecurity

Although the research on cybersecurity culture is still in its infancy, there is growing consensus that a techno-centric approach to information security governance is inadequate and myopic.[14] Security experts and thought leaders have expressed the view that "security can no longer be isolated as a technical problem with a technical solution; it must be prioritized as a critical business concern."[15] A deeper, more holistic, and human-centered approach, anchored in culture, is essential to tackle cybersecurity-related hurdles and challenges.[16]

Several studies have been conducted to determine ideal forms of organizational culture that are supportive of information security management goals.[17] There are others that have focused on understanding how to build and strengthen the information security culture.[18] Influence of specific cultural traits and dimensions on cybersecurity governance has also been the subject of investigation. Studies examining the impact of technology, people, and procedure-specific factors on information security management also indirectly inform the role of organizational culture in bringing about the desired security compliance behaviors. High-reliability organization studies have also informed security culture research.[19]

With attackers exploiting human vulnerabilities, procedural loopholes, and technological deficiencies, the strategic preparation and response must be multi-pronged, requiring the involvement and commitment of both internal and external stakeholders. Achieving interorganization and extra-organization wide buy-in requires a change in mindset that can be brought about and reinforced through a cultural change.[20]

An organizational culture that stimulates loyalty and oneness is likely to mitigate the risk of attacks from insiders. A 2016 IBM study found that 60% of the breaches are triggered by unhappy employees who have an axe to grind.[21] According to social bond theory, a person is likely to commit a crime if the bonds of attachment, commitment, and involvement are weak.[22] A cohesive and controlling culture with well-designed incentives and sanctions, and robust enforcement processes, will be an effective deterrent to insider threats.

One particular empirical study finds control-focused organizational culture emphasizing effectiveness and consistency conducive to realizing the information security management goals of integrity, availability, and accountability.[23] Studies also emphasize the important role of the senior leadership in developing and instilling an information security–friendly organizational culture. While C-suite executives recognize the significance and importance of information security, the friction or difference lies in their approach to translating the security sentiment into reality.[24]

Organizational security culture can be strengthened over time by crafting an information security policy and ensuring the employees are extremely familiar with the policy document.[25] By providing guidelines on ideal and desired practices, the security policy can help influence social norms and values and thereby make the culture more security conscious. Implementing and institutionalizing the recommended controls for securing data, devices, networks, storage locations, and people (through training) also strengthen the security culture.[26] Studies have also found that highly trained and visible incident response teams enhance awareness of the organizational commitment to information security, which in turn reinforces the security culture.[27]

4.3 High-Reliability Organizational Culture Traits

While the organizational culture literature sheds light on winning traits and characteristics, it is the organizational safety and high-reliability organization (HRO) studies that are most relevant for identifying the key dimensions of a high-performance cybersecurity culture. In high-risk industries and operations such as nuclear plants, chemical manufacturers, airlines, hospitals, and infectious disease research laboratories, organizations are expected to operate at a very high level of reliability because the cost of a single error could be catastrophic.[28] So, the cultural traits and attributes that enable HROs to minimize errors will be ideally suited for cybersecurity management, as the consequences of cyberattacks can be equally devastating.

One such HRO is the U.S. Naval Nuclear Propulsion Program. The program was commissioned in the 1950s to examine the feasibility of using nuclear power (instead of diesel) as a new source of energy that would allow submarines to stay submerged for longer periods of time and thereby avoid detection. These onboard nuclear reactors must be operated with great caution because one mistake could result in complete destruction of the vessel and the death of all crew members. In addition, the radiation released from such accidents can have a catastrophic impact on the environment and the people within that environment. Creating a high-reliability environment where such accidents would not happen was clearly the priority for Admiral Hyman Rickover, the pioneer of the nuclear navy program. He was extremely successful: during his 30-year stint at the helm of the program, there was no incident of a nuclear catastrophe, and that unblemished record continues to this day. "In more than 60 years of existence, the nuclear propulsion program that he helped launch hasn't suffered a single incident."[29]

Rickover's success has been attributed to an organization culture anchored on six key principles—integrity, depth of knowledge, procedural compliance, forceful backup, questioning attitude, and formality in communications.[30] The "integrity" principle speaks to the level of commitment displayed by the submariners in managing operations. The nuclear submarine officers are fully dedicated to safely and efficiently running and maintaining the onboard nuclear equipment. This single-minded and focused dedication to ensuring operational efficiency and safety is a trait that would go a long way in supporting the cybersecurity goals of an organization.

The nuclear naval culture also values a high level of preparedness, which is reflected in a) thorough and rigorous training and assessment programs; b) numerous internal controls and checks and balances in place to prevent any kind of operational missteps; and c) empowering of employees to promptly raise alarms and draw attention to problem situations. As will be discussed in later chapters, such preparedness traits are essential to building and sustaining a robust information security mechanism.

Finally, the principles of *procedural compliance* and *formality in communications* reflect a highly disciplined and meticulous approach to safety on board the nuclear-powered vessels. Similarly, a disciplined approach of following through with the cybersecurity strategy and action plans; continuous monitoring of attack surfaces, vectors, and defense mechanisms; effective communication and enforcement of policies; continuous performance assessment and improvement; and frequent security audits and drills are essential to cybersecurity effectiveness.

Thus, the six principles driving the high-reliability environment at the U.S. Naval Nuclear Propulsion Program can be broadly mapped (Figure 13) into three high-performance information security cultural dimensions (or traits) of commitment, preparedness, and discipline.

These three high-performance cultural dimensions also find support in other case studies and empirical studies. For instance, under the leadership of Sergio Nacach, Kimberly-Clark's Andean region was able to establish a "winning" culture of people who were totally committed to results. Empathy and community were the cornerstones of this committed culture and were reflected in the people-focused and people-friendly attitude both within and outside the organization. In the words of the organization's supply chain manager: "It is a culture of sincerity, where anyone can say whatever crosses his or her mind. There is a culture to achieve and exceed the goals, a winning culture of people totally committed to the results."[31]

The leadership at Infrastructure Development Finance Corporation (IDFC) embarked on a journey to develop a high-performance organizational

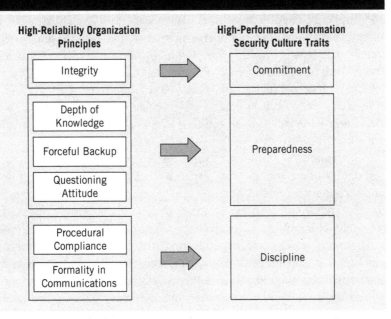

Figure 13   Mapping High-Reliability Organization Principles
to High-Performance Information Security
Culture Traits

High-Reliability Organization Principles

- Integrity
- Depth of Knowledge
- Forceful Backup
- Questioning Attitude
- Procedural Compliance
- Formality in Communications

High-Performance Information Security Culture Traits

- Commitment
- Preparedness
- Discipline

culture in 2009. Their focus was to create a culture of oneness to help unify the various business units. Growth through acquisitions had saddled the company with several disparate business unit cultures, and IDFC's "One-Firm" initiative was aimed at creating a shared sense of purpose and values. Building such an integrated culture led to greater collaboration across units, thereby enhancing the level of preparedness. The cultural transformation resulted in a revenue increase, improvements in customer service quality, and growth in market share.[32]

Establishing a culture of preparedness is also well documented in emergency and disaster management literature.[33] Numerous studies on disaster preparation and recovery have examined the critical success factors and made recommendations on how best to prepare for the different types of possible calamities. Enhancing general awareness, conducting vulnerability assessments, and having in place well-rehearsed action plans are the distinctive characteristics of organizations that have a strong culture of preparedness.[34]

Tribune Publishing, a highly reputed media organization and owner of the newspaper *Chicago Tribune,* went through a cultural transformation following a 1985 strike by its production unions. The crisis created an opportunity for the organization to reflect on its current state and operating style and craft a new path forward. The management team made a commitment to a customer-focused operating philosophy, to establishing stronger vendor relationships, and to meeting its printing goals. They embraced a more disciplined approach to performance measurement by aligning the system with corporate mission, values, and goals. The cultural transformation results were quite impressive—productivity improved by 25% and the *Chicago Tribune* also realized tens of millions of dollars in annualized advertising revenue savings.[35]

To examine the validity of high-performance cultural traits from the standpoint of cybersecurity governance, data was gathered from primary and secondary sources. A multimethod approach of literature review, focus groups, and expert interviews was used to collect data. Representatives from for-profit and non-profit organizations participated in this study. To ensure a rich and diverse perspective, information security experts from technology user and technology provider firms were interviewed. Industries ranging from healthcare and public health to supply-chain management, higher education, security and information management solutions, and financial technology were in the surveyed sample. Qualitative analysis was used to validate the information security relevancy of the three high-performance cultural traits and also to identify the associated cybersecurity success factors and best practices. These traits and success factors are discussed in the following chapters.

NOTES TO CHAPTER 4 ———————————————

1. Ifinedo, P. (2012). Understanding Information Security Policy Compliance: An Integration of the Theory of Planned Behavior and the Protection Motivation Theory. *Computers and Security*, 31, 83–95.
2. CompTIA. (2018, April 16). *Building a Culture of Cybersecurity: A Guide for Corporate Executives and Board Members*. https://www.comptia.org/content/white-papers/building-a-culture-of-cybersecurity-a-guide-for-corporate-executives-and-board-members
3. Fairfield-Sonn, J. W. (1993). Moving beyond Vision: Fostering Cultural Change in a Bureaucracy. *Journal of Organizational Change Management*, 6(5), 43–55.

4. Quick, J. C. (1992). Crafting an Organization Culture: Herb's Hand at Southwest Airlines. *Organizational Dynamics*, 21(2), 45–56.
5. Schein, E. (1983). The Role of the Founder in Creating Organizational Culture. *Organizational Dynamics*, Summer 1983, 13–28.
6. Barney, J. B. (1986). Organizational Culture: Can It Be a Source of Sustained Competitive Advantage? *Academy of Management Review*, 11, 656–65.
7. Gerstner, L. (2002). *Who Says Elephants Can't Dance?* HarperCollins.
8. Peters, T. J. and Waterman Jr., R.H. (2003). *In Search of Excellence*. HarperCollins.
9. Prajogo, D. I. and McDermott, C. M. (2011). The relationship between multi-dimensional organizational culture and performance. *International Journal of Operations and Production Management*, 31(7), 712–35.
    Kotter, J. P. and Heskett, J. L. (1992). *Corporate Culture and Performance*. The Free Press.
    Sorensen, J. B. (2002). The strength of corporate culture and the reliability of firm performance. *Administrative Science Quarterly*, 47(1), 70–91.
10. Prajogo, D. I. and McDermott, C. M. (2011). The relationship between multi-dimensional organizational culture and performance. *International Journal of Operations and Production Management*, 31(7), 712–35.
11. Sawner, T. E. (2000). *An Empirical Investigation of the Relationship between Organizational Culture and Organizational Performance in a Large Public Sector Organization* [Unpublished doctoral dissertation], The George Washington University.
12. Mannion, R. Davies, H. T. O., & Marshall, M. N. (2005). Cultural Characteristics of 'High' and 'Low' Performing Hospitals. *Journal of Health Organization and Management*, 19(6), 431–39.
13. Gordon, G. G. and DiTomaso, N. (1992). Predicting Corporate Performance from Organizational Culture. *Journal of Management Studies*, 29(6), 783–98.
14. Gcaza, N., von Solms, R., Grobler, M. M., & van Vuuren, J. J. (2017). A General Morphological Analysis: Delineating a Cyber-Security Culture. *Information and Computer Security*, 25(3), 259–78.
15. CompTIA. (2018, April 16). *Building a Culture of Cybersecurity: A Guide for Corporate Executives and Board Members*. https://www.comptia.org/content/white papers/building-a-culture-of-cybersecurity-a-guide-for-corporate-executives-and-board-members
16. Gcaza, N., von Solms, R., Grobler, M. M., & van Vuuren, J. J. (2017). A General Morphological Analysis: Delineating a Cyber-Security Culture. *Information and Computer Security*, 25(3), 259–78.
17. Chang, S. E. and Lin, C. (2007). Exploring Organizational Culture for Information Security Management. *Industrial Management and Data Systems*, 107(3), 438–58.
    Tang, M., Li, M., & Zhang, T. (2016). The Impacts of Organizational Culture on Information Security Culture: A Case Study. *Information Technology Management*, 17, 179–86.
18. Chen, B. (2018, October 21). Fostering a Culture of Cybersecurity. *Forbes*. https://www.forbes.com/sites/forbestechcouncil/2018/08/28/fostering-a-culture-of-cybersecurity/?sh=22c9b940183a
19. Roberts, K. (1990). New Challenges in Organization Research: High Reliability Organizations. *Industrial Crisis Quarterly*, 3, 111–25.

Roberts, K. and Rousseau, D. M. (1989). Research in Nearly Failure-Free, High-Reliability Organizations: Having the Bubble. *IEEE Transactions on Engineering Management*, 36(2), 132–39.

Pidgeon, N. F. (1991). Safety Culture and Risk Management in Organizations. *Journal of Cross-Cultural Psychology*, 22(1), 129–40.

Roberts, K. and Rousseau, D. M. Research in Nearly Failure-Free, High-Reliability Organizations: Having the Bubble. *IEEE Transactions on Engineering Management* 36(2), 132–39.

20. Harnish, R. (2017, September 21). What It Means to Have a Culture of Cyber-security. *Forbes*. https://www.forbes.com/sites/forbestechcouncil/2017/09/21/what-it-means-to-have-a-culture-of-cybersecurity/?sh=43800de1efd1

21. Zadelhoff, M. V. (2016, September 19). The Biggest Cybersecurity Threats Are Inside Your Company. *Harvard Business Review*, 2–4.

22. Hirschi T. (1969). *Causes of delinquency*. University of California Press.

23. Chang, S. E. and Lin, C. (2007). Exploring organizational culture for information security management. *Industrial Management and Data Systems*, 107(3), 438–58.

24. Chen, B. (2018, October 21). Fostering a Culture of Cybersecurity. *Forbes*. https://www.forbes.com/sites/forbestechcouncil/2018/08/28/fostering-a-culture-of-cybersecurity/?sh=22c9b940183a

25. Veiga, A. D. (2016). Comparing the Information Security Culture of Employees Who Had Read the Information Security Policy and Those Who Had Not. *Information and Computer Security*, 24(2), 139–51.

26. Sager, T. (2020, April 2). Developing a Culture of Cybersecurity with the CIS Controls. *Center for Internet Security*. Retrieved April 2, 2020 from https://www.cisecurity.org/blog/developing-a-culture-of-cybersecurity-with-the-cis-controls/

27. Rosenthal, B. (2020, April 2). Why and How to Create a Culture of Cybersecurity. *National Cybersecurity Alliance*. Retrieved April 2, 2020 from https://staysafeon-line.org/blog/createculture-cybersecurity/

28. Medeiros, J. J. and Pinto, W. (2009). High Reliability Organizations and Operational Risk Management. *Brazilian Business Review*, 6(2), May–August 2009, 165–80.

29. Winnefeld Jr., J. A., Kirchhoff, C., & Upton, D. M. Cybersecurity's Human Factor: Lessons from the Pentagon. *Harvard Business Review*, September 2015, 1–11.

30. Ibid.

31. Pfeffer, J. and Anderson, M. (2009, March 16). *Kimberley-Clark Andean Region: Creating a Winning Culture*. Stanford Graduate School of Business Case.

32. Narayanan, V. G. and Muthuram, V. (2014, March 23). *Building a High Performance Culture at IDFC*. Harvard Business School Case.

33. Kapucu, N. (2008). Culture of Preparedness: Household Disaster Preparedness. *Disaster Prevention and Management*, 17(4), 526–35.

34. Pielke Sr., R. A. and Pielke Jr., R. A. (1997). *Hurricanes: Their Nature and Impact on Society*. Wiley Publishing.

35. Frame, R. M., Nielsen, W. R., & Pate, L. E. (1989). Crafting Excellence Out of Crisis: Organizational Transformation at the Chicago Tribune. *Journal of Applied Behavioral Science*, 25(2), 109–22.

CHAPTER

5

Commitment

Cyber threats present a unique challenge and dilemma for organizations. No amount of investment or level of preparedness can ensure complete immunization from such attacks. But that uncertainty cannot justify a reactive or chaotic approach to the problem. If media reports are to be believed, the first attack is often not good enough for many organizations to further shore up their defenses. As described in the following vignette, it took multiple attacks for UnityPoint Health, one of the largest medical care providers in the United States, to boost its information security defense mechanisms.

Unitypoint Health Falls Prey to Multiple Phishing Attack

UnityPoint Health was the target of multiple phishing attacks in 2018. The first breach, which happened in April 2018, compromised staff email accounts and exposed 16,000 patient records. In July, UnityPoint Health systems was hacked again and this time 1.4 million patient records were accessed. Sensitive data ranging from patient identity and contact information to Social Security numbers, credit card records, treatment details, lab results, and insurance data were stolen.

According to law enforcement and forensic investigators, the hackers had targeted UnityPoint Health's business email systems. Numerous phishing emails were sent, and one employee fell for the messages that seemed to be coming from an executive of the healthcare organization. Once the malware had been installed, the perpetrators gained access to the internal email accounts for almost three weeks. They were trying to divert vendor and payroll payments to their own accounts.

Surprisingly, it took multiple attacks for UnityPoint to implement security measures such as conducting mandatory phishing education, adding monitoring and detection tools, and implementing multifactor authentication.[1] A class action lawsuit was filed against the company (after the first

(Continued)

successful phishing attack), and the plaintiffs alleged that the company was negligent in adequately securing sensitive patient records and had waited more than two months to notify the victims.

The risk of not taking necessary precautionary measures is significant. The very existence of an organization can be in jeopardy as a result of a major breach. So management must be genuinely and completely committed to securing the organization.

Developing and successfully implementing a robust and comprehensive security plan demand a high level of sustained commitment at all organizational levels and even among the value chain partners. Although the tone has to be set at the top, every organizational member must do their part to keep the organization secure. Humans continue to be both the strongest and weakest link of a cyber defense system. So, without their genuine commitment, an organization won't be successful in mitigating risks. Qualitative analysis of primary and secondary data reveals seven cybersecurity readiness success factors (as shown in Figure 14) that are reflective of a high level of commitment. Each of them is discussed below.

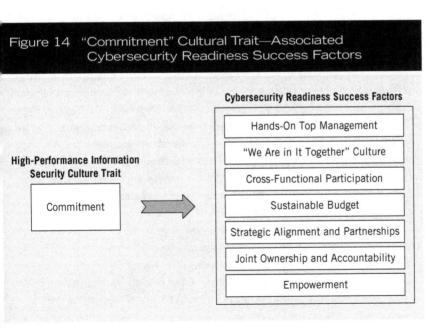

Figure 14 "Commitment" Cultural Trait—Associated Cybersecurity Readiness Success Factors

Cybersecurity Readiness Success Factors

High-Performance Information Security Culture Trait

Commitment

- Hands-On Top Management
- "We Are in It Together" Culture
- Cross-Functional Participation
- Sustainable Budget
- Strategic Alignment and Partnerships
- Joint Ownership and Accountability
- Empowerment

5.1 Hands-On Top Management

For cybersecurity governance to be truly effective, top management needs to be very hands-on in its approach—from making every effort to learn about the organization's vulnerability points and defense mechanisms to participating in security review discussions and proactively engaging with, and serving on, different security governance committees. A suggested best practice for the C-suite executives is to participate in incident-response simulated exercises, so they can gain a better understanding of the types of attacks, the appropriate responses, roles, and cost implications. Even though simulated, such firsthand experience can go a long way in establishing a top-down security-focused culture.[2] The 2018 Information Systems Audit and Control Association (ISACA) report emphasizes the need for senior leadership to serve as champions and evangelists of cybersecurity preparedness. The report states:

> Organizations with successful cybersecurity cultures tend to have C-suite executives who reinforce behavioral norms when they lead by example. They appoint—or become—a senior-level champion, participate in town hall discussions, allocate budgetary support, hire consultants, and do the research to assess the enterprise's risk and capabilities.[3]

It is quite alarming when a survey reveals that only 40% of C-level executives have an in-depth understanding of cybersecurity protocols.[4] This finding is consistent with anecdotal evidence and other research reports, which suggest that top management does not take the lead, ownership, or responsibility in ensuring strong cybersecurity governance.[5] A study involving the healthcare industry confirmed this lack of senior leadership attention to data security strategies. The majority of respondents said that cybersecurity strategy discussion is never on the board of directors' meeting agenda.[6] Another study reports that despite being briefed regularly on cybersecurity state of affairs, board of directors of companies do not act promptly or decisively. They are reactive in their stance and approach to cybersecurity incidents.[7]

Senior leadership, especially the CEO, can't afford to take a backseat when it comes to cyber governance. They have to be in the driver's seat and knowledgeable about cybersecurity matters. Ultimately, the CEO is answerable to various stakeholders, including governing bodies such as the U.S. Congress. Richard Smith, former CEO of Equifax, was called in to testify before the House Energy and Commerce Committee and respond to breach-related questions.[8]

Not only is the reputation of the senior leadership on the line but also their jobs. The Equifax CEO, along with several other senior executives, resigned after a massive breach that compromised data on 143 million customers. Target Corp's CEO and chief information officer (CIO) resigned after the company and its board of directors were sued by a shareholder for compromising the personal information of more than 60 million customers.[9]

Legal sanctions in the form of stiff penalties and potential jail time should also motivate top management to actively engage in securing strategic assets. To further bolster information security governance, Senator Ron Wyden of Oregon introduced the Consumer Data Protection Act (CDPA) bill that proposes jail time of up to 20 years for executives who are found guilty of gross negligence—"knowingly signing off on incorrect or inaccurate annual certifications of their companies' datasecurity practices."[10] Appendix 4 provides a summary of the sanctions and penalties associated with the different cybersecurity and privacy laws and regulations.

A survey of the National Association of the Board of Directors (NACD) found the majority of respondents recognizing the adverse impact of cyberattacks not only on stock prices but also on the reputation of the company and its board of directors.[11]

Though the bar for convicting a board of directors is quite high, that does not absolve board members from their responsibility of providing informed oversight. There is a growing recognition that

> cybersecurity can no longer be the concern of just the IT department. Within organizations, it needs to be everyone's business—including the board's.[12]

When top management proactively takes every possible precaution to protect sensitive data because it is the right thing to do and not because there is a legislative requirement, that's when the organization takes a huge step forward in earning customer confidence and trust.

The senior leadership needs to support every aspect of cybersecurity governance—from strategic planning to education and training, hiring of talent, mobilizing organization-wide support, instituting appropriate roles and responsibilities, and remediating vulnerabilities. They need to recognize that cybersecurity investment is a strategic priority, necessity, and competency.[13] No stone should be left unturned, so the organization is able to effectively answer the question that stakeholders are likely to ask after a successful attack: "What did this institution do to prepare?"

Following is a set of guiding questions to gauge the extent of top management involvement and support.

Top Management Involvement and Support: Guiding Questions

1. Is top management intimately familiar with the organization's security vulnerability points?

2. Is top management intimately familiar with the organization's information security defense mechanisms?

3. Is top management actively engaged in cybersecurity planning and strategizing?

4. Do members of the top management team serve on cybersecurity governance committees?

5. Does top management take the lead, ownership, or responsibility in ensuring strong cybersecurity governance?

6. Does the senior leadership support the following aspects of cybersecurity governance?

   a. Strategic planning

   b. Education and training

   c. Hiring of talent

   d. Mobilizing organization-wide support

   e. Instituting appropriate roles and responsibilities, and

   f. Remediation of vulnerabilities

5.2 "We-Are-in-It-Together" Culture

While top management needs to lead the way, information security needs to be everyone's concern. Strong partnerships need to be forged among all stakeholders. Creating a "We Are in It Together" culture is a very important success factor, especially in a highly mobile and global environment where employees equipped with mobile devices are traveling around the world and companies are partnering with third-party service providers. So, not only do employees of an organization have to do their part, even business partners must be on board with the security plans and protocols. A traditional technology-centric "protect the perimeter" approach is no longer adequate to deal with the borderless and evolving scope of cyber threats and attacks.[14]

Developing and sustaining the "togetherness" mindset is easier said than done. A multipronged approach of creating awareness, building emotional capital, and incentivizing behavior is recommended. Through effective and sustained communication, organizational members must be made aware of how breaches happen, the direct and indirect consequences (to them) of the attacks, and what they can do to protect and secure critical data and systems. Emotional capital is built over a period of time by creating a work environment where employees a) feel valued and develop a sense of belonging, b) take pride in their work, c) are having fun, and d) perceive leadership to be genuine and authentic.[15]

In organizations that exude a culture of camaraderie and cohesion, everyone is driven, motivated, and committed to learn and follow through with the prescribed protection, defense, and recovery procedures.[16]

Following is a set of questions to evaluate organization-wide commitment and togetherness to secure digital assets.

"We-Are-in-It-Together" Culture: Guiding Questions

1. Are employees eager and motivated to participate in information security training and awareness programs?

2. Are employees eager and motivated to join information security initiative teams?

3. Do the results of tests indicate motivated employees who are striving hard to learn and apply the learned security awareness skills?

4. Are supply chain partners and service providers eager and motivated to comply with the prescribed information security plans and protocols?

5.3 Cross-Functional Participation

A successful and effective cybersecurity program cannot be developed or executed solely by the IT or information security function. Every aspect of cyber governance—from risk assessment to strategy formulation and alignment, vulnerability evaluation, implementation of controls, data classification and governance, software development, training, disaster recovery planning, and committee oversight—can benefit from strong cross-functional participation.

Partnership among representatives from business, information systems, legal, ethics, and compliance is key to developing a comprehensive understanding of an organization's cyber risk exposure and tolerance. Representatives from different functions must also weigh in on the information security risk implications associated with different strategic and operational business initiatives.

Such cross-functional participation is also essential for an in-depth assessment of vulnerabilities and determination and implementation of appropriate controls. For instance, Human Resources will work closely with the security team to prevent unauthorized access and also the prompt revocation of access privileges as soon as employment is terminated. Legal will provide guidance and oversight to ensure the regulatory guidelines and compliance requirements are being followed.[17]

When it comes to data sensitivity classification and prioritization, input from the various functional units is essential. Determining data protection roles, responsibilities, and ownership must also be a collaborative endeavor, especially if the goal is to mobilize organization-wide support and involvement.

Effective data governance is contingent on a good working relationship among data owners, stewards, and custodians. Senior-level business executives generally serve as the data owner for a particular data set relating to their organizational function. While they are responsible and accountable for data security, privacy, and quality, the day-to-day governance activities such as access, storage, and backup decisions are handled by the data stewards, who are the subordinates of the data owners. The IT staff play the role of data custodians and are responsible for executing the data governance decisions ranging from managing user access to complying with regulations and standards; maintaining appropriate data classification and security levels; and running systems, networks, and servers. Thus, business and IT must work in close cooperation to secure organizational data.

In acquisition and divestiture situations, security professionals and business executives (across business functions) from involved organizations must work together to evaluate data protection implications and make prudent calls on tightening controls, eliminating redundancies, and ensuring compatibility.

In many companies, there exists a huge disconnect between the security and development teams. While the developers are encouraged and incentivized to speed up the software creation process, the security team is required to ensure the product is robust and has little or no vulnerabilities. As one particular industry report highlighted, "Many information security engineers don't understand software development—and most software developers don't understand security. Developers and their managers are focused on delivering features and meeting time-to-market expectations, rather than on making sure that software is secure."[18] Prior research finds that the application layer (and not network layer) is the real weak spot and rushing the development and implementation of applications is adding to the security vulnerability problem.[19] So it is imperative that these two very important functions develop a high level of awareness and respect for each other's work and partner up to produce high-quality and secure software.

Disaster recovery planning is another security activity that requires significant coordination and collaboration among all organizational units. Information security teams must also work hand-in-hand with business units to determine and customize training requirements. Information governance committees providing oversight to various information security initiatives will also benefit from a strong partnership between senior business and technology leaders.

Thus, through cross-functional involvement, the silo mindset is likely to be replaced with a more holistic view of the organization's information security needs. Such shared understanding is essential for creating and sustaining a truly engaged and committed security culture. Following are guiding questions to assess the extent of cross-functional participation.

Cross-Functional Participation: Guiding Questions

1. Is there cross-functional involvement in cyber governance activities such as:

   a. risk assessment

   b. cybersecurity strategy formulation and alignment

   c. vulnerability evaluation

   d. implementation of controls

   e. data classification and governance

   f. software development

   g. training

   h. disaster recovering planning

   i. oversight committees

2. Are representatives from the following functions actively involved in cyber governance activities (stated above)?

    a. Operations/Manufacturing

    b. Human Resources

    c. Marketing and Sales

    d. Logistics

    e. Procurement

    f. Legal

    g. Accounting

    h. Others (please specify)

5.4 Sustainable Budget

Is your organization spending enough on cybersecurity? How much is enough? These are million-dollar questions, the answers to which are likely to vary across firms and industries. Investing in cybersecurity is seldom viewed as an exciting proposition, for there are no "real" returns in terms of revenue or profits. There is also no guarantee of immunity from attacks. So, it is not surprising when research reports suggest that security budgets are below par. A study of the cybersecurity state of affairs in the public sector reveals that insufficient funding is one of the three challenges plaguing state and local governments since.[20] A healthcare industry–focused study finds that the IT security budget is about 3% of the total annual IT organizational budget and has remained stagnant since 2016.[21] One of the expert respondents aptly summed up the funding challenge—"justifying the ROI is always a challenge. There is only so much funding you get based on FUD (fear, uncertainty, and doubt)."

However, lack of adequate investments could increase vulnerability and susceptibility to attacks, which in turn could jeopardize organizational success and survival. Deciding on a cybersecurity budget and sustaining it over a period of time are thus challenges that firms must face head-on. The funding must be sustained over the long term, as it takes time to build robust defense capabilities. Organizational commitment toward a strong cybersecurity defense is also reflected in the allocated funding.

With the number of data breaches escalating in the United States and with CEOs losing their jobs over successful attacks, there is a growing recognition of the significance of cybersecurity investments. According to a 2017 *Wall Street Journal* report, cybersecurity is emerging as the top investment focus for U.S. CEOs. So it is reasonable to hope that having in place a sustained and adequate budget for cybersecurity management could cease to be a major hurdle and become an intrinsic part of an organization's culture of commitment.

Following is a set of questions for gauging organizational commitment to providing a sustainable cybersecurity budget.

Sustainable Budget: Guiding Questions

1. To what extent is investment in cybersecurity initiatives considered strategic?

2. To what extent is top management committed to adequately funding cybersecurity initiatives?

3. During the last five years, has cybersecurity funding been on the rise or decline?

4. During the last 12 months, how much has been invested on external resources (such as consultants and third-party service providers) to develop and implement cybersecurity initiatives?

5. During the last 12 months, how much has been invested in internal resources (such as new hires, training, etc.) to develop and implement cybersecurity initiatives?

6. During the last 12 months, how much time has been invested in understanding or managing the implementation of policies and procedures related to cybersecurity?

5.5 Strategic Alignment and Partnerships

A strategic and mature approach to securing the organization is contingent upon effective alignment with the overall goals and priorities of the organization. Such alignment needs to first happen at the top levels of the organization. The senior leadership must view cybersecurity as a strategic necessity and capability, to provide the necessary support and championing.

Information security leaders must also recognize that there is more to the organization than security. While securing data and related assets is critical, the controls should not become an impediment to growth and operating efficiency. Finding the right balance and alignment between business and security goals is key.

One way of achieving this alignment is by requiring all security initiatives be owned by leaders of business units. It is through direct involvement and participation that business leaders will be able to shape the information security agenda for the organization and also support the implementation of necessary controls. Another alignment mechanism is the process for evaluating and selecting information security projects. A business case must be made for the proposed project, where the proposer provides a quantitative and qualitative justification for the security investment. While the quantitative impact analysis will focus on business value creation, the qualitative description will highlight how the proposed security measures will enhance the organization's ability to realize its stated mission and goals.

Alignment is also achieved when data security implications feature in every strategic and operational decision-making process. To effectively integrate information security into governance processes and structures, information security leaders must have a seat on the various governance committees such as information governance committee, data governance committee, risk management committee, board of directors, and board of trustees.

Partnering with the right set of third-party service providers is also critical to effective cybersecurity governance. There are a variety of security services available, ranging from virtual private networking (VPN), to vulnerability detection, network monitoring, identity access management, AI-driven malware detection, cloud-based security information-and-event-management (SIEM) systems, penetration testing, and training. Identifying, selecting, and managing the vendors that meet organizational security standards and expectations are centric to effective cyber governance. A recent study recommended that government agencies team up with the corporate sector and educational institutions to resolve their talent and competency shortage issues.[22]

Following is a set of questions for assessing strategic alignment and partnership.

5.6 Joint Ownership and Accountability

High-performing organizational cultures recognize that cybersecurity is a business issue of strategic significance; it is not just a technology matter that can be outsourced to a security team within or outside the company. Every phase and aspect of cyber governance must have senior-level executives sponsoring and owning the initiatives along with the technology leaders.[23] By establishing milestones and tollgates, cybersecurity preparedness activities can be closely monitored. It is also worth adopting an appropriate awards system that recognizes outstanding data security efforts and practices on the part of organizational members and units.

The Choice Hotels data breach was caused by vendor negligence. The hotel chain's customer data were sitting on the vendor server without protection for four days. Approximately 700,000 customer records were stolen, and the hackers were seeking a ransom to return control of the customer database. Though the vendor was fired, the action does not remedy the harm caused to the victims. With their identities stolen, the affected customers were susceptible to a variety of cyber threats ranging from phishing attacks to fraudulent account openings and credit card transactions. Emphasizing the need for shared responsibility and commitment, Elad Shapira, a senior executive and security expert, advised that "companies need to be aware that outsourcing a business unit to a third party does not relieve them also from the security burden. They need to ensure that their partner has the right level of security before engaging with them, and if already engaged with them, to demand a minimum-security standard."[24]

Businesses and their IT service providers should come to a clear understanding on data protection and ownership expectations and codify that commitment in the form of a service level agreement (SLA). Generally, a customer will seek the highest level of protection and uninhibited ownership rights on the data stored and managed by third-party service providers. The SLA provisions must clearly spell out the vendor's rights and responsibilities in managing and using client data and also the data purge policy. For instance, the contract language should specify the period for which client data can be stored before deletion, especially after the service relationship ends.

The European Central Bank suffered a breach when the Banks' Integrated Reporting Dictionary (BIRD) website was compromised. An external service provider was hosting the site. Equally alarming is that the breach was not detected until several months after the attack, during routine maintenance work.[25] Shared accountability might have motivated the vendor to be more vigilant and put in place robust access controls.

Bangladesh Bank was the victim of a major heist when $81M was siphoned off by intruders to private accounts held in some Asian banks. By stealing access credentials to the SWIFT (Society for Worldwide Interbank Financial Telecommunication) platform, the perpetrators were able to direct the Federal Reserve Bank of New York to automatically execute the fund transfer. Neither SWIFT nor the Federal Reserve Bank of New York was willing to accept any responsibility or blame for the attack.[26]

Some questions to gauge organizational commitment toward joint ownership and responsibility are presented below.

Joint Ownership and Accountability: Guiding Questions

1. To what extent are cybersecurity planning and implementation teams headed by senior business executives?

2. To what extent are senior level business executives sponsoring and owning cyber governance initiatives?

(Continued)

(Continued)

3. Is a tollgate approach in place to manage the implementation of cybersecurity programs?

4. Is senior leadership sign-off required before a cybersecurity project can move on to the next phase?

5. Do performance review systems include assessment of cybersecurity involvement and effectiveness?

6. To what extent do SLA agreements with business partners and vendors include explicit data protection expectations and consequences for noncompliance?

5.7 Empowerment

Appointing and empowering the chief information security officer (CISO) is a definite reflection of commitment and a step in the right direction toward creating and maintaining a security-focused culture.[27] Chief security officer and director of information security are other common titles for the CISO role. Though there are different opinions and perspectives on whether the CISO should report to the CIO or the CEO, there can be no disagreement on appropriately equipping the CISO with resources and decision-making powers so they can be effective.[28]

In many organizations, the CISO reports to the CIO and the information security function is part of the overall IT function. Considering that technology is an enabler of security measures, housing those measures within the IT function makes sense. In such a structural arrangement, however, information security function fades into the background from a profile and significance standpoint.[29] Also, such an arrangement makes it politically difficult for the security personnel to blow the whistle on IT personnel. To maintain the independence and objectivity of the security function and enhance its strategic significance, the CISO should have their own budget and report directly to the CEO.[30] To maintain a certain degree of independence, in some organizations the CISO reports to the audit committee or the risk management committee.

There is growing recognition that the CISO is much more than a risk or technology officer. They are business enablers and must be involved in strategic and value creation activities.[31] Considering that every business initiative has information security implications, it is important for the CISO to be intimately familiar with the business model and operations. Such awareness and knowledge will help craft and implement business-friendly security strategies and policies. Business-friendly does not imply being soft on security measures; the idea is to strike the right posture that makes it feasible to take informed risks. Whether it is the development and implementation of artificial intelligence–enabled applications, leveraging the cloud platform, deploying Internet of Things (IoT) devices, or establishing a highly mobile environment, the CISO has a significant partnering role in enabling such digitization initiatives. Thus, CISOs must be empowered to facilitate innovation, actively engage in all strategic initiatives, and be treated as a peer at the C-level.

Ideally, the CISO should be part of the C-level team or at least have direct access to the top management. One recommended best practice is for top management to proactively engage with and involve the CISO in every business initiative. It is important to recognize that cybersecurity is not an IT issue but a business issue. Structural mechanisms need to be in place for business/operating units to partner with the security and IT team to deal with cyber threats and challenges. A 2016 survey found that in 31% of the companies represented in the sample, there was no designated leader with the sole focus on cybersecurity.[32] Following is a set of questions to assess the extent to which the CISO is empowered to succeed.

Empowerment: Guiding Questions

1. To what extent is the CISO involved in the strategic decision-making processes?

2. Does the CISO report directly to the CEO?

3. Does the CISO report directly to the audit committee?

4. Does the CISO report directly to the risk management committee?

5. Is the CISO part of the senior leadership team?

6. Is the CISO provided an independent operating budget?

In summary, organizational commitment for effective cybersecurity governance requires active involvement and support of all organizational members including business partners. Top management is expected to set the tone and lead by example. Commitment is also reflected in the willingness to provide sustained financial and other forms of support. A focused and integrated approach to cybersecurity governance is yet another important dimension of commitment. It is through strategic alignment and partnership that an organization can present a unified front in securing sensitive information and other strategic organizational assets. Yet another aspect of commitment is when all organizational members (including business partners) have a stake in the game—a certain level of responsibility and accountability to protect critical data and systems. Finally, the leadership must commit to helping the chief information security officer (CISO) and their team succeed. The CISO should not be treated as a scapegoat, that is, someone to put blame on when there is a breach.

NOTES TO CHAPTER 5 —————————

1. Donovan, F. (2018, July 31). Phishing Attack Exposes PHI of 1.4M UnityPoint Health Patients. *Health IT Security*. Retrieved September 9, 2019 from https://healthitsecurity.com/news/phishing-attack-exposes-phi-of-1.4m-unitypoint-health-patients#:~:text=July%2031%2C%202018%20%2D%20Iowa%2D,may%20have%20compromised%20their%20PHI.&text=Electronic%20medical%20record%20and%20patient,in%20the%20attack%2C%20stressed%20UnityPoint.
2. McKinty, C. (2017, April 26). The C-Suite and IT-Need to Get on the Same Page on Cybersecurity. *Harvard Business Review*, 2–4.
3. "Narrowing the Culture Gap for Better Business Results," ISACA 2018 report.
4. Sweeney, B. (2016, September 13). Cybersecurity Is Every Executive's Job. *Harvard Business Review*, 2–4.
5. Visner, C. (2016, November 15). Cybersecurity Is Everyone's Responsibility—And It Starts at the Top. *CSO*. Retrieved December 11, 2020 from https://www.csoonline.com/article/3140924/cybersecurity-is-everyones-responsibility-and-it-starts-at-the-top.html
6. HIMSS. (2016, March 30). *"Addressing Healthcare Cybersecurity Strategically."* https://www.himsslearn.org/addressing-healthcare-cybersecurity-strategically
7. Parent, M. Murray, G., & Beatty, D. R. (2019, September 1). Act, Don't React: A Leader's Guide to Cybersecutiry. *Rotman Management Magazine*, 69–73.
8. Chalfant, M. (2017, September 13). Equifax CEO Formally Called to Testify before Congress. *The Hill*. https://thehill.com/policy/cybersecurity/350517-equifax-ceo-formally-called-to-testify-before-congress
9. Arnold, C. (2017, September 26). *Equifax CEO Richard Smith Resigns after Backlash over Massive Data Breach*. NPR. Retrieved August 10, 2019 from https://thehill.com/policy/cybersecurity/350517-equifax-ceo-formally-called-to-testify-before-congress
10. Chatterjee, D. (2019, February 17). Should Executives Go to Jail over Cybersecurity Breaches? *Journal of Organizational Computing and Electronic Commerce*, 1–3.

11. Rothrock, R. A., Kaplan, J., and Van der Oord, F. (2018). The Board's Role in Managing Cybersecurity Risks. *MIT Sloan Management Review*, Winter 2018, 12–15.

12. Rothrock, R. A., Kaplan, J., & and Van Der Oord, F. (2018). The Board's Role in Managing Cybersecurity Risks. *MIT Sloan Management Review*, 59 (2),12–15.

13. Bailey, T., Kaplan, J., & and Rezek, C. (2014, June 20). Why Senior Leaders Are the Front Line against Cyberattacks. *McKinsey & Company*.

14. Bailey, T., Del Miglio, A., & and Richter, W. (2014, May). The Rising Strategic Risks of Cyberattacks. *McKinsey Quarterly*, 1–6.

15. Huy, Q. and Shipilov, A. (2012). The Key to Social Media Success within Organizations. *MIT Sloan Management Review*, 54(1), Fall 2012, 74–81.

16. Visner, C. (2016, November 15). Cybersecurity Is Everyone's Responsibility— And It Starts at the Top. CSO. Retrieved December 11, 2020 from https://www .csoonline.com/article/3140924/cybersecurity-is-everyones-responsibility-and-it- starts-at-the-top.htm

17. Nagele-Piazza, L. (2018, November 28). Create a Cross-Functional Team to Combat Data Security. *SHRM*. Retrieved June 15 2019 from https://www.shrm .org/resourcesandtools/hr-topics/technology/pages/cross-functional-team-to- combat-data-security-issues.aspx

18. Bird, J., Johnson, E., & Kim, F. (2015). *State of Application Security: Closing the Gap*. SANS Institute Report. Retrieved July 17, 2020 from https://techbeacon .com/sites/default/files/gated_asset/sans-state-application-security-2015-report- survey-closing-gap_0.pdf

19. Morgan, S. (2015, September 2). Is Poor Software Development the Biggest Cyber Security Threat? *CSO Online*. Retrieved December 11, 2020 from https:// www.csoonline.com/article/2978858/is-poor-software-development-the- biggest-cyber-threat.html#:~:text=The%20U.S.%20Department%20of%20 Homeland,biggest%20cyber%20threat%20of%20all.&text=%5B%20Keep%20 up%20with%208%20hot,(and%204%20going%20cold)
Quevedo, A. (2016, September 21). How Cybersecurity Teams Can Convince the C-Suite of Their Value. *Harvard Business Review*, 2–5.

20. Ward, M. and Subramanium, S. (2018). *States at risk: The cybersecurity impera- tive in uncertain times*. 2020 Deloitte-NASCIO Cybersecurity Study. Retrieved July 18, 2020 from https://www2.deloitte.com/content/dam/insights/us/articles/ 6899_nascio/DI_NASCIO_interactive.pdf

21. Leventhal, R. (2018, March 16). Cyber Attacks Increase as IT Security Budgeting Remains Static, Report Finds. *Healthcare Innovation*. Retrieved May 14, 2018 from https://www.hcinnovationgroup.com/cybersecurity/news/13030218/cyber- attacks-increase-as-it-security-budgeting-remains-static-report-finds

22. Ward, M. and Subramanium, S. (2018). *States at risk: The cybersecurity imperative in uncertain times*. 2020 Deloitte-NASCIO Cybersecurity Study. Retrieved July 18, 2020 from https://www2.deloitte.com/content/dam/insights/us/articles/6899_ nascio/DI_NASCIO_interactive.pdf

23. Dang-Pham, D., Pittayachawan, S., and Bruno, V. (2016). "Impacts of Security Climate on Employees' Sharing of Security Advice and Troubleshooting: Empirical Networks," *Business Horizons*, 59, 571–584.

24. Shapira, E. quoted in Seals, T. (2019, August 15). Choice Hotels Breach Showcases Need for Shared Responsibility Model. *Threat Post*. Retrieved August 18, 2019 from

https://threatpost.com/choice-hotels-breach-shared-responsibility-model/147383/

25. Winder, D. (2019, August 16). European Central Bank Breach: ECB Confirms Hack and Shuts Down Website. *Forbes*. Retrieved August 19, 2019 from https://www.forbes.com/sites/daveywinder/2019/08/16/european-central-bank-breach-ecb-confirms-hack-and-shuts-down-website/?sh=2a0fe186594b

26. Zetter, K. (2016, May 17). That Insane, $81M Bangladesh Bank Heist? Here's What We Know. *Wired*. Retrieved July 9, 2020 from https://www.wired.com/2016/05/insane-81m-bangladesh-bank-heist-heres-know/

27. Dang-Pham, D., Pittayachawan, S., & Bruno, V. (2016). Impacts of security climate on employees' sharing of security advice and troubleshooting: Empirical networks. *Business Horizons*, 59(6), 571–584.

28. Optiv. (2014, November 12). *Empowering the CISO*. Retrieved June 19, 2019 from https://www.optiv.com/blog/empowering-the-ciso

29. Hooper, V. and McKissack, J. (2016). The Emerging Role of the CISO. *Business Horizons*, 59, 585–91.

30. Dunn, B. (2019, March 15). The Evolving Role of the Federal CISO in 2019. *Morning Consult*, Retrieved June 19, 2019 from https://morningconsult.com/opinions/the-evolving-role-of-the-federal-ciso-in-2019/

31. Somaini, J. (2018, July 31). The Evolving Role of the CISO: From Risk Manager to Business Enabler. *SecurityRoundtable.org*. Retrieved August 19, 2018, https://www.securityroundtable.org/evolving-role-of-the-ciso-risk-manager-to-business-enabler/

32. Bell, G. (2016, October 25). Good Cybersecurity Doesn't Try to Prevent Every Attack. *Harvard Business Review*, 2–4.

CHAPTER

6

Preparedness

Preparedness refers to an organization's game plan and execution mechanism to secure five things: data, networks, devices, locations, and people. Time and again, organizations are found wanting in their level of preparation and face gross negligence charges in the court of law. According to experts, to seek legal restitution, the plaintiff organization must be able to prove it had strong multi-factor authentication (MFA) in place, robust authorization mechanisms, flawless auditing systems, and were in compliance with relevant laws and regulations.[1] This chapter provides guidance on adopting a systematic and thorough approach to information security management. It begins with a vignette that describes a major breach incident where Marriott International faced a class-action lawsuit and was charged with lack of preparedness and negligence.

The Marriott Breach That Exposed 500 Million Applicants and Customer Information

On November 30, 2018, Marriott International suffered a massive data breach that compromised about 500 million customer records. Data ranging from customer contact information to passport numbers, payment card details, Starwood loyalty account information, and reservation information was accessed. While some of the personally identifiable information was encrypted, the company is not sure if the hackers also stole the decryption codes.[2]

An IT company managing the Starwood guest reservation database detected the breach and informed Marriott on September 8.[3] Further investigations revealed that a malware, a remote access Trojan (RAT), was on the Starwood IT system. This malicious code enables hackers to stealthily gain access to a system and then control the computer.

One wonders how prepared Marriott was to deal with such attacks. Did it have a multi-factor authentication system in place? Did it regularly conduct penetration testing to detect and fix its vulnerabilities? Furthermore,

(Continued)

(Continued)

it took Marriott almost three months to acknowledge the breach and inform its customers. Not surprisingly, a federal class-action lawsuit has been filed against the company; the plaintiffs have claimed that "Marriott did not adequately protect guest information before the breach and, once the breach had been discovered, 'failed to provide timely, accurate, and adequate notice' to guests whose information may have been obtained by hackers."[4]

Honesty, transparency, and promptness are key to damage control and Marriott failed to exhibit those traits when dealing with this situation. According to one cyber expert, "The key to rebuilding confidence is to be 'upfront, open and honest' from the start: 'This builds trust in a company.'"

So, what does it take to achieve a high level of information security preparedness? This section draws upon research findings and information security management frameworks and standards such as National Institute of Standards and Technology (NIST), ISO 27001, and Payment Card Industry-Data Security Standard (PCI-DSS) to identify and discuss the success factors (Figure 15) associated with a highly prepared organization. These factors relate to four key dimensions of preparedness—identify, protect, detect, and respond and recover.

6.1 Identify

The identify phase of the security preparedness process entails review, reflection, and assessment of an organization's role and purpose, risk tolerance and exposure levels, and types of vulnerabilities. Each of these elements is discussed in the following subsections.

6.1.1 Organizational Role Recognition

An effective cybersecurity strategy cannot be created in a vacuum. It must be developed in relation to the organization's role in the broader business environment. For instance, public and public-sector organizations that support critical infrastructure services (such as water, energy, financial services, health care, and transportation) must be extra vigilant and take a very responsible and thorough approach to cybersecurity preparedness. Especially those industries that rely on industrial control systems (ICS) and other operational technologies are extremely vulnerable to nation-state attacks conducted by well-funded and skilled teams of cybercriminals.

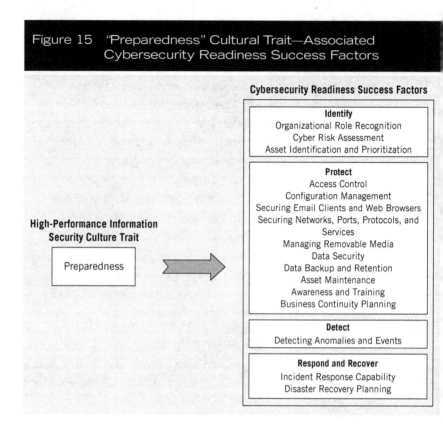

Relentless attack on critical infrastructure firms and industries is a global phenomenon. The Ukrainian power grid was compromised in 2015, causing power disruption for several hours. The same grid was again breached in 2016 and this time the attackers were able to break into the operational environment. Saudi Arabia's national oil company Aramco has been attacked several times since 2012. Banks in Asia and Latin America have also been compromised over the years. The WannaCry ransomware attack in 2017 caused significant disruption and damage to Britain's National Health Services. Energy and transport organizations in Europe, the United States, Russia, and Ukraine were hit by the virus NotPetyamalware in 2017. SCADA systems in Ukraine were targeted with VPNFilter malware in 2018.[5] According to David Emm, principal security researcher, Kaspersky Lab, "the difference between an attack on a single organization and an attack on critical national infrastructure is there could be a real-world effect across an entire country."[6]

Given the volume of sensitive data handled by public sector organizations, it is not surprising that they are the targets of constant attacks. Nothing would please the nation-state attackers more than compromising the electricity grid, contaminating the water supply, or causing the financial markets to fail. A global study found several vulnerabilities and challenges faced by government organizations. These include lack of highly skilled security personnel, inadequate budget, and reliance on manual processes. The President's National Infrastructure Advisory Council was tasked with assessing the cybersecurity defense capabilities of the public and private sector. Based on a "review of hundreds of studies and interviews with 38 cyber and industry experts," the council came to the following conclusion in its 2017 report:

> We believe the U.S. government and private sector collectively have the tremendous cyber capabilities and resources needed to defend critical private systems from aggressive cyber attacks— provided they are properly organized, harnessed, and focused. Today, we're falling short.[7]

In light of these reports indicating a relative lack of preparedness, organizations must commit to improving their preparedness level. They can't afford to be chaotic and disoriented in managing cybersecurity risks. The cybersecurity strategy must be aligned and integrated with the overall goals and responsibilities of the organization. Effective strategy formulation and execution is contingent on clear articulation of vision and organizational goals. Organizations must have in place strategic and tactical teams (with cross-functional representation) that will assist with supply chain role recognition, risk assessment, cybersecurity strategy formulation and alignment, and identification of threat scenarios.

Following are a set of questions to guide organizational role recognition and alignment of cybersecurity goals.

Organizational Role Recognition: Guiding Questions

1. Does the leadership recognize the organizational role and responsibility within its supply chain and beyond? Is such recognition explicitly documented in the cybersecurity strategic plan?

2. Are the organizational goals, mission, and objectives explicitly documented in the cybersecurity strategic plan?

3. Is it clearly stated (in the cybersecurity strategic plan) how the cybersecurity strategy is aligned with the overall organizational strategy?

4. Is there a cross-functional team in place to assist with supply chain role recognition, risk assessment, cybersecurity strategy formulation and alignment, and identification of threat scenarios?

6.1.2 Cyber-Risk Assessment

Exemplar organizations will factor in cyber-risk implications alongside other risks when making prioritization decisions on what digital assets to protect and which initiatives to undertake. They adopt a systematic and meticulous approach where they a) identify risks and tolerance levels, b) evaluate likelihood of occurrence and potential impact, c) assess strategic and operational initiatives by examining risk implications, and d) take preemptive action to mitigate the risks.[8]

Risks that organizations encounter can be categorized in different ways. One such classification would include financial, brand and reputation, environmental, legal, people, technology, and systems risks. A sample rubric for scoring the impact of any organizational initiative or project on the different risk types is presented in Table 4 (see on pg 82). The likelihood of occurrence of such risks and the organization's tolerance level is presented in Figure 16 (see on pg 83).[9]

To explain how the risk evaluation system will work, let's consider the four initiatives described in Table 5 (see on pg 84).

Initiative 1, implementing and leveraging a customer relationship management (CRM) system, is assumed to have a risk score that places it above the risk tolerance level set by the organization. So, the organization has a choice of either pursuing or abandoning the project. If the decision is to go ahead with the project, the preemptive risk mitigation strategies would include: a) using strong hashing algorithms to encrypt customer data; b) establishing robust access controls; and c) regular monitoring and testing.

Initiative 2 is about enhancing operational efficiency by implementing an enterprise class resource planning system (ERP). Such ERP implementations are fraught with challenges and delays and not many organizations are successful in effectively assimilating and deploying them. Let's assume this initiative also falls beyond the organization's risk tolerance level, and compared to initiative 1, the probability of occurrence of the anticipated risks are higher. If the organization still decides to persist with initiative 2, the proactive risk mitigation strategies would be similar to those recommended for initiative 1.

Initiative 3, the artificial intelligence (AI)–driven precision manufacturing initiative, is well within the risk tolerance level and is relatively safe bet for the organization to pursue. Once again, the recommended cyber-risk mitigation action plan entails securing the data, network, and systems, along with rigorous monitoring and testing.

Impact Bands				
Risk Categories	Low (1)	Moderate (2)	High (3)	Very High (4)
Financial	0–1 Million	1–5 Million	5–10 Million	10–15 Million
Brand and Reputation	Limited adverse impact.	Significant/community/ shareholder concern.	Regular adverse national coverage. Repeated shareholder concern.	Major adverse national coverage.
Environmental	Negligible damage.	Minor environmental damage that is below any legally reportable level.	Reportable but temporary environmental impact. Noncompliance with regulatory requirements leading to a warning or reprimand with no financial impact.	Significant environmental damage and leads to complaints and fines for damages.
Legal	Minor legal vulnerability that is likely to be resolved without litigation or prosecution.	Moderate legal vulnerability that is likely to be resolved without litigation or prosecution.	Material legal vulnerability that is liable to prosecution.	Material legal vulnerability that is liable to prosecution. The potential for negative consequence is significant.
People	Minor adverse impact. There might be a few disgruntled workers.	Moderate adverse impact. There might be several unhappy employees across business units.	Significant adverse impact. Unhappy employees are likely to resist work and contemplate a protest and possibly sue the company.	Significant adverse impact. Unhappy employees are most likely to resist work and sue the company.
Systems and Technology	Minor impact on the functioning of the existing technology infrastructure.	Moderate impact on the functioning of the existing technology infrastructure.	Significant impact on the functioning of the existing infrastructure. Could require a major overhaul.	Significant impact on the functionating of the existing infrastructure. Will require a major overhaul.

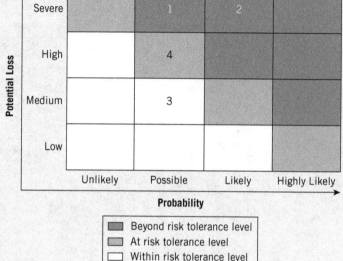

Figure 16   Risk Probability Matrix

Source: Adapted from Boehm et al. (2018).

Initiative 4 is focused on protecting student data. Universities can't afford to have breaches that compromise personally identifiable information (PII) and payment details associated with student records. This critical project falls within the risk tolerance level and is likely to be pursued. The proactive risk mitigation strategies are similar to those discussed for the other initiatives.

This hypothetical example was meant to provide a general idea on how the process works. More detailed and sophisticated approaches involve identifying, aggregating, and evaluating cyber risks at different levels of the organization, and assigning ownership and responsibility for the mitigation strategies.[10] Other best practices include use of a) scientific methods and techniques to conduct probabilistic risk assessments, b) sound data quality management methods to filter erroneous data, c) consistent and defensible methods to score and quantify the risk impacts and, d) dashboards that provide real-time updates on threat levels, counter-risk initiative implementation status, actual impact of such initiatives, and more.[11]

Thus, a holistic and comprehensive approach to cyber risk management and reporting entails a) identification and aggregation of asset

	Objective	Strategic Initiative	Potential Risks	Key Risk Indicators	Preemptive Mitigation Strategies
1.	Grow market share	Invest in a customer relationship management system to develop customized up-selling, cross-selling, and marketing strategies.	Confidential customer data falls in the wrong hands (perpetrators and competitors).	• Data breach • Loss in customer confidence • Drop in sales • Loss of market share • Lawsuits and settlement • High customer attrition	• Strong encryption • Dual-Factor Authentication • Adhering to the principle of least privileged access • Use of virtual private network for remote access • Network segmentation • Invest in high availability and fault-tolerance systems • Regular monitoring and testing
2.	Improve operational efficiency	Invest in enterprise-class resource planning systems to streamline processes, consolidate databases, and automate workflows.	Confidential data falls in the wrong hands (perpetrators and competitors); possibility of fraudulent transactions and ID theft.	• Data breach • Fraudulent transactions; Financial loss	• Strong encryption • Dual-Factor Authentication • Adhering to the principle of Least Privileged Access • Use of Virtual Private Network for remote access • Network segmentation • Invest in high availability and fault-tolerance systems. • Regular monitoring and testing

	Objective	Strategic Initiative	Potential Risks	Key Risk Indicators	Preemptive Mitigation Strategies
3.	Improve productivity	Use of robotic technology to automate manufacturing.	Machine malfunction due to manipulation of execution logic.	• Machine failure • Loss in production output • Production delays • Increase in material scrap generation	• Strong encryption • Dual-Factor Authentication • Adhering to the principle of Least Privileged Access • Use of Virtual Private Network for remote access • Invest in high availability and fault-tolerance systems • Network segmentation • Regular monitoring and testing
4.	Secure sensitive customer data	Investing in advanced security technologies to protect systems and databases that store customer data.	Confidential data falls into the wrong hands (perpetrators and competitors); possibility of fraudulent transactions and ID theft.	• Data breach • Fraudulent transactions • Financial loss • Tarnished reputation	• Strong encryption • Dual-Factor Authentication • Adhering to the principle of Least Privileged Access • Use of Virtual Private Network for remote access • Network segmentation • Invest in high availability and fault-tolerance systems • Regular monitoring and testing

vulnerabilities, risk types, tolerance and appetite levels; b) analysis and evaluation of risk relevance and impacts; c) quantification and scoring of risk impacts; d) prioritizing threats and putting in place appropriate defense measures; and e) constant monitoring of the current state of affairs by using reporting tools such as a digital risk dashboard. Following are some guiding questions to assess the extent to which a risk-based approach is driving an organization's cyber-risk mitigation plans and programs.

Cyber-Risk Assessment: Guiding Questions

1. Does the organization engage in a comprehensive and periodic evaluation of its risk tolerance levels and vulnerabilities?

2. Are cross-functional teams with representation from senior leadership engaged in such risk evaluation?

3. Are tools such as a cyber-risk matrix and dashboard in use to monitor and manage threat levels?

4. Are key risk indicators for each strategic initiative determined and monitored?

6.1.3 Asset Identification and Prioritization

It is hard to manage or defend the unknown. If an organization is clueless about the nature and types of digital assets that need protection, their respective locations, and worth, it is difficult to engage in effective asset management. A study conducted by the Ponemon Institute found the majority of respondents (80%) citing "lack of visibility into the attack surface, knowing what systems are part of their IT environments, as the number one issue in their inability to prevent business-impacting cyberattacks."[12]

Many organizations don't recognize or value the need to create and maintain a comprehensive catalog of their digital assets. Daniel Miessler, a cybersecurity expert, brings to light such misplaced organizational priorities:

> Companies pay hundreds of thousands a year to keep snacks in the break rooms. They pay to send people to training and conferences that usually have very few tangible benefits. And we dump millions into marketing campaigns that we can't tie to sales results. But pay 100K a year to have a list of what we're actually defending? Nope. Too expensive. Wasteful, really.[13]

Clarity and awareness of where these informational and digital assets reside and what types of data they store, process, access, and transmit are essential to developing and implementing an appropriate protection strategy. Security solutions providers offer agentless automated tools that can help organizations continuously uncover and keep track of all authorized and unauthorized hardware and software. Figure 17 presents a generic list of hardware and software discovered by security software solutions. These tools also identify the risks and vulnerabilities associated with each of the discovered devices.[14]

Figure 17   A Generic List of Discovered Hardware and Software

Laptops

Servers

Printers

Adapters

Scanners

Routers

iPhones

Switches

iPads

VOIP Phones

Smart TVs

Software

Data Center Hardware and Software

Projectors

Security Cameras

An appropriate asset classification scheme should be in place to prioritize the level and extent of protection. In military organizations, the classification levels are top secret, secret, confidential, and unclassified. Highly sensitive, sensitive, internal, and public are classification labels used by many business organizations. The criteria for categorizing the sensitivity of data could include a) financial and other consequences from modification, loss, or exposure, b) usefulness of the data, c) age of the data, and d) cost of acquiring the data.[15]

An information security–conscious organization must make a thorough effort to identify and inventory all physical systems and devices as well as software applications and platforms. It is considered a best practice to have a complete inventory and blueprint of the network; detailing the locations and specifications of all the devices—servers, workstations, laptops, desktops, and other communication and transmission devices—on the network.[16] The hardware inventory records should reflect details such as network address, hardware address, machine name, owner and department name for each device, and whether the asset has received approval to be connected to the network. Software records should include the name, version, publisher, and install date.

Hardware assets that are not connected to the networks must also be recorded from the standpoint of completeness. Recording of unauthorized assets will help in getting them removed or quarantined. Preferably, the authentication system, tied into the hardware device inventory data, should ensure only authorized devices are able to connect to the network. Client certificates should also be used for authenticating hardware devices on the network.

Authorized and unauthorized software must be recorded, and the inventory list should be regularly reviewed and updated. The authorized software inventory must include only applications and operating systems that are currently supported by the vendor. Unsupported software must be suitably tagged and listed separately. Unauthorized software must be removed.

It is a good practice to use application whitelisting technology to ensure that only authorized software executes and all unauthorized software is blocked. The application whitelisting software should be appropriately configured to only allow authorized software libraries to load and authorized digitally signed scripts to run on corporate devices and systems.

Yet another important control measure is to identify software that is required for high-risk business operations and run them on separate (physically or logically segregated) networks and systems.

Hardware and software inventory tools should be used to facilitate the identification and recording process and help maintain an integrated recording and tracking system. It is recommended that organizations use active and passive discovery tools to identify hardware devices connected to the network and update the inventory list. Dynamic Host Configuration Protocol (DHCP) and IP address management tools should also be used for hardware inventory identification and updates.

When preparing the digital assets catalog, it is also essential to include information systems and platforms that reside outside an organization's managed domains but connect with internal systems to exchange data and messages.

Although it is desirable to comprehensively capture all hardware and software assets, this might be hard to do in a highly global, decentralized, virtual, and mobile work environment. Prioritizing critical digital assets and ensuring the high-priority items are closely monitored would be a reasonable and defensible course of action for an organization.

In addition to being in the know of critical assets, knowledge of what (and how) data flows between networks, applications, and systems is also important. Documenting communication and data flows helps with monitoring of network traffic and early detection of cyber threats and attacks. Hackers engage in gathering information about an organization's systems and data during the reconnaissance phase. So for organizations not to keep track of their own communication and data flows would be a serious security flaw. Whereas mapping of all information flows is ideal, the reasonable scenario would be to document and secure flows of strategic significance.[17]

Following is a list of questions to gauge and guide the asset identification and prioritization state of affairs.

Asset Identification and Prioritization: Guiding Questions

1. Are hardware and software assets of the organization inventoried?

2. Do the hardware inventory records capture comprehensive details such as network address, hardware address, machine name, owner and department name for each device, and whether the asset has received approval to be connected to the network?

3. Do software records include comprehensive details such as name, version, publisher, and install date?

4. Are hardware devices that are not connected to the networks also recorded in the asset inventory?

(Continued)

(Continued)

5. Is an authentication system in place to ensure only authorized devices are able to connect to the network?

6. Are client certificates used to authenticate hardware devices on the network?

7. Are active and passive discovery tools being used to identify hardware devices on the network and suitably update the hardware inventory list?

8. Are Dynamic Host Configuration Protocol (DHCP) and IP address management tools being used for hardware inventory identification and updates?

9. Is unauthorized and unsupported software identified, recorded, and removed on a regular basis?

10. Is application whitelisting technology used to ensure only authorized software executes and all unauthorized software is blocked?

11. Is software, used for running high-risk business operations, identified and run on segregated networks and systems?

12. Are hardware and software tools such as asset inventory recording and tracking systems in use? Are these systems integrated?

13. Are external systems and devices that reside outside an organization's managed domains but connect with internal systems included in the digital assets inventory?

14. Are organizational communication and data flows mapped?

15. Are resources (e.g., hardware, devices, data, and software) prioritized based on their classification, criticality, and business value?

16. Are suitable organizational criteria used to classify the level of data sensitivity?

6.2 Protect

From controlling unauthorized access to encrypting data, managing system and device configurations, developing an asset maintenance plan, and training people, there are several initiatives that must be undertaken to secure and protect sensitive data and associated digital assets. The overall goal is to have several layers of security and create a relatively robust and impenetrable security infrastructure. Figure 18 (see on page 92) depicts a defense-in-depth strategy that leverages numerous physical, technical, and administrative controls. This information security strategy is often referred to as the "castle approach." During medieval times, castles were secured by building moats, ramparts, drawbridges, towers, and more. The enemy had to penetrate several layers of security to get inside the castle.

Several of the security defense mechanisms to secure data, networks, devices, locations, and people are discussed in the following subsections.

6.2.1 Access Control

Access control measures are aimed at ensuring that unauthorized individuals and other entities (such as computer systems) cannot gain access to data, applications, networks, and other resources. There are three essential steps to controlling access: identification, authentication, and authorization. Usernames and smart cards are the two most common ways of uniquely identifying an entity requesting access. Typically, authentication factors fall under three categories—something you know, such as a password; something you are, as indicated by biometric characteristics like fingerprints, retina and voice scans; and something you have, for example a token fob, smart cards, or an app like Duo on a smartphone. Thus, a multi-factor authentication (MFA) would be any combination of the three factors, such as a password and fingerprint scan or a password and a code. Finally, authorization can take the form of mandatory access control (MAC) systems and discretionary access control systems.

There are two fundamental principles that drive authorization best practices—principle of least privilege (PoLP) and separation of duties. According to PoLP, the default level of access will be set to the minimum needed for the employee to perform their job. By limiting scope of access, the organization can mitigate the risk of insider attacks from disgruntled employees. The principle of least privilege also limits the ability of an external hacker to gain widespread access after compromising a particular employee's account.

Separation of duties is another form of access control to ensure that sensitive activities such as vendor account creation and payment authorizations are handled by two different individuals. This mitigates the risk of a fraudulent purchase transaction where payment is made to a fake vendor.

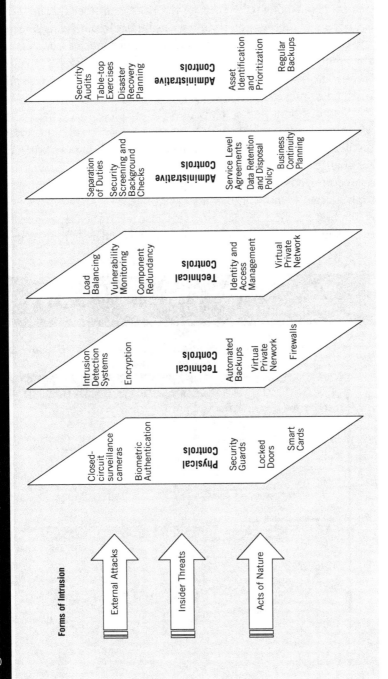

Figure 18 Defense-in-Depth Approach

Thorough screening and background checks during the recruiting process could potentially alleviate the risks of insider threats. Educating employees about their roles and responsibilities in protecting sensitive data and complying with related organizational rules, policies, and controls are also important control measures to minimize the risks of unauthorized access. The organization must also be prompt in revoking access privileges when an employee leaves the organization.

Sound monitoring systems must be in place to ensure the granted access privileges are still valid. It is through regular account reviews that privilege creep can be detected. Privilege creep can happen when employees change roles and gain new access privileges without losing the previous permissions. Automating the process of access privilege review using sophisticated identity and access management (IAM) solutions is considered a best practice. Service providers such as Oracle (see Figure 19) offer such solutions with extensive functionalities ranging from secure single

Figure 19   Oracle's Identity and Access Management Dashboard

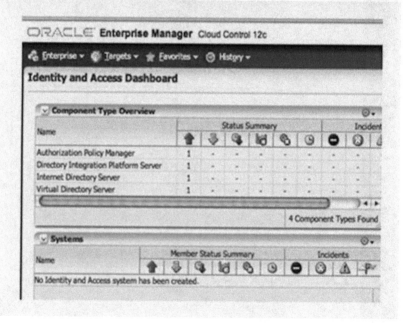

Source: Oracle.com

sign-on, authorization controls using attribute-based policies, adaptive multi-factor authentication (MFA), user management, automated customer lifecycle workflows, seamless integration with enterprise directories, and access gateways.

Other forms of access control include requiring employees take mandatory vacations and practicing job rotation. When an employee is on vacation, their access to networks and systems are suspended and another personnel is assigned to the job as a substitute. This approach could often bring to light unauthorized activities carried out by the vacationing employee. By periodically rotating personnel from one role to another, especially in sensitive positions, it makes it difficult for someone to engage in fraudulent behavior for a prolonged period and also cover up their digital footprints.

Remote access must be secured by mandating the use of an authorized virtual private network (VPN) service provider, implementing strong password controls and multi-factor authentication (MFA). The Wi-Fi networks with the strongest encryption level (e.g., WPA3) should be used. Access credentials of third-party service providers must be constantly reviewed and scrutinized.

Another recommended approach to securing critical data and systems from unauthorized access is network segmentation.[18] According to the PCI data security standards, credit card holder data should be separated from the rest of network. Similarly, point-of-sale systems and databases should be on a completely separate network from that accessible by third-party service providers. The Target breach could have possibly been avoided if its network comprising of customer systems and databases was segregated from other networks that are accessible by Target's suppliers.[19] In addition to reducing the probability of unauthorized access, network segmentation also prevents single point of failure.[20]

Managing administrative privileges is yet another very important access control measure. First and foremost, it is a good practice to automate the process of reviewing administrative accounts to ensure that only authorized individuals have administrative level access. The administrative accounts should only be used for elevated activities and not for Internet browsing, email, and other regular user activities.

Multi-factor authentication and encryption are important ways of securing administrative access. Strong and unique passwords should also be required for administrative level accounts. Dedicated and segregated machines must be used for hosting administrative accounts and conducting higher-level system administration functions; such machines should not be connected to the Internet and must not be used for email, composing documents, and other routine user-level activities. Systems must also be suitably configured to send an alert notification every time there is an unsuccessful account to log into an administrative account. Such alerts must also be triggered when any changes are made to administrative group membership. Finally, access to scripting tools such as Python and Microsoft PowerShell must be restricted to only administrative or development users.

Physical access control measures to secure data centers and server rooms include locked doors, closed-circuit surveillance cameras, security guards, and the previously discussed biometrics-enabled identification systems.[21]

Following are a set of questions to serve as a checklist for robust access control measures.

Access Control: Guiding Questions

1. Are policies and procedures in place to manage authorized access to devices and systems?

2. Is multi-factor authentication (MFA) in place?

3. Are access logs maintained and periodically reviewed?

4. Are access permissions properly managed by incorporating the principles of least privilege and separation of duties?

5. Are access privileges regularly reviewed and updated?

6. Does the organization conduct thorough screening and background checks during the hiring and recruiting process?

7. Are employees continuously reminded (through education and training programs) of their roles and responsibilities in protecting sensitive data and complying with organizational access control policies?

8. Are access privileges promptly revoked at the time of voluntary or involuntary termination of jobs?

(Continued)

(Continued)

9. Is network integrity protected, incorporating network segregation where appropriate?

10. Are firewalls used to segregate and secure critical network segments?

11. Is remote access secured and monitored by using tools such as virtual private networks?

12. Is Wi-Fi network with the strongest encryption (e.g. WPA3) in use?

13. Are Identity and Access Management solutions in use to automate the access control monitoring process?

14. Is access to server rooms and data centers physically secured with locked doors?

15. Are closed-circuit surveillance cameras in place to monitor traffic in server rooms and data centers?

16. Is multi-factor authentication system in use to ensure authorized access to server rooms and data centers?

6.2.2 Configuration Management

The purpose and focus of configuration management is to achieve a high level of system interoperability and functionality without compromising on security. From addressing how the various information system components (e.g., servers, workstations, routers, switches, operating systems, and applications) will be configured to deciding on their physical and logical arrangement, setting a baseline configuration, and implementing security controls, the scope of configuration management is quite vast. It is a continuous process of planning, identification and implementation of configuration settings, controlling configuration changes, and monitoring to keep up with organizational growth and security needs.

Many organizations will often rely on the configuration standards set by industry groups such as the Center for Internet Security.[22] This resource provides access to detailed configuration settings for the different elements of the IT infrastructure such as operating systems, network devices, mobile devices, server software, web browsers, and other application platforms. While some companies adopt these standards as is and treat them as baseline benchmarks, others will suitably customize them.

Through effective configuration management, an organization can ensure integrity of its technology assets and improve incident response effectiveness, disaster recovery, timely development of suitable software solutions, and compliance with policies and regulations.[23]

Lack of proper configuration of hardware and software can be, and has been, the cause of major breaches such as the ones suffered by Capital One and Equifax. Whether hosted/on-premise or remote, organizations should not rely on the default configuration set by the manufacturers or vendors. The factory or default settings are normally geared toward easy use and deployment—not security. The onus is on the user organization to become familiar with the different security settings and appropriately configure the devices. Considering there are numerous settings options, this is a complex and challenging task and needs to be carried out with great care and diligence. Even after establishing a strong initial security configuration, there must be a process in place to continually check the settings and avoid security "decay." Device and software configurations and settings are often tweaked during updates and installations; they must be reset to their original high-level option upon completion of the install.

In addition to conforming to approved configuration standards, secure images and templates of all system settings must be maintained for resetting purposes. The master images and templates must be stored on highly secure servers, and integrity-monitoring tools should be used to reduce the likelihood of unauthorized changes to the images. Organizations are strongly encouraged to use Security Content Automation Protocol (SCAP)-compliant configuration management tools to automate, verify, enforce, and monitor the security settings process. These tools also send out alert notifications when they detect unauthorized configuration activities and changes. Figure 20 presents a screen shot of an audit summary generated by Tenable's SCAP tool.

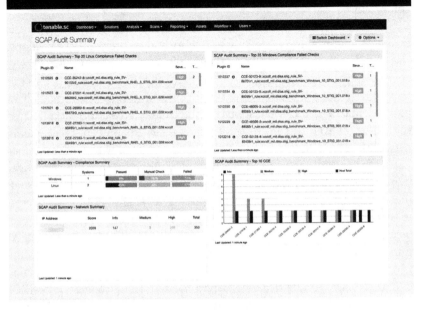

Figure 20   Tenable's SCAP Audit Summary Dashboard

Following is a set of guiding questions to effectively manage system configurations.

Configuration Management: Guiding Questions

1. Are configuration specifications in place for all systems, devices, and networks?

2. Has a baseline configuration been established?

3. How frequently are configuration settings reviewed, monitored, and updated?

4. Are automated tools/solutions in use to facilitate configuration management?

6.2.3 Securing Email Clients and Web Browsers

Users are often enticed and spoofed into opening a rogue email with a malware attachment, or they get tricked into clicking a link that takes them to a phishing website. It took a single click to cause the most massive data breach in history, when each and every Yahoo user account was compromised.

Considering the heavy use of email systems and Web browsers, it is extremely important to take every step to try and secure these applications. Use of fully supported and the latest version email clients and web browsers is an important security measure. Systems should be appropriately configured to prevent the deployment of unauthorized browsers, email client plugins, and add-on applications. Only authorized scripting languages should be allowed to run in web browsers and email clients. Leveraging network-based URL filters to prevent access to certain websites is another important control. The organization should subscribe to URL categorization services to be in the know about uncategorized sites and also block them. Domain Name System (DNS) filtering services should also be used to block access to malicious sites. All email attachments entering the organization's email gateway should be blocked if the file types are deemed unnecessary for the business. To reduce the possibility of spoofed or modified emails from valid domains, organizations should implement Domain-based Message Authentication, Reporting and Conformance (DMARC) policy and verification. All URL requests should be logged and reviewed to identify monitor, detect, and prevent malicious attacks. Finally, using sandboxing to analyze inbound email attachments and blocking of attachments that represent certain (unnecessary) file types are useful security vigilance measures.

Below is a set of questions to help organizations comprehensively secure emails and web browsers.

Email and Web Browser Protections: Guiding Questions

1. Is the organization using the latest and fully supported versions of email clients and web browsers?

2. Are systems appropriately configured to prevent the deployment of unauthorized browsers and email client plugins?

3. Are only authorized scripting languages running in web browsers and email clients?

(Continued)

(Continued)

4. Does the organization subscribe to URL categorization services?

5. Are network-based URL filters used to prevent access to certain websites?

6. Are Domain Name System (DNS) filtering services used to block access to malicious sites?

7. Are inbound email attachments screened for malware?

8. Has the organization implemented a Domain-based Message Authentication, Reporting and Conformance (DMARC) policy?

6.2.4 Securing Networks, Ports, Protocols, and Services

Multiple layers of security controls enhance the robustness of networks to combat attacks. For instance, an organization could use a virtual private network (VPN) connection to provide a secure tunnel for transmitting data. In addition, by implementing a TLS encryption that comes with the HTTPs at the application later and using virtual local area networks (VLANs) to segment the networks, three layers of security have been added to protect against eavesdropping type attacks. Another example of a layered approach to security would be the use of VLANs to segment networks along with media access control (MAC) address filtering and port security. A third example of a multilayered defense system would be the use of a router access control that filters traffic before they reach the stateful inspection firewall. If any of the malicious traffic gets past the firewall, they have to contend with an intrusion protection system that sits behind the firewall.[24]

Remotely accessible network ports and poorly configured web servers, mail servers, DNS servers, and file and print services are ideal targets for cyberattacks. As noted by an expert, these vulnerable entry points can be used by attackers to "listen in, watch for credentials, inject commands via [man-in-the-middle] attacks, and ultimately perform Remote Code Executions (RCE)."[25] While some network ports are good entry points, others provide ideal escape routes. For instance, TCP/UDP port 53, used for DNS traffic and rarely monitored, is often exploited by hackers to get out the door by converting stolen data into DNS traffic.[26]

Securing ports and associated services entails a multipronged approach that includes use of approved ports and protocols, regular automated scans to detect unauthorized ports, use of filtering tools with a default-deny rule to block unauthorized traffic, and implementation of application firewalls in front of critical servers. Lack of a proper firewall was identified as a potential reason for the breach of Bangladesh Bank's computer systems and the embezzlement of 81 million dollars.[27]

Artificial intelligence (AI)–driven next-generation firewalls deliver proactive threat protection with high-performance inspection of traffic. Use of such solutions achieves the dual goals of protection without costly downtime and unsatisfactory user experience. Fortinet, Palo Alto Networks, Cisco, and Checkpoint are some of the many service providers that offer such firewall capabilities.

Organizations should also consider adopting a single door serial layered approach to network security. This is a relatively foolproof protection method where a threat has to deal with multiple controls one after another. In comparison, a multidoor parallel scenario is more vulnerable as the attack vector could possibly sneak in through a less secure access point.

Following is a set of questions to assist organizations in effectively securing their network ports, protocols, and services.

Securing Networks, Ports, Protocols, and Services: Guiding Questions

1. Is a defense-in-depth strategy followed to secure the data transmission and communication networks?

2. Is there an approval system in place to ensure only a select set of network ports, protocols, and services are activated?

3. Are automated scans performed regularly to detect unauthorized open ports?

4. Are host-based firewalls with a default/deny rule in place to block unauthorized traffic?

5. Are AI-driven next-generation firewalls being used to inspect and filter traffic without degrading user experience?

6. Are port-filtering tools in use to block unauthorized traffic?

7. Is a serial-layered approach used to secure access to organizational networks and systems?

6.2.5 Managing Removable Media

Protecting removal media (e.g., USB drives, SD cards, and optical media) is an integral and key component of an organization's cybersecurity preparedness program. Numerous and devastating cyberattacks have been launched by compromising portable media. Dark Tequila, a malware that has been targeting banks and consumers in Mexico since 2013, was spread through USB devices. Hackers like to use USB devices to attack networks not connected to the Internet; the Stuxnet campaign in 2009 and 2010 that targeted Iran's nuclear facilities was launched through USB devices. Norsk Hydro, a Norwegian aluminum manufacturer, was a recent victim of a ransomware attack that cost the company millions. The perpetrators were able to launch this attack by infecting just one portable device. According to industry reports, 25% of malware is spread through USB devices. Thus, transient cyber assets—devices that are not connected to the network all the time—are a major information security vulnerability for organizations.[28]

Many companies, such as IBM, have banned the use of all USB drives and other portable storage devices; employees are encouraged to use cloud-based data file sharing and storage services. Other not-so-extreme measures include disabling auto-run on optical and USB drives, restricting usage on certain devices, using a standalone virus scanning PC, and educating users. There should be a policy in place clearly documenting how portable devices will be protected, and a monitoring process must be in place to ensure compliance.[29]

Following is a set of questions to help establish a checklist for managing removable media.

Managing Removable Media: Guiding Questions

1. Is an inventory of removal media and portable devices maintained and periodically reviewed and updated?

2. Are policies in place to govern usage of portable storage devices?

3. Are auto-run features disabled on optical and USB drives?

6.2.6 Data Security

The different methods for securing critical data-in-transit and data-at-rest are discussed below:

Encryption. Encryption remains one of the best ways of securing data at rest or in motion. Complex algorithms (rules for coding and decoding data), also known as keys, are used for scrambling and unscrambling data. When the same key is used to encrypt and decrypt data, the method is known as *symmetric encryption,* and when different keys are used, the method is referred to as *asymmetric encryption.* Some of the popular data encryption algorithms are AES, RSA, Triple DES, and Twofish. These encryption methods vary in capability and perform differently on different types of infrastructure. Similarly, encryption tools also vary in capability: some are better at encrypting or decrypting small volumes of data, others excel when it comes to large amounts of data. So, an organization must perform with due diligence to identify and implement the appropriate encryption method and tool. It is also considered a best practice to identify and encrypt all types of sensitive data. The encryption key must be secured, and there are multiple ways of accomplishing this important security measure. Regular review of data encryption performance is also a reflection of a mature approach to cybersecurity preparedness. Maintaining comprehensive logs and audit trails linked to accessing encrypted data is yet another important element of a robust data protection plan.[30] When selecting an appropriate encryption mechanism, it is important to ensure that it will easily integrate with any third-party application. Frequently backing up encrypted data and also restoring the backed-up data to check for accuracy is another best practice.[31]

Documents containing sensitive data must be encrypted with a persistent file-level security policy. Such a policy indicates who can access the file and what they can do with it. Effectively enforcing the policy ensures only authorized users are able to access and edit files and thereby protect against data leaks.[32]

Organizations should also consider products and solutions that support end-to-end encryptions; that is, the data are encrypted at all times. Virtru is a security solutions provider that offers the "Host Your Own Keys and Maintain Control of Your Data" option. By subscribing to this self-control option, firms can protect their data keys from any third party including governments who can blind-subpoena service providers.[33]

Digital Signatures and Digital Certificates. Digital signature is an encryption technique used for authentication and to achieve the data integrity goal of nonrepudiation. Non-repudiation means the creator of the message cannot dispute that they did create the message and it was not forged. Similar to the traditional wet signature, a digital signature is "an electronic, encrypted stamp of authentication on digital data."[34] It is generated by using a complex algorithm (hashing function) that converts the original document into a set of characters, also known as digital digest. The digital digest is encrypted with the private key of the creator who sends the corresponding public key to the recipient to decrypt the document. Figure 21 presents a step-by-step enumeration of the digital signature creation-and-use process. This form of electronic authentication, commonly used for financial transactions and software distributions, is legally acceptable and binding in many countries.[35] PandaDoc, DocuSign, Lightico, and RevvSales are some notable digital signature software providers.[36]

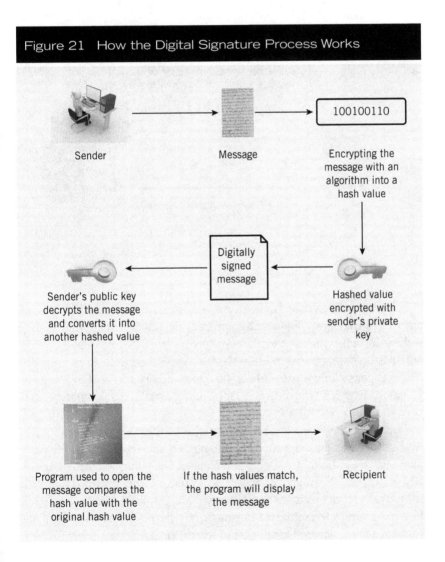

Figure 21   How the Digital Signature Process Works

Sender

Message

100100110

Encrypting the message with an algorithm into a hash value

Sender's public key decrypts the message and converts it into another hashed value

Digitally signed message

Hashed value encrypted with sender's private key

Program used to open the message compares the hash value with the original hash value

If the hash values match, the program will display the message

Recipient

Figure 22   Use of Digital Certificate to Securely Access a
Website

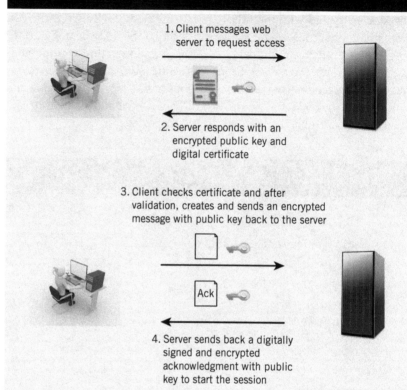

1. Client messages web
   server to request access

2. Server responds with an
   encrypted public key and
   digital certificate

3. Client checks certificate and after
   validation, creates and sends an encrypted
   message with public key back to the server

Ack

4. Server sends back a digitally
   signed and encrypted
   acknowledgment with public
   key to start the session

Digital certificates serve the purpose of a passport or driver's license to authenticate an entity. Figure 22 graphically depicts a server authenticating a client by reviewing the client's secure socket layer (SSL) digital certificate and then accepting the connection request. An SSL certificate from a reputed provider goes a long way in enhancing the credibility and trust of a website. Comodo, DigiCert, Entrust, GeoTrust, and GlobalSign are reputable SSL certificate providers.[37]

Software developers can request a digital certificate from a Certificate of Authority (CA) that is approved by established and reputed software companies such as Microsoft, Adobe, and Google. Operating systems are generally set to check the digital certificate of a vendor before downloading their software. Users can register complaints with the certification authority if they find the downloaded software to be malicious; the CA can revoke the digital certificate of the accused vendor if the complaint is found to be valid.[38]

Digital certificates are more trusted than digital signatures because they are approved by a recognized organization. A digital signature is a form of self-identification; in other words, "the only entity confirming the identity of the publisher is the publisher itself." Browsers and operating systems are likely to trigger a warning message when a user is trying to download software from a vendor who has a digital signature but not a certificate.[39]

Data Masking. Masking the data is an effective way of reducing the exposure of sensitive data such as personally identifiable information (PII). By creating characteristically intact but inauthentic replicas of highly sensitive data, data masking protects the integrity of the data. Tests performed on masked data will produce the same results as those performed using the authentic data. Some of the common data masking techniques include encryption, character scrambling, nulling out or deletion, substitution, and shuffling.[40] Internal Revenue Service regulations allow employers to mask Social Security numbers by displaying only the last four digits and replacing the first five with *x*s (Example: xxx-xx-5678) or asterisks (Example: ***-**-5678).[41]

Data masking is a requirement in many regulated industries. Organizations obfuscate the highly sensitive data before using it for training, development, or testing purposes. DATPROF, IRI FieldShield, and Accutive Data Discovery and Masking are examples of popular tools that can automate the masking process.[42]

Steganography. Steganography is a type of data masking technique that hides sensitive information within an image file that is undetectable to the naked eye. While cryptography conceals the contents of a message, steganography conceals the very fact that a message has been communicated. In addition to the widely used image steganography, there are other types of steganography—text, audio, and video steganography.[43] QuickStego, Xiao Steganography, OpenStego, and Camouflage are popular steganography tools.[44]

Data Loss Protection Tools and Technologies. Data loss protection (DLP) solutions are also worthy of consideration. These technologies use rules to detect and stop sensitive information such as intellectual property, financial data, and employee or customer details from reaching the wrong hands. Symantec DLP, Code42, and Trend Micro Smart Protection are some examples of DLP software that can be used to secure data in use, in motion, and at rest.[45]

Principle of Least Privilege. By adopting the Principle of Least Privilege (PoLP) to data access, an organization can reduce the risk of unauthorized access to sensitive data. Such a policy mandates that by default each user will have bare minimum access to the data needed to perform their respective roles.

EMail Domain Restrictions. Yet another effective way of preventing data leaks is by placing restrictions on email domains that employees have access to; thereby, the organization is able to minimize the probability and risk of sensitive data (being shared via attachments) falling in the wrong hands.

Managing Personal Device Usage. Placing restrictions on how employees can use their personal devices at work is also an important element of data leak prevention strategy. In many organizations, employees cannot have access to corporate systems and data from their personal devices. In other organizations, two different environments are created within the same mobile devices, one storing personal data and apps and the other hosting enterprise data and apps. By allowing employees to create dual personas, organizations are able to achieve the dual goals of keeping employees happy by allowing use of their preferred mobile devices and also being able to secure and remotely monitor corporate data and applications.[46] Requiring usage of strong passwords, automatically locking out access when incorrect password is used a few times (typically three or more), and remotely wiping off sensitive data and applications when the device is lost, stolen, sold, or sent to a third party for repairs are some other best mobile device security best practices.[47] Mobile device users must also be required to use a virtual private network (VPN) connection to access corporate systems and data and a dual-factor authentication (DFA) mechanism must be in place. Performing regular backups of data stored on mobile devices is also a critical data security measure.

Managing Data-in-Transit Visibility. Maintaining visibility of data-in-transit is critical from the standpoint of monitoring: authorized personnel need to know where the data is going or coming from, both within and outside the organization. A recommended best practice is to adopt a managed file transfer (MFT) platform that would not only provide complete visibility but also protect data in transit or at rest, provide tracking and audit capabilities, enable data wiping and sanitization, set and monitor security standard violation alerts, and generate compliance reports.[48]

Creating Employee Awareness. Creating employee awareness about the consequences of data leaks and how such leaks can be prevented can help mobilize support that is essential for the other elements of the data security plan to be successful. More details on how to effectively enhance awareness is discussed in a subsequent section on awareness and training.

Managing Data on Non-Critical Systems. Due diligence must also be exercised to ensure that sensitive data are not residing in non-critical systems. Thoroughly checking and cleaning up such systems and associated devices is key to preventing leakage of critical data.

Data Integrity Checks. Organizations must also consider deploying tools to check and report unauthorized changes to hardware, software, and information. Parity checks, cyclical redundancy checks, and cryptographic hashes are examples of integrity mechanisms that should be part of an organization's arsenal to detect malicious attacks.[49]

Separating of Production, Development, and Testing Environments. Production, development, and testing environments must be kept separate to mitigate the risk of sensitive data (in production servers) falling in the wrong hands. Another reason for keeping the environments separate is to avoid contamination of production data with test data. Since development and testing involve a lot of debugging, one incorrect program or code could cause the server performance to be compromised and also erroneously modify production data.[50]

Data Disposal Management. Proper disposing of data is also an integral element of data security. There are multiple methods of destroying data, from overwriting to degaussing (i.e., erasing the magnetic field) and disk shredding. It is important that organizations have a well-thought-out and clearly documented data disposition plan and follow it. With growing and extensive use of third-party managed cloud-based services, organizations need to be all the more cautious that the vendor is following through with the agreed-upon data destruction plan.[51] Following is a list of questions to guide management in adopting a multipronged approach to securing sensitive data.

Data Security: Guiding Questions

1. Are appropriate encryption tools in use to secure data-at-rest and data-in-transit?

2. Is the performance of the encryption tools regularly reviewed and are changes made as deemed necessary?

3. Is data-in-transit protected?

---

4. Is a persistent file-level security policy in place when encrypting sensitive data?

5. Are steganography tools used to hide the transmission of sensitive data?

6. Are data loss protection technologies being used to secure data in use, in motion, and at rest?

7. Is the Principle of Least Privilege in place to restrict access to sensitive data?

8. Are sensitive data masked using one of the recommended methods such as character scrambling, nulling out or deletion, substitution, and shuffling?

9. Is encrypted data frequently backedup?

10. Are periodic tests conducted to ensure the data backup method is satisfactory?

11. Is a policy in place to govern use of personal mobile devices?

12. Are mechanisms such as creating dual personas, use of strong passwords, remote wipe-off capability, regular backups, and secure remote access in place to manage use of mobile devices?

13. Are appropriate tools such as a managed file transfer (MFT) platform in place to provide complete visibility but also to protect data in transit or at rest, provide tracking and audit capabilities, enable data wiping and sanitization, set and monitor security standard violation alerts, and generate compliance reports?

14. Are integrity checking mechanisms used to verify software, firmware, and information integrity?

15. Are the development and testing environments kept separate from the production environments?

16. Does the organization have a well-thought-through and clearly documented data disposal plan?

17. Are users regularly made aware of the consequences of data leaks and trained on how to prevent such leakages?

6.2.7 Data Backup and Retention

Probably the most foolproof method of preparing for data breaches is to frequently back up sensitive data and carry out regular tests to ensure the backed-up data is easily retrievable.[52] It is rather alarming when a survey finds that 32% of IT administrators don't regularly test the reliability of their data restoration process.[53]

Although online backups might be more convenient and the accepted norm, periodically saving data to storage devices that are not connected to the Internet is an essential component of a robust strategy. There should be multiple backup sources—virtual and physical. An offsite data backup and storage solution is a prudent move to offset potential threats to the main operations center. The frequency of backup will depend on the nature and criticality of data. Sensitive transactional data must be backed up daily, preferably real-time. Weekly backup might be fine for data that are not used or updated frequently.[54]

How long should data be retained? What is the appropriate data retention policy? The organization must carefully and thoroughly deliberate on these questions and take into consideration regulatory requirements. For instance, the Sarbanes-Oxley Act (SOX) requires that receivables and payables ledgers and tax returns must be saved for seven years and customer invoices must be retained for five years. SOX also mandates that payroll records and bank statements be kept forever.[55] According to the Payment Card Industry (PCI) Data Security Standard (DSS), merchants should only store the information required to complete the transaction. If the 16-digit card number is stored, it should be destroyed as soon as it is no longer required.[56] Article 5(e) of the General Data Protection Regulation (GDPR) stipulates that "data should only be retained for as long as is required to achieve the purpose for which data were collected and are being processed." Exception is granted when data needs to be retained "for archiving purposes in the public interest, scientific or historical research purposes or statistical purposes."[57] Recital 39 of GDPR further articulates that the data controller must conduct periodic reviews to ensure that data is securely erased when no longer required.[58]

Retention policies also prescribe how data should be destroyed. Specialized tools must be used to securely wipe data off hard drives, flash drives, and other storage media before the storage devices are destroyed. In addition to the built-in disk clean-up utility that comes with the operating systems, DBAN, Eraser, Disk Wipe, CCleaner, Darik's Boot, and Nuke are popular hard drive eraser tools.[59]

In both the Adult Friend Finder and Ashley Madison site breaches, the organizations were accused of data management malpractice because they did not properly secure confidential customer data. In the Ashley Madison case, the hackers published a huge amount of sensitive data that was supposed to have been deleted. They justified their action by claiming that Ashley Madison lied to its customers about vigorously protecting its data. Supposedly, the company did not comply with the offer to delete customer personal accounts completely for $19. The attack team also claimed that Ashley Madison failed to comply with the promise of deleting sensitive data such as purchase transaction details, credit card information, and the real names and addresses of customers.[60]

It is imperative that companies clearly spell out their customer data storage and deletion policies and follow through with them. The service level agreements (SLAs) with managed service providers must include data backup, storage, and purge provisions.

Following is a set of guiding questions to help implement a reliable data backup strategy and process.

Data Backup and Retention: Guiding Questions

1. Is data being automatically backed up to multiple storage locations?

2. Is data being automatically backed up to physical and virtual storage locations?

3. Is a copy of the backed-up data maintained in an offline storage space?

4. Is the frequency of data backup determined after thorough and careful deliberation?

5. Is the data restoration method regularly tested for reliability?

6. Did the organization implement appropriate data retention and purge policy after thorough and careful deliberation?

7. Is there an appropriate oversight mechanism, such as the role of the data controller, to ensure the date retention and purge policies are being followed?

8. Are data storage and purge expectations clearly documented in the SLAs?

6.2.8 Asset Maintenance

A clearly defined set of procedures must be in place to maintain and manage the hardware and software assets of an organization. Whether it is scheduling regular system maintenance or performing periodic checks of the different types of software such as operating systems and applications, there must be a formal documented approach in place. Logs and records also must be kept of hardware and software repair activities so that there is complete awareness of what the issues were, how they were resolved, and who resolved the issues. From a security standpoint, such repair and maintenance logs are very important because viruses can be installed by those engaged in such activities. Detecting unauthorized access will be difficult in the absence of detailed records. Periodic maintenance and review are also important from the standpoint of ensuring that all hardware and software are highly secure and robust. Evidence of regular hardware and software maintenance, review, and update activities is also important from an auditing standpoint.

Organizations with a mature digital asset maintenance process will constantly be monitoring hardware and software for vulnerabilities and viruses. For instance, malware is known to find its way to the boot sector, file allocation tables, and in .com and .exe files. Hence, scanning these locations on a regular basis is an extremely important maintenance activity.

In addition, making sure the recommended patches and updates are installed in a timely manner is a very important element of the upkeep operations. Patching or fixing a software means adjusting parts of the program code to reduce vulnerabilities to different types of attacks. Since attack methods are forever evolving, it is impossible for any software development team to predict every possible security loophole and fix them before the software is released. It is through software updates that engineers maintain operating systems and applications as well as the devices that run them.[61]

A list of questions to guide digital asset maintenance is presented below.

Asset Maintenance: Guiding Questions

1. Is the process for maintaining and updating hardware and software clearly documented?

2. Are logs maintained to track the maintenance, update, and repair activities?

---

3. Are automated tools in use to constantly monitor digital assets and detect unauthorized access or malware?

4. Is a software patch management system in place to automate the update process?

6.2.9 Awareness and Training

Humans continue to be the weakest cybersecurity link. As one security analyst puts it, "The system is only as secure as its weakest link, and that is very often its people."[62] They are the target of phishing and ransomware attacks, the predominant cause for breaches.[63] While email is the most popular medium for launching phishing attacks, hackers are also deploying other means (such as AI-enabled phone scams, social media, pop-ups, ads, instant messaging, browser extensions, and freeware) to get employees to share their access credentials.[64]

There are numerous breach incidents where hackers were able to compromise employee credentials via different forms of phishing campaigns. The eBay attack is one such example and is discussed in the following vignette.

A Phishing Attack on eBay

In May 2014, eBay requested 145 million users to change their passwords because of a breach discovered earlier in the month. Though no financial information was compromised, hackers did steal encrypted passwords and other personal account details such as names, emails, physical addresses, phone numbers, and birth dates. Evidence suggests that the attackers gained access using the credentials of three corporate eBay employees between late February and early March.[65]

Customers complained about the delay in notification about the breach. Emails about the breach and recommended password changes reached customers a few weeks after the global e-commerce corporation discovered the incident. In defense of eBay, it is quite common for an attack on large companies to go unnoticed for weeks due to a lack of obvious clues. Additionally, investigators advise companies to refrain from disclosing information before fully understanding the extent of the attack.

(Continued)

(Continued)

Immediate communication could be more harmful than helpful, as hackers may attempt to cover their trace or leave "back doors" to return to the system after investigations occur.[66]

Prior to the breach, eBay and PayPal security systems were considered "state of the art." Although hackers copied a large part of the eBay database, customers' PayPal accounts were encrypted and stored on a separate network, making it difficult for attackers to connect personal and financial information. Sources predict that the breach occurred due to "social engineering" where a company insider was tricked into handing over important information to a hacker posing as a trusted eBay insider. Regardless, top eBay executives claimed that the company reacted to the breach as soon as it was detected and planned to develop a more robust security system.[67]

Research finds that corporate cybersecurity training and awareness programs are not proving to be effective. Lack of customization and personalization makes the offerings less engaging and employees "feel bored with such training programs and lack enthusiasm to participate in them."[68] The traditional approach of getting people to watch videos followed by assessments lacks hands-on interaction; in addition, it is relatively easy to find workarounds to pass the tests without carefully watching the video content. So, how do you make security training fun and effective? The following are some important attributes of a successful and engaging learning program:

Accountability. Cybersecurity training performance should be an important component of an employee's performance assessment.

Fun. Both content and delivery must be humorous and engaging. Use of dramatic scenarios, games, and funny videos are some of the ways of making the training a fun and valuable experience. Use of gamification is a very popular and effective training method. Project Ares is an example of an online AI-enabled cyber learning platform that provides participants an immersive gaming experience. They receive training and then enter battle rooms (Figure 23) to detect and repel attacks. As the trainees engage in cyber battles, they receive tips and advice from Athena, an AI-driven chat bot.[69]

Hands-on. Role-playing, simulation, testing, and hacking contests are ways to make the training as hands-on as possible. Phishme Simulator is a

Figure 23   Project Ares Battle Room Dashboard

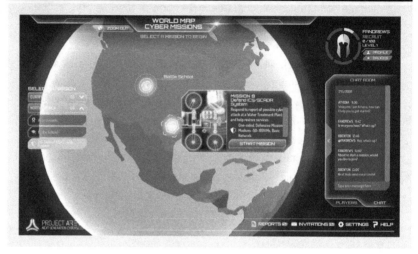

Source: circadence.com. Reproduced by permission.

training tool offered by Cofense, a third-party security service provider, to reduce the probability of employees becoming victims of phishing attacks. Such tools are designed to enhance knowledge and skill level through continuous training and practice. Many organizations conduct their own customized training programs to reduce phishing-related vulnerabilities.

Interactivity. To make the experience collaborative, engage participants by asking them to share security-related stories and scenarios. They should also be encouraged to come up with solutions to the discussed security challenges. The more you can get employees to feel they are part of the solution, the greater is the likelihood of successful compliance with security policies and directives.

Just-in-Time Training. The content must be current and focused on ensuring employees don't make the same mistakes. They should receive coaching and help as soon as vulnerabilities are detected, or they have failed a certain security test.

Personalization. People learn best when the training can be linked to their personal interests, lives, and work needs. In other words, get each employee to recognize how a particular security threat can impact and adversely affect their professional lives, either directly or indirectly by adversely impacting firm operations and performance. What is in it for me? Why should I care? These are the kinds of questions that need to be addressed when setting the stage for the training program.

Reinforcement. Training should never be a one-time or one-shot experience. There needs to be repetition and reinforcement to enhance the level of understanding and the ability to apply the learned skills. Continuous training is key to ensuring that organizations are at a high level of human readiness to thwart cyberattacks. Immersive Labs provides a training platform to enhance organizational cyber intelligence and also stress-test decision-making capabilities during cyberattack-related crises. Business and technology leaders and other organizational employees not only learn about the latest attack types and how to deal with them but also get to apply the knowledge in simulated crisis conditions.

Reward. Through a mix of tangible and intangible rewards, organizations are likely to succeed in achieving the desired security behavior and thereby bring about a gradual transformation in the security culture. Both individuals and security teams need to be recognized for various information security management outcome scenarios—such as no-breach over a certain time period and quick and effective incident response and disaster recovery.[70]

In summary, the goal of the training program should be to instill in each and every employee a deep sense of awareness of the different types of threats and how to protect sensitive data and other critical assets from potential attacks. As one security expert aptly stated, "Teach all employees what cybercrime looks like and how it is likely to affect them."[71] Such awareness and understanding will come from frequent and sustained training. A one-shot training exercise might be economically viable but not effective.[72]

Following is a list of questions to guide managerial decision making on information security-related awareness and training.

Awareness and Training: Guiding Questions

1. Is cybersecurity training performance an important component of an employee's assessment?

2. Is the training customized to employee roles and needs?

3. Is the cybersecurity training continuous?

---

4. Are the content and delivery interactive and engaging? Are dramatic scenarios, games, and funny videos used to make the training program a fun and informative experience?

5. Are techniques such as role-playing, testing, and hacking contests used to make the training interactive and hands-on?

6. Are all users informed and trained?

7. Do privileged users understand their roles and responsibilities?

8. Do senior executives understand their roles and responsibilities?

9. Do third-party stakeholders (e.g., suppliers, customers, partners) understand their roles and responsibilities?

10. Do physical and information security personnel understand their roles and responsibilities?

6.2.10 Business Continuity Planning

Related to cybersecurity risk assessments, business continuity planning (BCP) focuses on understanding the various adversity scenarios that could bring operations to a halt. From system failures to earthquakes, viral attacks, terrorism, hacking, and employee turnovers, organizations have to be prepared for all kinds of incidents, some caused intentionally, others being acts of nature. The significance of BCP cannot be overemphasized, especially under the current coronavirus pandemic conditions.

Business continuity planners will adopt a very meticulous approach to identify all possible operational disruption risks and conduct a business impact assessment (BIA). The BIA analyses will help identify the threats, quantify their impacts, and rank order them based on expected loss amounts. Then, for each of the threats, the planners will identify suitable preventive or control measures. These measures fall under two broad categories: technical and administrative.

The focus of technical measures is to increase the fault tolerance of devices and systems. One such technical control is to build in device and component redundancy and thereby avoid single points of failure. Having a cluster of servers instead of relying on a single server, using multiple firewalls instead of one, and using multiple sources to power data centers are examples of redundancies to maintain continuity of operations.

Organizations are also known to implement a redundant array of inexpensive disks (RAID) to protect themselves from storage device failures. Disk mirroring is one form of RAID (level one) implementation, where the server contains two storage disks, each being a mirror image of the other. Each of these disks contains identical data. Thus, if the primary disks fail, the system will automatically switch to the backup disk. Disk striping is another form of RAID (level five) implementation where the system writes to three or more disks and parity blocks are included across the disks. The parity information helps in regenerating the failed disk's contents.

Load balancing is another recommended fault tolerance method where the computing load is spread across multiple servers. Failure of a single device is unlikely to result in total disruption as the burden of service performance is shared across multiple machines.

Organizations should also be prepared to support remote work by offering the necessary network bandwidth and also have in place a reliable virtual private network service. Employees must also receive training and guidance to use secure connections and storage locations and be vigilant to different forms of phishing and other attacks.

In addition to technical control measures, organizations must have in place administrative controls such as succession planning to protect itself from loss of skilled and experienced personnel. By offering job enrichment programs and other rewards and opportunities, companies should make proactive efforts to earn the loyalty and trust of their employees. A happy workplace and culture can go a long way in retaining top talent and also protect the company from insider attacks.

Having backup sites in place is another form of administrative control to maintain continuity of operations. These sites take the form of data centers and office locations that are suitably equipped with systems and personnel. When companies experience denial-of-service type attacks that freeze up their networks and systems or they experience natural disasters such as hurricanes, floods, and earthquakes, it pays off to have these backup sites in geographically dispersed locations. They are able to maintain continuity of operations from these alternative locations.

Clarity on leadership roles and responsibilities during times of crisis is very important. A tested plan outlining who is responsible for what and when must be in place. Teams who will be leading the recovery must also be formed, with clear demarcation of their scope of operation. To ensure a strong coordinated response, the teams must train collaboratively to become more familiar with their respective roles. Communication strategies that specify the format and delivery of different types of crisis recovery messaging are also crucial. According to one senior information security leader, "overcommunicating was a game changer," as he was guiding his organization's response to the pandemic. Communicating creatively, focusing on what to do rather than what not to do, and being transparent and prompt with sharing updates are some other recommended best practices.[73] Finally, coordinating with vendors to synchronize and align their continuity plans is an integral component of business continuity planning.

Presented below is a set of questions to guide the implementation of a robust business continuity plan.

Business Continuity Planning: Guiding Questions

1. Is there a cross-functional team of business continuity planners?

2. Is a business impact analysis (BIA) methodology in place to drive BCP efforts?

3. Are multiple systems and devices in use to protect against single points of failure?

4. Is the company using RAID or similar technology to protect against storage device failures?

5. Do servers come with multiple power sources and are powered by two independent power providers?

6. Are server clustering and similar technologies in use to implement load balancing?

7. Are appropriate technologies in use to support and secure remote work?

8. Are training programs offered to enhance the remote work skill level of employees?

9. Is there a succession plan, especially for the highly skilled information security personnel?

10. Are job enrichment programs in place to motivate employees and help them realize their potential?

(Continued)

(Continued)

11. Has the company invested in backup sites that can ensure continuity of operations during crisis?

12. Are leadership roles and responsibilities to guide business recovery efforts clearly identified and documented?

13. Are communication strategies formulated that specify the format and delivery of different types of crisis recovery messaging?

14. Are the business continuity plans of vendors in sync with those of the company?

15. Is the business continuity plan tested on a regular basis?

16. Is the business continuity plan periodically subjected to a tabletop test?

6.3 Detect

Conducting reconnaissance activities to gather cyber threat–related intelligence must feature in an organization's information security defense strategy. Tracking abnormal network traffic patterns, unusual messages from suspicious sources, and atypical transaction activity in unfamiliar locations are all part of a cyber intelligence gathering exercise. Through such monitoring and detection activities, organizations become more aware of the nature and types of cybersecurity threats and can proactively deal with them. The fundamental principle is: "You need to understand your threat before you can protect against it."[74] Awareness of who the likely threat actors are; what assets they are planning to target; and when, where, and how they plan to carry out their mission helps in determining appropriate protection measures.

Unless detection and proactive defense capabilities are strengthened, organizations are likely to be victims of multiple cyberattacks. The following vignette presents the story of one such organization, the Alaska Department of Health and Social Services, which experienced multiple breaches and was found in violation of Health Insurance Portability and Accountability Act (HIPAA) and Alaska Personal Information Protection Act (APIPA) regulations.

Alaska's Department of Health and Social Services Again Falls Victim to a Cyberattack

Alaska's Department of Health and Social Services (ADHSS) suffered a significant data breach when an employee unsuspectingly clicked on an email attachment that seemed legitimate. The malware that got installed on the employee's laptop was a variant of the Zeus/Zbot Trojan virus and is designed to steal information. The unauthorized software gave the attackers access to the laptop between April 26 and April 30, 2018, and allowed them to steal electronic protected health information (ePHI). The sensitive data included first and last names, dates of birth, phone numbers, Medicaid/Medicare billing codes, criminal justice information, health billing information, Social Security numbers, driver's license numbers, pregnancy status, incarceration status, and other confidential information. Between 500K to 700K individuals were affected by the breach.

Preliminary investigation revealed that the virus was able to bypass multiple layers of security and get the infected laptop connected to Russia-based IP addresses. The antivirus (AV) software could not detect the malware because it was a day one attack, i.e., it was carried out before the AV software could be updated with the Trojan's signature.

The Federal Bureau of Investigation (FBI) is still examining the nature and extent of the breach and the associated violations of the Health Insurance Portability and Accountability Act (HIPAA) and the Alaska Personal Information Protection Act (APIPA). Incidentally, this agency experienced another data breach in 2009 and was found guilty of a HIPAA violation. A penalty of $1.7 million was imposed due to "failure to conduct a comprehensive risk analysis to identify vulnerabilities that could be exploited to gain access to PHI, insufficient device and media controls, and a lack of staff training on data security."

The focus of detection processes and mechanisms needs to be on the three cardinal goals of information security—protecting confidentiality, ensuring integrity, and maintaining availability. Every effort must be made to prevent unauthorized access, insulate sensitive data from destruction, modification, or degradation, and ensure that systems are up and running and providing timely information to authorized personnel.[75]

A mature cyber intelligence gathering process is comprised of four phases: planning, collection, processing and analysis, and dissemination.

Determining the cyber intelligence requirements of an organization is an extremely important first and foundational step. Based on the organization's needs, a strategy for how best to collect and analyze the data will be formulated. Finally, the sharing of threat-related insights also entails decisions relating to reporting format, timing, and recipients.

Threat intelligence providers gather different types of data and from various sources. For instance, analysis of malware will reveal the attack code, IP addresses, and domain names and can be used to update firewalls and detection systems, as well as contribute to an understanding of the threat actors' tactics and procedures. A security information and event management (SIEM) tool is a source of information regarding the client organization's infrastructure, nature of network traffic, and so on. Member-only hacking forums such as the Deep Web are yet another source for insights and scoops on the latest tools and services offered and requested by cybercriminals. Then there is the Dark Web, which refers to online marketplaces hosted on anonymity-focused networks where perpetrators buy and sell goods and services. Stolen data such as login credentials, credit card and medical data, and intellectual property are available for sale. Monitoring various messaging and social media platforms is yet another way of keeping track of threat activities ranging from potential targets to attack method and tactics. Insights on attack plans and capabilities can also be gained from code repositories and paste sites. Code repositories such as GitHub and BitBucket are often a go-to resource for the software development team. These host platforms support sharing of ideas and collaboration among software engineers and developers.[76] Paste site or Pastebin is another useful resource for programmers who will often share blocks of code to help their professional community or seek debugging help. ControlC, Hastebin, and Just Paste Me are some popular code paste platforms.[77] Finally, there are numerous other information sharing platforms such as:

- The UK National Cyber Security Centre's (NCSC) Cyber Security Information Sharing Partnership (CiSP)

- The Financial Services Information Sharing and Analysis Center (FS-ISAC)

- AlienVault's Open Threat Exchange (OTX), a crowd-sourced platform used by participants in 140 countries

- US-CERT's (United States Computer Emergency Response Team) Automated Indicator Sharing (AIS) platform

- The Asia Pacific (APAC) Intelligence Centre based in Singapore

Organizations that are seriously committed to proactively gather and act on operational, tactical, and strategic security intelligence have in place a Security Operations Center (SOC). The SOC team is charged with gathering threat intelligence data from various sources and acting on them. They are expected to keep the organization informed of threat urgency levels and guide appropriate action. This group is also entrusted with the responsibility of deciding on external service providers who would aid intelligence gathering, vulnerability testing, and defense activities. The selection process must be rigorous and service provider performance closely monitored and regularly reviewed.[78]

With the advancements in artificial intelligence and big data analytics, today's threat detection and response (TDR) solutions are quite sophisticated. By monitoring and mining network traffic and user behavior data, these tools are able to detect anomalies and abnormal patterns (which often go undetected by firewalls and antivirus software) and raise an alarm. When the automatic alert is triggered, the responsible security team personnel are able to evaluate the seriousness of the threat, eliminate false positives, and respond. The nature of response can range from conducting more in-depth forensic analysis to banning malicious files, quarantining affected devices, and stopping malicious processes.[79]

Splunk's on-premise and cloud-based Security Information and Event Management (SIEM) platform[80] is representative of the state-of-the-art software solutions that leverage structured and unstructured data to offer security monitoring, advanced threat detection, incident investigation and response, and other security operation services.

Considering the plethora of sophisticated detection tools, an organization must have a clear and deliberate plan on what to use and how to create an integrated technology architecture to optimize detection effectiveness.[81] In the absence of a holistic plan, organizations end up with numerous and disparate tools and managing them becomes a challenge. Often the functionalities are overlapping with each tool offering certain types of detection capabilities, which range from endpoint detection and response, to network traffic analysis, to malware sandboxes, and cyber threat intelligence. According to cybersecurity expert and analyst J. Oltsik:

> Each of these tools must be deployed, configured, and operated daily. Furthermore, each tool provides its own myopic alerting and reporting. Security analysts are then called upon to stitch together a complete threat management picture across endpoint security tools, network security tools, threat intelligence, etc.

This is a manual process slog that doesn't scale. Little wonder then why malware is often present on a network for hundreds of days before being discovered.[82]

Organizations are best served by investing in an integrated detection and response platform. Check Point, Splunk, Cisco, Fidelis, FireEye, McAfee, Palo Alto Networks, Symantec, and Trend Micro are representative of vendors offering such integrated capabilities. Supplementing the integrated platform with "best-of-breed" tools that provide unique capabilities is always an option.

Maintaining, monitoring, and analysis of audit logs are another important detection control. Data breaches often go undetected for long periods because organizations do a poor job of maintaining comprehensive logs and regularly analyzing and reviewing the results.

Logging capabilities on all systems and networking devices must be enabled. The settings should be appropriately configured so that the log report includes detailed information ranging from event source to data, user, timestamp, source address, and destination address. To ensure timestamp consistency, it is recommended that all servers and network devices retrieve information from at least three synchronized time sources. There should be a process in place, preferably automated, to regularly collect, suitably aggregate, and transmit log data to a central log management system for analysis and review.

Following is a list of questions to guide the planning and implementation of detection processes and tools.

Detecting Anomalies and Events: Guiding Questions

1. Is there a formal and well-documented cyber intelligence gathering process in place?

2. To what extent is the cyber intelligence gathering plan comprehensively written, addressing each of the four phases—planning, collection, processing and analysis, and dissemination?

3. To what extent are the various intelligence-gathering sources clearly identified and a plan in place on how to leverage those resources?

---

4. Does the organization deploy a Security Information and Event Management (SIEM) platform for security monitoring, advanced threat detection, incident investigation and response, and other related services?

5. Is a security operations center (SOC) and team in place to lead the threat intelligence gathering initiatives?

6. Is a formal and rigorous process in place to select external expertise to assist with intelligence gathering and threat detection activities?

7. Considering the plethora of sophisticated detection tools, is a rigorous process in place to implement an integrated detection and response platform?

8. Is a baseline of network operations and expected data flows for users and systems established and managed?

9. Are detected events analyzed to understand attack targets and methods?

10. Are event data aggregated and correlated from multiple sources and sensors?

11. Is there a process in place to determine the impact of events?

12. Are incident alert thresholds established?

13. To what extent are roles and responsibilities for detection well defined to ensure accountability?

14. How often are detection processes tested?

15. Is event detection information communicated to appropriate parties?

16. How often are detection processes reviewed and updated?

6.4 Respond and Recover

With the threat of cyberattack constantly looming over their heads, organizations must be ever prepared to effectively deal with a real threat incident.

The ability to a) quickly identify and isolate affected devices and systems, b) expeditiously restore normal business operations, c) meticulously gather evidence and secure the attack domain for further investigation, and d) effectively communicate with various stakeholders—customers, employees, regulators, business partners, and investors—are some attributes of a highly prepared and response-ready organization.[83] The next two subsections are devoted toward understanding how to develop and sustain incident response and disaster recovery capabilities.

6.4.1 Incident Response Capability

According to investigation reports, the massive Equifax breach was caused by the negligence of a senior management person who didn't take necessary action upon receiving good intelligence. As discussed in Chapter 3, one of the lessons from the Equifax incident is to develop the discipline and routine of promptly reviewing intelligence reports and making informed decisions on whether to act or not.

The effectiveness of an organization's incident response capability (IRC) depends on many factors—from senior management commitment and mindset to organization-wide support, suitable governance structures and mechanisms, appropriate technology solutions, adequate resources, and well-trained personnel.

Crisis management preparation must be driven by a top management mindset that recognizes cybersecurity to be more than an IT issue and requires the expertise and involvement of personnel from multiple functions and varied skillsets. Technical and forensic skills are essential to detect the source and cause of the cyberattack. Legal representation will guide organizational response from the standpoint of dealing and communicating with law enforcement, customers, employees, shareholders, regulatory agencies, business partners, and investors. Communications personnel must also be part of the cross-functional crisis management team to drive the messaging plan. Members from the various operating units will enlighten the crisis management team on the business implications of the attack. From a technology standpoint, both proactive and responsive tools must be available to the team to mitigate the possibility of similar attacks in the future. The personnel assigned to deploy, support, and maintain these tools must be well trained. If third-party services are going to be utilized, then the individual or team dealing with the external agency must have the experience and ability to provide strong oversight.

Thus, establishing a cross-functional incident response (IR) team is an important step from a governance standpoint. Roles, responsibilities, and reporting relationships must be clearly defined to ensure that everyone on the team knows what they are expected to do and when. Preferably, the IR team should be led by a senior business leader either operating at the C-level or reporting directly to a C-level executive.

A step-by-step approach to dealing with threat incidents must be documented and rehearsed. For instance, the following is a generic set of actions that should be triggered following an incident:

- Document the incident details such as who reported it, how it was uncovered, and who alerted the relevant personnel.

- Investigate the cause of the incident and take immediate steps to prevent further damage.

- Identify and isolate affected systems and/or devices.

- Quarantine the area of the incident and the digital assets involved for evidence gathering by relevant authorities such as the Federal Bureau of Investigation (FBI).

- Gather and analyze the evidence to get to the root of the cause and source of attack.

- Strengthen network security and protocols, enhance monitoring, review and modify policies, and implement any other necessary measures to boost security.

- Document the findings and the steps taken in response to the attack.

- Promptly and clearly communicate with all affected stakeholders, regulatory agencies, and the general public.

Many of the listed actions might need to be taken simultaneously and not necessarily in the order above. The established procedure must be periodically tested and modified on an as-needed basis. Measures to evaluate IR effectiveness must also be in place.

Below is a set of questions to enable organizations assess and develop their ability to effectively respond to threats and attacks.

6.4.2 Disaster Recovery Planning

In the absence of a good disaster recovery plan (DRP), organizations can be in huge trouble. A recent survey finds 93% of the companies without a DRP are out of business within a year of a catastrophic data loss incident. On the other hand, 96% of the surveyed companies with a robust backup and disaster recovery plan survived a ransomware attack. Yet, 75% of the small businesses polled were without any DRP.[84]

When developing a DRP, first and foremost, the planning team must brainstorm and list the various possible threat scenarios. Each threat type is likely to vary in how the organization is impacted and the appropriate steps that need to be taken to restore normal operations. The potential disaster scenarios must be rank ordered based on risk and business impact analysis.[85]

Many organizations, generally the larger ones, tend to separate incident response plans (IRPs) from disaster recovery plans (DRPs). At a high level, both have the same goals, namely to provide a game plan and roadmap to quickly and effectively recover from an adverse incident or event. From a tactical standpoint, however, IRP is focused on getting to the bottom of the incident through intelligence gathering and analysis, while DRP comprises a set of activities to recover from the incident and restore normalcy. For certain firms, IRP tends to focus on information security events, while DRP is triggered when the organization is facing large-scale disasters such as earthquakes, hurricanes, and acts of terror. Considering that cyberattacks, similar to other catastrophic events, can have the potential of shutting down the entire business operation, it is important to develop and manage these plans in a highly collaborative manner.[86]

Organizations with both IRPs and DRPs must reduce ambiguity by clearly articulating and documenting how the plans support and complement each other. There must also be an explicit understanding of circumstances and scenarios when IRP or DRP is triggered and the transition points. Both teams must work closely together and conduct joint training exercises to develop a strong understanding of their respective roles and responsibilities.[87]

The following are some key elements of a comprehensive disaster recovery plan:

Comprehensive Asset Inventory. The organization must maintain a detailed and comprehensive inventory of its digital assets—both hardware and software. Such a list needs to include description, photos, location details, serial numbers, and organizational control numbers. Pictures showing location of the equipment before and after the preparation for potential disasters (such as natural calamities) also provide evidence of organizational efforts to take protective measures. Relevant contract and vendor contact information should also feature in the asset inventory list. Maintaining a list of passwords to access the different devices, systems, and applications is also a good practice. Such meticulous documentation is extremely useful from the standpoint of protection, restoration, and filing insurance claims.[88]

Communication Plan. It is extremely important to clearly articulate and document assignments, roles, and responsibilities of all individuals and teams in the event of a disaster. Nothing should be merely assumed. To the extent feasible and possible, every detail of how individuals and teams will act, communicate, and report must be explicitly stated in the plan document. Relevant employee, vendor, supplier, and customer contact information and details of multiple/alternate communication methods (such as emails, phones, and social media platforms) must also be included.[89]

Organizations must also have a written plan on how to communicate with the entire workforce, the media, and the general public. Online portals are often used to update all concerned about the state of recovery.

Roles and Responsibilities. Everyone involved with disaster recovery operations must have complete clarity as to their respective roles and responsibilities. For easy and quick identification, it is recommended that assigned personnel be listed by name and not their regular job titles. Since the disaster recovery role is likely to be different from the day-to-day operational role, listing team members by titles can get confusing. Contact information must be kept current. Listing of backup members is equally important.[90]

Tolerance Levels. It is important to set the acceptable recovery point objective (RPO) and recovery time objective (RTO) for all systems and applications, especially for the mission-critical ones. Desirably the recovery time should be no more than a few milliseconds, but that may not be a realistic goal. It is imperative that planners carefully deliberate and decide on these two metrics for each tiered set of applications. Generally, the Tier 1 applications need to be up and running immediately, Tier 2 within eight to ten hours, and Tier 3 within a few days.[91]

Backup Sites. Organizations must be prepared with one or two backup site locations from where they can start operating the mission-critical systems if the main operational site goes down. These recovery sites must be set up with trained personnel and devices and systems to be functional as soon as disaster strikes and takes down the main production systems. There are three types of backup sites: hot, warm, and cold sites. Hot sites are fully equipped with all the necessary hardware, software, network, and internet connectivity; even data are regularly backed up or replicated on the hot site systems. Such a site can exist physically in a data center or at a branch/satellite office location, or virtually in the cloud. The hot site is expected to be up and running immediately. On the other hand, the warm and cold sites, the cheaper options, are reasonably equipped and staffed and will take a few days to be functional.

The disaster recovery team must have a clear understanding of where they need to be when there is an incident. There must be adequate space at the alternate sites to accommodate the assigned personnel.

Service Level Agreements with Service Providers. If external service providers are involved in deploying computing operations, the service level agreements (SLAs) with each of these service providers must explicitly state the level of service expected from the contractors in the event of a disaster. Desirably, there should be penalties for not meeting the contracted expectations.

Regular Testing. The DR plan must be tested periodically to ensure that the recovery performance meets expectation. Using measures such as the Recovery Point Objective and Recovery Time Objective, the testing process must comprehensively evaluate the effectiveness of the plan. The methodology and frequency of testing must be documented in the plan document and followed. There are tools that can be used to automate DR testing without disrupting production systems. It is also important to test the performance of the assigned personnel using simulated disasters and drills.

Following is a set of guiding questions to ensure that the key elements of a disaster recovery plan are addressed and in place.

Disaster Recovery Planning: Guiding Questions

1. Is a comprehensive asset inventory maintained to identify the various vulnerability points?

2. Are the various threat scenarios identified and rank ordered (based on risk and business impact analysis) prior to developing recovery strategies?

3. Are recovery performance measures (such as the Recovery Point Objective and Recovery Time Objective) for mission-critical and noncritical applications and systems clearly defined?

4. Are the roles and responsibilities of the DRP team members clearly articulated and documented?

5. Are details on how individuals and teams will act, communicate, and report explicitly depicted in the plan document?

6. Do the Incident Response and Disaster Recovery teams work in close cooperation and conduct joint training exercises?

7. To the extent applicable, are business partners (such as customers and vendors) kept informed of the recovery plan?

8. Is there a written communication plan that details how the entire workforce, media, and the general public will be kept informed and updated during the disaster recovery process?

9. Are backup sites, whether hot, warm, or cold, in place?

10. Do service level agreements (SLAs) with vendors explicitly detail the expected level of service and support during disasters?

11. Is the Disaster Recovery Plan (DRP) regularly tested and updated as needed?

Thus, there are several elements to a comprehensive approach to preparedness—from identifying the critical assets to coming up with a risk-based protection prioritization scheme, implementing multi-factor authentication measures, managing access privileges, encrypting data, following reliable backup methods, securing networks and ports, engaging in customized and immersive training exercises, deploying sophisticated detection capabilities, and formulating and rehearsing business continuity and disaster recovery plans. Doing them well can be a challenging and overwhelming endeavor. Without a deep-rooted conviction and belief in the value of being thoroughly prepared, organizations cannot achieve and sustain a high level of preparedness.

NOTES TO CHAPTER 6

1. Chapple, M., Stewart, J. M., & and Gibson, D. (2018). *Certified Information Systems Security Professional, Official Study Guide, 8th ed.* John Wiley & Sons.
2. Gressin, S. (2018, December 4). The Marriott Data Breach. *Federal Trade Commission.* Retrieved September 9, 2019 from https://www.consumer.ftc.gov/blog/2018/12/marriott-data-breach.
3. O'Flaherty, K. (2019, March 11). Marriott CEO Reveals New Details About Mega Breach. *Forbes.* Retrieved December 16, 2020 from https://www.forbes.com/sites/kateoflahertyuk/2019/03/11/marriott-ceo-reveals-new-details-about-mega-breach/#e5ce8b6155c0.
4. Del Valle, G. (2019, January 11). *Marriott's Data Breach May Be the Biggest in History. Now It's Facing Multiple Class-Action Lawsuits.* Vox. Retrieved September 9, 2019 from https://www.vox.com/the-goods/2019/1/11/18178733/marriott-starwood-hack-lawsuit
5. Hosn, H. (2018, October 26). *Three Key Steps to Help Protect National Infrastructure.* Secureworks. Retrieved June 3, 2019 from https://www.secureworks.com/blog/three-key-steps-to-help-protect-national-infrastructure
6. Quoted in Staff, M. (2019, February 27). *Critical Infrastructure Attacks: Nations Are Not Ready.* Raconteur. Retrieved June 13, 2019 from https://www.raconteur.net/technology/critical-infrastructure-cyberattacks
7. Cybersecurity and Infrastructure Security Agency. (2017, August). *Securing Cyber Assets: Addressing Urgent Cyber Threats to Critical Infrastructure.* https://www.cisa.gov/sites/default/files/publications/niac-securing-cyber-assets-final-report-508.pdf
8. Bailey, T., Barriball, E., Dey, A., & Sankur, A. (2019, March 8). What Is Supply Chain Risk Management? A Practical Approach to Supply Chain Risk Management. *McKinsey & Company.* https://www.mckinsey.com/business-functions/operations/our-insights/a-practical-approach-to-supply-chain-risk-management#
9. Boehm, J., Merrath, P., Poppensieker, T., Riemenschnitter, R., & and Stahle, T. (2018, November 19). Cyber risk measurement and the holistic cybersecurity approach. *McKinsey & Company.* https://www.mckinsey.com/business-functions/risk/our-insights/cyber-risk-measurement-and-the-holistic-cybersecurity-approach

10. Xactium. *6 Meaningful Approaches to Risk Aggregation* [White paper].

11. Kulwal, M. (2019, June 15). *Best Practices on Risk Aggregation* [White Paper]. RiskSpotlight. www.riskspotlight.com

12. Barker, I. (2019). *90 Percent of Critical Infrastructure Hit by Cyberattacks*. Betanews. Retrieved June 13, 2019 from https://betanews.com/2019/04/05/critical-infrastructure-cyberattacks/#:~:text=A%20new%20survey%20of%20professionals,experiencing%20two%20or%20more%20attacks.

13. Miessler, D. (2018, December 31). *If You're Not Doing Continuous Asset Management, You're Not Doing Security*. Danielmiessler.com. Retrieved June 13, 2019 from https://danielmiessler.com/blog/continuous-asset-management-security/

14. ARMIS. (2020). *Cybersecurity Asset Management: Device Discovery and Risk Assessment* [White Paper]. https://www.armis.com/resources/iot-security-white-papers/cybersecurity-asset-management-white-paper/

15. Chapple, M., Stewart, J. M., & and Gibson, D. (2018). *Certified Information Systems Security Professional, Official Study Guide, 8th ed*. John Wiley & Sons.

16. Rothke, B. (2019, April 16). *9 Keys to Getting the Most Out of Your Vulnerability Management Solution*. BeyondTrust. Retrieved June 4, 2019 from https://www.beyondtrust.com/blog/entry/9-keys-to-getting-the-most-out-of-your-vulnerability-management-solution

17. Francis, P. (2018, June). *Security Think Tank: Use Data Flow Information to Protect Systems*. Computer Weekly. Retrieved June 13, 2019 from https://www.computerweekly.com/opinion/Security-Think-Tank-Use-data-flow-information-to-protect-systems

18. Godfrey, J. (2015, January 15). *Best Practices and Tips for Network Segmentation*. Algosec. Retrieved June 12, 2019 from https://www.algosec.com/blog/best-practices-tips-network-segmentation-use-cases-professor-wool/

19. Olzak, T. (2016, April 25). Keep Your Critical Systems Safe. *CSO Online*. Retrieved June 12, 2019 from https://www.csoonline.com/article/3060058/keep-your-critical-systems-safe.html

20. Reichenberg, N. (2014, March 20). *Improving Security via Proper Network Segmentation*. Security Week. Retrieved June 12, 2019 from https://www.securityweek.com/improving-security-proper-network-segmentation

21. Walkowski, D. (2019, August 22). *What Are Security Controls?* Education. Retrieved August 21, 2020 from https://www.f5.com/labs/articles/education/what-are-security-controls
    Mullahy, T. (2019, September 27). *5 Physical Controls Your Business Needs*. Total Security Advisor. Retrieved August 21, 2020 from https://totalsecurityadvisor.blr.com/facility-security/5-physical-security-controls-your-business-needs/

22. https://www.cisecurity.org/, accessed on July 28, 2020.

23. Johnson, A., Dempsey, K., Ross, R., Gupta, S., & Bailey, D. (2011, August). *Guide for Security-Focused Configuration Management of Information Systems*. National Institute of Standards and Technology. https://csrc.nist.gov/publications/detail/sp/800-128/final

24. Chapple, M., Stewart, J. M., & and Gibson, D. (2018). *Certified Information Systems Security Professional, Official Study Guide, 8th ed*. John Wiley & Sons.

25. Geer, D. (2017, April 24). *Securing Risky Network Ports*. Network World. Retrieved October 11, 2019 from https://www.networkworld.com/article/3191513/securing-risky-network-ports.html

26. Ibid.

27. Bukth, T. and Huda, S. M. S. (2017, January 4). *The Soft Threat: The Story of the Bangladesh Bank Reserve Heist*. SAGE Business Cases.

28. Bigman, R. (2019, May 28). *Transient Devices Require Strict Control Measures as Regulatory Compliance Requirements Grow*. SC Media. Retrieved July 22, 2019 from https://www.scmagazine.com/home/opinion/executive-insight/transient-devices-require-strict-control-measures-as-regulatory-compliance-requirements-grow/ https://www.scmagazine.com/

29. Burt, J. (2018, October 1). *USB Devices Still a Threat to Businesses, Kaspersky Finds*. Informa Tech. Retrieved July 22, 2019 from https://www.securitynow.com/author .asp?section_id=715&doc_id=746429

30. Pal, K. (2015, July 15). *10 Best Practices for Encryption Key Management and Data Security*. Techopedia. Retrieved June 5, 2019 from https://www.techopedia.com/2/30767/security/10-best-practices-for-encryption-key-management-and-data-security

31. Tozi, C. (2020, February 17). *Data Encryption 101: The Quick Guide to Data Encryption Best Practices*. Precisely. https://www.precisely.com/blog/data-security/data-encryption-101-guide-best-practices

32. FASOO. *NIST Cybersecurity Framework Can Help Protect Against Data Leaks*. Retrieved June 6 2019 from https://en.fasoo.com/nist-cybersecurity-framework-can-helpprotect-against-data-leaks/

33. Vitru. *Encryption Key Management: Host Your Own Keys and Keep Control of Your Data*. Retrieved July 8, 2020 from https://www.virtru.com/encryption-key-management/

34. AET. *The difference between a digital signature and digital certificate*. Retrieved July 2020 from https://www.aeteurope.com/news/digital-signature-digital-certificate/

35. Ibid.

36. GetApp. *Best Signature Software*. Retrieved July 2020 from https://www.get app.com/p/sem/digital-signatures-software?t=Best%20Signature%20Software &camp=adw_search&utm_content=g&utm_source=ps-google&utm_campaign=COM_US_Desktop_BEElectronic_Signature&utm_medium=cpc&account_campaign_id=1541494274&account_adgroup_id=877327209 33&ad_id=409684450497&gclid=Cj0KCQjwg8n5BRCdARIsALxKb96w4My--cdiH4TNaMxiwUWCC5N4bP1OxxiVEfxV3HJ80-ct99Ny2TUaAgzuEALw_wcB

37. Soni, V. (2018, January 11). Top 10 reliable SSL Certificate Providers in 2020. *ZNETLIVE*. Retrieved August 11, 2020 from https://www.znetlive.com/blog/top-10-reliable-ssl-certificate-providers/

38. SoftwarePublisherCertificate. *Introduction to Code Signing*. Retrieved August 2020 from http://www.softwarepublishercertificate.com/#

39. Ibid.

40. Watts, S. (2018, June 22). Data Masking: An Introduction. *BMC Blogs*. Retrieved August 2020 from https://www.bmc.com/blogs/data-masking/

41. American Payroll Association. (2019, December 7). *IRS Finalizes Rules to Allow Employers to Mask SSNs on Employees' W-2s*. Retrieved August 2020 from https://www.americanpayroll.org/news-resources/apa-news/news-detail/2019/07/12/irs-finalizes-rules-to-allow-employers-to-mask-ssns-on-employees-w-2s#:~:text=APA%20Merchandise-,IRS%20Finalizes%20Rules%20to%20Allow%20Employers,SSNs%20on%20Employees'%20W%2D2s&text=The%20IRS%20has%20finalized%20regulations,7%2D3%2D19%5D.

42. SoftwareTestingHelp. (2020). *10 Best Data Masking Tools and Software in 2020*. Retrieved November 13, 2020 from https://www.softwaretestinghelp.com/data-masking-tools/

43. Pujari, A. and Shinde, S. (2016, July-August). Data Security Using Cryptography and Steganography. *Journal of Computer Engineering*, 18(4), Ver. V, 130–139.

44. Medium. (2017, January 3). *Top 5 steganography software which are absolutely free*. Retrieved August 9, 2020 from https://medium.com/@gizest/top-5-steganography-software-which-are-absolutely-free-8e5686a901b

45. G2. *Where you go to buy software*. Retrieved July 2020 from www.g2.com.

46. Hein, D. (2109, October 25). 7 Essential Mobile Security Best Practices for Businesses. Mobile Management Solutions Review. https://solutionsreview.com/mobile-device-management/7-essential-mobile-security-best-practices-for-businesses/

47. P. DeBeasi, P. (2011, February 1). Best Practices for Enterprise Mobile Device Security. *ComputerWeekly*. Retrieved July 20, 2019 from https://www.computerweekly.com/tip/Best-practices-for-enterprise-mobile-device-security

48. Globalscape. (2018, May 10). What is the Best Way to Protect Your Data? Retrieved July 20, 2019 from https://www.globalscape.com/blog/what-best-way-protect-your-data

49. National Institute of Standards and Technology. *National Vulnerability Database*. Retrieved June 6, 2019 from https://nvd.nist.gov/800-53/Rev4/control/SI-7

50. Munjal, V. (2018, July 8). *Why should we have separate development testing and production-environments*. Linux Together. Retrieved June 6, 2019 from https://linuxtogether.org/why-should-we-have-separate-development-testing-and-production-environments/

51. Violino, B. (2012, February 6). The In-Depth Guide to Data Destruction. *CSO Online*. Retrieved December 16, 2020 from https://www.csoonline.com/article/2130822/the-in-depth-guide-to-datadestruction.html

52. AgileIT. (2017, August 3). *Data Backup Best Practices: Avoid These 6 Disaster Recovery Fails*. https://www.agileit.com/news/data-backup-best-practices/

53. Ibid.

54. Dobran, B. (2018, February 22). *Data Backup Strategy: Ultimate Step by Step Guide for Business*. PhoenixNAP. Retrieved August 13, 2019 from https://phoenixnap.com/blog/data-backup-strategy-guide-business

55. Myerson, J. (2019, June 13). *4 Steps to Remain Compliant With SOX Data Retention Policies*. TechTarget Network. Retrieved August 5, 2020 from https://searchcompliance.techtarget.com/tip/Four-steps-to-consolidate-SOX-data-retention-and-deletion-processes

56. ControlCase. *What are the 12 requirements of PCI DSS Compliance?* https://www.controlcase.com/what-are-the-12-requirements-of-pci-dss-compliance/

57. HIPAA Journal. (2018, May 17). *Do You Have a GDPR Data Retention Policy?* Retrieved August 5, 2020 from https://www.hipaajournal.com/gdpr-data-retention-policy/#:~:text=GDPR%20data%20retention%20is%20covered,collected%20and%20are%20being%20processed

58. Ibid.

59. Tiwari, A. (2019, August 24). *6 Best Hard Drive Eraser Tools for Your PC: Wipe Hard Drive In 2019*. Fossbytes. Retrieved August 5, 2020 from https://fossbytes.com/best-hard-drive-eraser-tools/

60. Panda. (2018, October 6). *A dating site and corporate cyber-security lessons to be learned.* Retrieved July 8, 2020 from https://www.pandasecurity.com/en/mediacenter/security/lessons-ashley-madison-data-breach/

61. Carfagno, D. (2019, August 19). *What Is a Security Patch?* Cybershark. Retrieved August 8, 2020 from https://www.blackstratus.com/what-is-a-security-patch/

62. Roman, J. (2014, May 21). *eBay Breach: 145 Million Users Notified.* Bank Info Security. Retrieved September 11, 2019 from https://www.bankinfosecurity.com/ebay-a-6858

63. Boulton, C. (2017, April 19). *Humans Are (Still) the Weakest Cybersecurity Link.* CIO. https://www.cio.com/article/3191088/humans-are-still-the-weakest-cybersecurity-link.html

64. Mushtaq, A. (2018, September 6). *How to Protect Against Human Vulnerabilities in Your Security Program.* Security. Retrieved June 12, 2019 from https://www.securitymagazine.com/articles/89382-how-to-protect-against-human-vulnerabilities-in-your-security-program

65. Finkle, J. and Deepa, S. (2014, May 27). *Cyber Thieves Took Data on 145 Million eBay Customers by Hacking 3 Corporate Employees.* Business Insider. Retrieved June 10, 2020 from https://www.businessinsider.com/cyber-thieves-took-data-on-145-million-ebay-customers-by-hacking-3-corporate-employees-2014-5#:~:text=Tech%20Contributors-,Cyber%20Thieves%20Took%20Data%20On%20145%20Million,By%20Hacking%203%20Corporate%20Employees&text=He%20said%20hackers%20got%20in,belonging%20to%20all%20eBay%20users.

66. Peterson, A. (2014, May 21). *eBay Asks 145 Million Users to Change Passwords After Data Breach.* Washington Post. Retrieved June 10, 2020 from https://www.washingtonpost.com/news/the-switch/wp/2014/05/21/ebay-asks-145-million-users-to-change-passwords-after-data-breach/

67. Quittner, J. (2014, May 30). *How the Once Impregnable EBay Fell Victim to Hackers (And You Can Too).* Inc. Retrieved June 10, 2020 from https://www.inc.com/jeremy-quittner/new-details-emerge-on-ebay-hack-attack.html

68. He, W. and Zhang, Z. (2019, July 29). Enterprise Cybersecurity and Awareness Programs: Recommendations for Success. *Journal of Organizational Computing and Electronic Commerce, 4,* 249–57.

69. CIRCADENCE. *What are your cyber security goals?* Retrieved July 18, 2020 from https://www.circadence.com/

70. Ibid.

71. Rosenthal, B. (2017, October 11). *When—and How—to Create a Culture of Cybersecurity.* National Cybersecurity Alliance. https://staysafeonline.org/blog/create-culture-cybersecurity/

72. Disparte, D. and Furlow, C. (2017, May 16). The Best Cybersecurity Investment You Can Make Is Better Training. *Harvard Business Review,* 2–4.

73. Violino, B. (2020, March 19). *A security guide for pandemic planning: 7 key steps.* CSOOnline. https://www.csoonline.com/article/3528878/a-security-guide-for-pandemic-planning-7-key-steps.html

74. CTIPs. *What is Cyber Threat Intelligence and How Is It Used?* [White paper]. CREST Threat Intelligence Professionals. Retrieved July 23, 2019 from https://www.crest-approved.org/wp-content/uploads/CREST-Cyber-Threat-Intelligence.pdf

75. LaPiedra, J. (2000-2002). *The Information Security Process: Prevention, Detection, and Response* [White paper]. SANS Institute. Retrieved July 27, 2019 from

https://www.giac.org/paper/gsec/501/information-security-process-prevention-detection-response/101197

76. Allen, Z. (2019, February 20). *Addressing Inherent Risks in Code Repositories*. Infosecurity. Retrieved August 21, 2020 from https://www.infosecurity-magazine.com/opinions/inherent-risks-code-repositories-1/

77. Stegner, B. (2019, November 11). *The 4 Best Pastebin Alternatives for Sharing Code and Text*. Make Use Of. Retrieved https://www.makeuseof.com/tag/4-alternatives-that-may-be-better-than-pastebin/

78. Ibid.

79. Lord, N. (2018, September 12). *What is Threat Detection and Response? Solutions, Benefits and More*. Digital Guardian. Retrieved July 28, 2019 from https://digitalguardian.com/blog/what-threat-detection-and-response-solutions-benefits-and-more

80. Splunk. *Bring Data to Every Security Challenge*. Retrieved July 2020 from https://www.splunk.com/en_us/enterprise-data-platform.html

81. Olstik, J. (2019, May 1). *5 Threat Detection and Response Technologies Are Coming Together*. CSO Online. Retrieved July 27, 2019 from https://www.csoonline.com/article/3391562/5-threat-detection-and-response-technologies-are-coming-together.html

82. Ibid.

83. Deloitte. (2016). *Cyber Crisis Management: Readiness, Response, and Recovery*. Retrieved July 28, 2019 from https://www2.deloitte.com/content/dam/Deloitte/global/Documents/Risk/gx-cm-cyber-pov.pdf

84. Dobran, B. (2018, August 16). 2019 *Disaster Recovery Statistics That Will Shock Business Owners*. PhoenixNAP. Retrieved July 30, 2019 from https://phoenixnap.com/blog/disaster-recovery-statistics

85. Stavridis, S. (2013, February 22). *A Guide to Disaster Recovery Planning*. CIO https://www2.cio.com.au/article/454491/guide_disaster_recovery_planning/

86. Keller, M. S. (2017, May 8). Deeper Dive: Incorporating Incident Response Into Disaster Recovery Plans. Baker Data Counsel. Retrieved December 16, 2020 from https://www.bakerdatacounsel.com/cybersecurity/deeper-dive-incorporating-incident-response-into-disaster-recovery-plans/

87. Kirvan, P. (2017, August 16). *Why You Need a Cybersecurity Incident Response Plan With DR*. TechTarget. Retrieved July 30, 2019 from https://searchdisasterrecovery.techtarget.com/tip/Use-a-cybersecurity-incident-response-plan-with-BC-DR

88. Schiff, J. L. (2016, July 5). *8 Ingredients of an Effective Disaster Recovery Plan*. CIO. Retrieved August 8, 2019 from https://www.csoonline.com/article/3091716/8-ingredients-of-an-effective-disaster-recovery-plan.html

89. Entech. (2018, April 16). *7 Key Elements of a Business Disaster Recovery Plan*. Retrieved August 8, 2019 from https://entechus.com/7-key-elements-of-a-business-disaster-recovery-plan/

90. Flesch, M. (2019, April 30). *Developing a Disaster Recovery Plan—5 Essential Elements*. Gordon Flesch Company. Retrieved August 8, 2019 from https://www.gflesch.com/elevity-it-blog/essential-elements-for-developing-a-disaster-recovery-plan

91. Schiff, J. L. (2016, July 5). *8 Ingredients of an Effective Disaster Recovery Plan*. CIO. Retrieved August 8, 2019 from https://www.csoonline.com/article/3091716/8-ingredients-of-an-effective-disaster-recovery-plan.html

Discipline

A disciplined approach to information security management is reflected in a) the meticulous formulation of governance policy and procedures, b) communication and enforcement of the policies, c) constant monitoring and testing of the plans, and d) continuous assessment of security plan performance. Each of these cybersecurity readiness success factors (Figure 24) is discussed in the following sections.

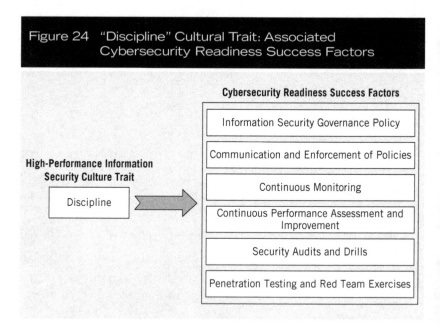

Figure 24   "Discipline" Cultural Trait: Associated Cybersecurity Readiness Success Factors

Cybersecurity Readiness Success Factors

Information Security Governance Policy

Communication and Enforcement of Policies

Continuous Monitoring

Continuous Performance Assessment and Improvement

Security Audits and Drills

Penetration Testing and Red Team Exercises

High-Performance Information Security Culture Trait

Discipline

7.1 Information Security Governance Policy

Organizations with a deliberate and thorough approach will have a clearly documented information security policy. This policy document should articulate the scope and goals of the company's information security strategy; how the strategy aligns with the overall organizational strategy, roles and responsibilities; information classification (from a confidentiality and sensitivity standpoint); directives for secure handling and protection of data; consequences for noncompliance; and more.[1]

Adhering to cybersecurity and data privacy laws should be a major goal of information security governance. The Health Insurance Portability and Accountability Act (HIPAA) of 1996, the California Online Privacy Protection Act of 2018, Consumer Privacy Protection Act of 2017, and the European Union's General Data Protection Regulation of 2018 are representative of many data privacy–related legislations. Working in collaboration with the legal department, the policy formulation team must identify the legal obligations and requirements spelled out by the various legislations and must put in place appropriate security controls. Appendix 4 provides a summary overview of cybersecurity and privacy laws and regulations.

Yoti, a cybersecurity solutions developer, grapples with the challenges of ensuring privacy of individual user data. They have implemented a range of measures to securely collect and store data. As part of due diligence, the company has consulted with international experts on human and consumer rights to guide the development and implementation of their data security policy.[2]

The policy document should also clarify the roles and responsibilities of the organization's personnel and its external partners. Within the organization, especially in large and professionally managed firms, the information security function will be headed by the chief information security officer (CISO) and will include personnel holding job titles such as directors, senior managers, and security professionals. Data owners, data custodians, end-users, and auditors are other roles that come with information security responsibilities.

Considering the growing use of third-party service providers, it is imperative that they be held to the same standard and expectations as the internal employees. Cybersecurity laws and regulations relevant to the organization and its implications on standards and practices must also be clearly spelled out in the information security policy manual. Formalized processes and procedures to manage cybersecurity risks and thereby accomplish the stated goals and mission must also be part of the policy documentation.

The standard elements of a comprehensive information security governance policy document include a) purpose, b) scope, c) objectives, d) authority and access control policy, e) asset and data identification and classification, f) roles and responsibilities, g) security awareness and training guidelines, h) vendor selection criteria, i) service level agreement guidelines, j) performance measures, and k) rewards and penalties.[3]

By providing a blueprint and road map to cybersecurity governance, such a policy document enhances overall awareness, transparency, and execution consistency and effectiveness. Security standards, baselines, guidelines, and procedures should also be crafted for effective implementation of the policies.

Following is a checklist to guide the formulation and documentation of a robust information security governance policy.

Information Security Governance Policy: Guiding Questions

1. Is the organizational policy on information security governance documented?

2. Is the security policy document comprehensive and comprised of the following representative elements?

   a. Purpose

   b. Scope

   c. Objectives

   d. Risk Tolerance Levels and Posture

   e. Asset and Data Identification and Classification Criteria

   f. Authority and Access Control

   g. Roles and Responsibilities

   h. Vendor Selection Criteria

   i. Service Level Agreement Guidelines

   j. Incident Response Plan

   k. Disaster Recovery Plan

   l. Training Guidelines

   m. Performance Measures

   n. Rewards and Penalties

   (Continued)

(Continued)

3. Are roles and responsibilities of information security personnel and information security responsibilities of other personnel clearly identified and documented?

4. Are security standards, baselines, guidelines, and procedures in place for effective implementation of the policies?

5. How frequently is the policy document reviewed and updated?

6. How frequently are the policy document elements tested to ensure they are actually in use?

7. Is a cross-functional team of senior leaders and experts involved in crafting the policy document and providing oversight?

7.2 Communications and Enforcement of Policies

In addition to crafting comprehensive security policies, disciplined organizations will make every effort to ensure that all organizational members and other stakeholders are extremely aware of the policies. Clear communication of expectations is essential to reinforce the organization's values and beliefs on how all stakeholders, at the individual or unit level, should conduct themselves to help mitigate cybersecurity risks. For instance, the Ownership and Responsibility policy would highlight the requirement of business and technology groups to partner and operate as a cohesive team and assume responsibility of the various security initiatives. The Noncompliance Consequences policy would clearly articulate the penalties for violating the established security codes of conduct and for not complying with the relevant regulatory requirements. Highly disciplined and meticulous organizations are also known to have Recovery and Business Continuity policies that clearly lay down procedures for recovering from different types of attacks.

Disciplined organizations will also have mechanisms in place to guarantee that the policies are in use and being enforced. Such mechanisms include a) requiring senior leaders own and be accountable for information security policy implementations, b) regular policy conformance reviews and audits, and c) awareness and training workshops.

Following is a set of questions to guide the communication and enforcement of information security policies.

Communication and Enforcement of Policies: Guiding Questions

1. Is there a communication plan in place for each type of information security policy?

2. Does the plan document clearly state how each type of policy communication will happen? For instance, who will be communicating the policy and to whom; what will be the scope of the messaging content; what will be the delivery style and content; and what media/platforms will be used to communicate?

3. For each information security policy, is ownership and accountability assigned to one or more senior leaders?

4. Are surprise tests and audits carried out to ensure appropriate use of the policies?

7.3 Continuous Monitoring

Just as the information security landscape continues to evolve with new threat actors and vectors, the state of an organization's security is also changing as it engages in a variety of sustenance and growth initiatives. Accordingly, organizations must discipline themselves to continuously monitor and evaluate vulnerabilities and defenses. Essentially, an organization has to protect itself from three types of attacks: external attacks, insider attacks, and supply chain or third-party ecosystem attacks. Hackers from anywhere could trigger external attacks. Insider attacks are often launched by disgruntled employees; many times, unsuspecting employees get compromised and unknowingly offer up necessary information for bad actors to access corporate systems and data. Attacks are also launched from breached systems of external vendors.[4]

Constant review of controls and configurations is also essential to protect the organization from self-caused security loopholes and lapses. The following vignette describes how a government organization fell short in securing sensitive individual and corporate data.

Oklahoma Department of Securities Data Leak

In December 2018, the Oklahoma Department of Securities learned about a firewall security vulnerability that had caused one of its storage servers to be publicly accessible for about a week. According to the UpGuard security analysts who detected the breach, the securities commission had left open an rsync server. Such servers are used for backing up data.

Three terabytes of sensitive data, from social security numbers to remote access credentials, FBI investigation details, and AIDS patients' data, were exposed. Shodan, a search engine for internet-facing IP addresses, first registered the storage server to be publicly accessible on November 30. UpGuard analysts who discovered the breach notified the agency on December 7, and the server was removed from public access on December 8.

The purpose of this state agency is to ensure that securities trading is conducted legally, and citizens are shielded from fraud. Given the organizational mission of protecting the public, it is rather surprising that the agency did not pay any heed to breach risk warnings such as the UpGuard Cyber Risk score of 171 out of 950. Use of an outdated web server that had reached the end of useful life in 2015 was one of the reasons for the low score. Between 2015 and the date of the discovery of the breach, namely, for a period of three and a half years, there were no server updates to address potential vulnerabilities.

Also concerning is the nature of response upon learning about the breach. According to Chris Vickery, head of research at UpGuard, the department did not follow up with a request for a thorough discussion with the security analysts who had detected the leak. Neither did it check to see what the researchers did with the downloaded data. The analysts were also shocked to find another poor security choice made by the department; it "had stored an encrypted version of one document in the same file folder as a decrypted version."[5]

An exemplary approach to continuous monitoring would include a) defining a strategy that clearly articulates the goals and scope of the security control assessment process, b) establishing measures and metrics to evaluate the effectiveness of the continuous monitoring program, c) implementing an efficient method of collecting and analyzing relevant data and generating reports, d) reporting the findings (at the desired level of granularity) along with recommendations to appropriate individuals or teams within the organization, and e) acting on the recommendations to improve the effectiveness of the continuous monitoring process.[6]

The following are some recommended good practices for continuous vulnerability management:

- Use a security content automation protocol (SCAP)–compliant vulnerability scanning tool to automatically and frequently scan all systems and devices.

- Use smart agents (running locally on each system) or remote scanners to perform vulnerability scanning.

- Dedicated accounts should be maintained for vulnerability scans, and each account should be tied to a specific device and IP address.

- Automated software update tools should be used to ensure all devices are running the most up-to-date version of the software.

- Vulnerability scan results must be constantly reviewed and compared to ensure timely remediation.

- A risk-based rating system must be in place to prioritize remedial actions.

A set of questions to guide the continuous monitoring plans and strategies of an organization is presented below.

Continuous Monitoring: Guiding Questions

1. Is there a documented strategy that clearly articulates the goals and scope of continuous monitoring?

2. Is a monitoring schedule in place (refer to Appendix 1 for a sample schedule) and being followed meticulously?

3. Are mechanisms in place to ensure conformance with the scheduled set of monitoring activities?

(Continued)

(Continued)

4. Are automated vulnerability scanning tools in use to facilitate continuous monitoring?

5. Are clearly defined measures and metrics in place to assess the effectiveness of the continuous monitoring program?

6. Are there efficient and effective methods in place to collect and analyze relevant data?

7. Are mechanisms in place to promptly act on the findings and recommendations?

The scope of information security monitoring is vast and includes a wide range of controls as depicted in Appendix 1. The frequency and scope of monitoring can change based on regulatory requirements and organizational needs.

7.4 Continuous Performance Assessment and Improvement

Data from expert surveys and literature reviews validate the significance of taking a proactive approach through continuous assessment of the current state of preparedness and performance and making necessary corrections and improvements. Such a preemptive mindset and approach is key in a highly dynamic environment where hackers are constantly presenting new and innovative forms of attacks.

Some commonly tracked security performance indicators are: a) dollar amount of savings from prevention of security attacks, b) dollar amount spent on resolving security issues, c) number of worker hours spent on resolving security issues, d) percentage of business partners with effective cybersecurity policies, e) mean time to detect and mean time to respond to attacks, and f) extent of compliance with regulatory requirements. Appendix 2 provides a sample list of information security performance measures.

Following is a set of questions to guide the continuous performance assessment and improvement process.

Continuous Performance Assessment and Improvement: Guiding Questions

1. Are Business Value Impact measures (such as the ones listed below) in place to holistically assess cybersecurity preparedness and performance?

   a) Dollar amount of damages and losses from security breaches

   b) Dollar amount of savings from prevention of security attacks

   c) Dollar amount spent on resolving security issues

2. Are Productivity Impact measures (such as the ones listed below) in place to holistically assess cybersecurity preparedness and performance?

   a) Number of worker hours spent on resolving security issues

   b) Number of worker hours lost due to disruption of operations

3. Are Nature of Incidence and Frequency of Occurrence type measures (such as the ones listed below) in place to holistically assess cybersecurity preparedness and performance?

   a) Number of security breaches

   b) Types of security breaches

4. Are Extent of Preparedness type measures (such as the ones listed below) in place to holistically assess cybersecurity preparedness and performance?

   a) Frequency of review of third-party accesses

   b) Percentage of business partners with effective cybersecurity policies

   c) Mean-Time-to-Detect and Mean-Time-to-Respond

   d) Number of days to deactivate former employee credentials

5. Are Audit- and Compliance-related measures (such as the ones listed below) in place to holistically assess cybersecurity preparedness and performance?

   a) Extent of compliance with ISO-27001 guidelines

(Continued)

(Continued)

    b) Number of outstanding high-risk findings open from last audit

    c) Extent of compliance with ISO-27001

    d) Extent of implementation and use of a vendor risk management program

6. Are Vulnerability Assessment measures (such as the ones listed below) in place to holistically assess cybersecurity preparedness and performance?

    a) Number of systems with known vulnerabilities

    b) Number of Secure Socket Layer (SSL) certificates configured incorrectly

    c) Volume of data transferred using the corporate network

    d) Number of users with "super user" access level

    e) Number of communication ports open during a given time period

    f) Frequency of access to critical enterprise systems by third parties

7. Is there a mechanism in place to regularly review the results and take necessary action?

7.5 Security Audits and Drills

Running regular security audits and drills are also the hallmarks of a disciplined execution culture. A real-time security audit is a best practice that allows an organization to make necessary adjustments to its defense strategies sooner rather than later. Such investigations also help identify certain vulnerabilities that could result in massive data leakage.

Organizations often undergo audits to ensure compliance with IT security standards. The International Organization for Standardization (ISO) has a checklist of security policies, controls, and guidelines in its family of ISO 27000 standards documentation.[7] HIPAA, SOX, and the Payment Card Industry (PCI) Data Security Standard (DSS) are representative of laws and regulations that specify information security compliance requirements (refer to Appendix 4).[8]

Using third-party expertise to conduct security audits is recommended. Leveraging security audit tools and platforms, such as SolarWinds

Security Events Manager, Netwrix Auditor, Nessus, and Nmap, would be a wise investment.[9] Audit details and reports should be properly maintained along with records that detail what actions were taken in response to the audit findings.

In addition to audits, highly disciplined organizations will also conduct security drills to test their ability to quickly and effectively recover from different types of attack scenarios. Such drills often take the form of tabletop exercises. These take the form of verbal and visual simulation of a cybersecurity crisis to test the organization's incident response plans.[10] The exercises are highly structured and interactive and require full participation of the involved personnel. They are also minimally disruptive to day-to-day operations and do not entail significant expenses.

Following is a set of questions highlighting the essentials of security audits and drills.

Security Audits and Drills: Guiding Questions

1. Does the organization conduct real-time security audits to detect vulnerabilities and threats?

2. Is there a formal process in place to guide the submission and review of the security audit report?

3. Is there documentation to record actions taken in response to security audit findings?

4. Does the organization conduct real-time security drills to assess preparedness for different types of attacks?

5. Is there a formal process in place to guide the submission and review of the security drill report?

6. Is there documentation to record actions taken in response to security drill findings?

7. Are tabletop exercises conducted regularly to test incident response plans?

The vignette below presents a brief overview of the First American data breach that could have potentially been avoided if a security audit mechanism was in place.

First American Corporation Data Leak, Which Compromised 900 Million Customer Records

First American Corporation, the largest real estate title insurance company, is alleged to have been careless and negligent in properly securing property transaction and customer information. The retail agent was supposedly assigning unique URLs to each property transaction record in a sequential order and did not secure the web addresses. As a result, anyone was able to access the customer information by simply entering the right URL into a browser. The security lapse was discovered by real estate developer Ben Shoval, who found that "by simply raising or lowering a single digit in the document URL sent to him loaded sensitive documents belonging to other people."[11]

Considered the second-largest data breach in history, 900 million real estate closing documents for the past 16 years, dating back to 2003, were exposed. A treasure trove of personal and financial information, including Social Security numbers, physical and email addresses, driver's license details, bank account numbers, wire transaction receipts, and tax records, were made easily available to criminals. The company was essentially offering customer personal data on a platter to data criminals and inviting them to carry out ID theft, financial fraud, and other kinds of cyberattacks. The leaked information could have easily fallen in the wrong hands. For instance, the criminal actors could sell the customer personal information on online hacker forums such as the Dark Web.

According to security experts, the leak could have easily been prevented by investing in a secure content management system (CMS) to catalog the data and by storing the records offline. The "security through obscurity" approach of randomly generated URLs assigned to documents and records is an acceptable approach if a) an algorithm is used to generate the URLs and b) additional security measures such as dual authentication and strong passwords are used.

First American, which is currently under investigation by the U.S. Securities and Exchange Commission, has hired an external security firm to investigate the leak and the extent of exposure and access. The company is also dealing with a class action lawsuit filed in the state of Pennsylvania. The data leak is also being investigated by the New York State Department of Financial Services (NYDFS). Considering that First American falls into a category of financial companies that are subjected to a higher standard for handing personal information, the NYDFS could potentially impose significant fines for "reckless" data security management.[12]

7.6 Penetration Testing and Red Team Exercises

Penetration testing is another proactive defense measure that not only identifies vulnerabilities but also exploits them to the fullest extent to assess the nature and extent of impact. So the scope of penetration testing is more expansive than vulnerability testing, as the latter only seeks to identify security weaknesses and loopholes.[13]

Penetration testing is carried out in five stages: planning and reconnaissance, scanning, gaining access, maintaining access, and analysis. The first stage is essentially focused on defining the scope and goals of the test, the testing methods to be used, and gathering necessary intelligence on the targeted system and application. The next stage entails the use of scanning tools to inspect the targeted application code and to gauge how the system will react to the planned attack test. The tester then launches the planned attack, such as a cross-site scripting, SQL injection, backdoors, or denial-of-service, in order to gain access, steal information, and disrupt operations. The next phase of the simulated attack would be to maintain a long-term presence in the exploited system and mine highly sensitive data. After accomplishing the set goals, the pen tester will prepare a report detailing the type of attack launched, the vulnerabilities exploited, the type of sensitive data accessed, and the length of time spent in the compromised system.[14]

A Red Team exercise or assessment is a more targeted form of penetration test. The main goal is to assess an organization's detection and response capabilities. Such exercises are generally for a longer duration than a penetration test and normally involve a team of people. For instance, "a member of the Red Team poses as a FedEx delivery driver and accesses the building. Once inside, the team member plants a device on the network for easy remote access. This device tunnels out using a common port allowed outbound, such as port 80, 443, or 53 (HTTP, HTTPS, or DNS), and establishes a command and control (C2) channel to the Red Team's servers. Another team member picks up the C2 channel and pivots around the network, possibly using insecure printers or other devices that will take the sights off the device placed. The team members then pivot around the network until they reach their goal, taking their time to avoid detection."[15]

Following is a set of questions that could serve as a checklist for conducting penetration testing and Red Team exercises.

Penetration Testing and Red Team Exercises: Guiding Questions

1. How often does the organization conduct (with or without the help of external agencies) penetration testing exercises?

2. Is there a formal process in place to guide the submission and review of the penetration testing report?

3. Is there documentation to record actions taken in response to penetration testing findings?

4. How often does the organization conduct (with or without the help of external agencies) Red Team exercises?

5. Is there a formal process in place to guide the submission and review of the Red Team exercise report?

6. Is there documentation to record actions taken in response to Red Team exercise report findings?

Planning and execution discipline are key to sustaining a high level of cyber readiness. An organization must have the discipline not only of planning rigorously but also of meticulously executing the plan. Whether it is the formulation and enforcement of security and communication policies, establishing a security controls monitoring routine, continuously looking for improvement opportunities, performing security audits, or penetration testing, the organization must strive to execute flawlessly.

Appendix 5 presents a summary list of administrative, technical, and physical controls to secure data, devices, networks, storage locations, and people. These controls reflect one or more of the three dimensions of a high-performance information security culture—commitment, preparedness, and discipline. Effectively implementing these controls is key to achieving a high level of cybersecurity readiness.

NOTES TO CHAPTER 7 ──────────

1. Pratt, M. K. (2020, March 4). How to write an effective information security policy. *CSO Online.* https://www.csoonline.com/article/3528773/how-to-write-an-effective-information-security-policy.html

2. Jarmai, K. & Stacherl, B. (2020). Yoti: Responsible innovation in cyber security. In SAGE Business Cases. 2020. 10.4135/9781529704303.

3. Kostadinov, D. (2020, July 20). Key Elements of an Information Security Policy. *Infosec.* https://resources.infosecinstitute.com/topic/key-elements-information-security-policy/

4. Olcott, J. (2017, May 18). 5 Things to Consider in Your Continuous Security Monitoring Strategy. *Bitsight.* Retrieved July 25, 2019 from https://www.bitsight.com/blog/5-things-to-consider-building-continuous-security-monitoring-strategy

5. UpGuard. (2019, January 16). *Out of Commission: How the Oklahoma Department of Securities Leaked Millions of Files.* Retrieved September 8, 2019 from https://www.upguard.com/breaches/rsync-oklahoma-securities-commission

6. FedRAMP. (2018, April 4). *FedRAMP Continuous Monitoring Strategy Guide Version 3.2.* Retrieved July 24, 2019 from https://www.fedramp.gov/assets/resources/documents/CSP_Continuous_Monitoring_Strategy_Guide.pdf

7. ISO. ISO/IEC 27001 *Information Security Management.* Retrieved August 21, 2020 from https://www.iso.org/isoiec-27001-information-security.html

8. DNSStuff.com. (2020, March 10). *What Is an IT Security Audit?* Retrieved August 21, 2020 from https://www.dnsstuff.com/it-security-audit

9. SolarWinds Worldwide. (2020, March 10). *13 Best Network Security Auditing Tools.* https://www.comparitech.com/net-admin/network-security-auditing-tools/

10. Parent, M. Murray, G., & Beatty, D. R. (2019, September 1). Act, Don't React: A Leader's Guide to Cybersecutiry. *Rotman Management Magazine,* 69–73.

11. Ikeda, S. (2019, June 10). Security Oversight at First American Causes Data Leak of 900 Million Records. *CPO Magazine.* Retrieved September 8, 2019, from https://www.cpomagazine.com/cyber-security/security-oversight-at-first-american-causes-data-leak-of-900-million-records/#:~:text=An%20ongoing%20data%20leak%20at,hack%20of%202013.

12. Ibid.

13. Hayes, K. (2016, June 23). Penetration Test vs. Red Team Assessment: The Age Old Debate of Pirates vs. Ninjas Continues. *Rapid7 Blog.* Retrieved October 12, 2019 from https://blog.rapid7.com/2016/06/23/penetration-testing-vs-red-teaming-the-age-old-debate-of-pirates-vs-ninja-continues/

14. Imperva. *Penetration Testing.* Retrieved October 12, 2019 from https://www.imperva.com/learn/application-security/penetration-testing/

15. Hayes, K. (2016, June 23). Penetration Test vs. Red Team Assessment: The Age Old Debate of Pirates vs. Ninjas Continues. *Rapid7 Blog.* Retrieved October 12, 2019 from https://blog.rapid7.com/2016/06/23/penetration-testing-vs-red-teaming-the-age-old-debate-of-pirates-vs-ninja-continues/

CHAPTER

8

Key Messages and Actionable Recommendations

This chapter presents a summary of key takeaways. They are organized under the three high-performance cultural traits of commitment, preparedness, and discipline.

8.1 Commitment

There are seven key indicators that reflect a high level of organizational commitment toward cyber readiness. Each is briefly reviewed below.

8.1.1 Hands-On Top Management

Top management should be genuinely committed to developing and enhancing cybersecurity competency of the organization. They should be driven by their genuine concern for protecting stakeholder interests and not adopt a check-the-box approach to regulatory requirements. In their quest to become more aware and knowledgeable, senior leaders should get involved in cybersecurity planning and execution initiatives. The senior leadership team in exemplary organizations are found to be on cybersecurity oversight and governance committees. They are also known to participate in security review discussions and disaster recovery exercises.

8.1.2 "We-Are-in-It-Together" Culture

Although there is no one best approach to developing a highly collaborative and supportive information security culture, organizations should consider deploying cybersecurity champions to enhance awareness and mobilize support throughout the organization. Such influencers will engage with organizational units and individual members to establish a common ground and sense of purpose. The leadership at Infrastructure Development Finance Corporation (IDFC) was successful in developing a high-performance environment by creating a culture of oneness. The disparate business units were united by a common set of goals and values.

A complementary approach is to build emotional capital by creating a work environment where employees a) feel valued, b) develop a sense of belonging and pride, c) are having fun, and d) perceive leadership to be genuine and authentic.[1] Herb Kelleher of Southwest Airlines was instrumental in establishing a very happy and motivated culture founded on three core values: humor, altruism, and "luv."[2]

8.1.3 Cross-Functional Participation

Cybersecurity should be everyone's responsibility and concern. Though a specific individual or team is generally responsible for cybersecurity governance, cross-functional involvement is key to galvanizing grassroots support. Committees and teams established for different cybersecurity initiatives and governance activities should have representation from diverse functional units. At a minimum, representation from the legal, technological, and at least one business function is recommended.

8.1.4 Sustainable Budget

Budget allocation for cybersecurity spending is often a reflection of an organization's commitment toward developing this core competency. A 2018 Deloitte–NASCIO Cybersecurity study finds insufficient funding to be a major challenge in state and city governments.[3] Another study that focused on the healthcare industry found the IT security budget relatively inadequate and stagnant since 2016.[4] Organizations should assign strategic priority to cybersecurity funding and establish sound mechanisms to periodically determine adequacy limits. Every effort should be made to sustain the funding level over the long run.

8.1.5 Strategic Alignment and Partnership

A firm's overall organizational goals should be aligned with cybersecurity goals to gain organization-wide commitment. Communication of such alignment is essential for greater awareness of the strategic importance of developing a high level of cyber readiness. Performance assessment at the unit and individual level should reward efforts and initiatives to achieve and maintain alignment. For instance, if a particular unit is proactive about identifying and mitigating cyber risks associated with its initiatives, the unit should be recognized and rewarded.

When engaging with external business partners such as technology service providers, it is imperative to gauge alignment (of service expectations) before signing any kind of service contract. For instance, if a due diligence report reveals that the company's data security standards and support expectations are unlikely to be met by the potential vendor, the firm should not strike a deal.

8.1.6 Joint Ownership and Accountability

Cybersecurity planning and implementation initiatives should have a senior leadership sponsor who will assume ownership and accountability for the initiative. A tollgate approach should be in place for governing information security initiatives. Senior leadership sign-off should be required for the project to move on to the next phase. The organizational performance review system should reward individuals and business units for cybersecurity-related activities and initiatives. When establishing performance agreements with external service providers, incentives and sanctions should be in place to encourage a high level of commitment (to secure and protect sensitive data and systems) on the part of the business partners.

8.1.7 Empowerment

The chief information security officer (CISO) and their team should be adequately empowered to be successful. It is recommended that the CISO function be provided an independent operating budget and report directly to the CEO, audit committee, or risk committee. The overall goal is to remove any kind of hindrance to performing the cyber governance activities fairly and objectively.

8.2 Preparedness

The key indicators of organizational preparedness are described in terms of an organization's ability to effectively conduct four key activities: a) risk-based identification and prioritization of critical assets and initiatives; b) securing sensitive data and related digital assets; c) detecting threats and attacks; and d) responding and recovering from breach incidents. Recommendations relating to each of these preparedness elements are summarized and itemized below.

8.2.1 Risk-Based Asset Identification and Prioritization

Deciding on which assets to secure and to what extent is not an easy task. A risk-based prioritization system to guide asset identification and prioritization is recommended. Key features of an effective cyber risk assessment and asset identification and prioritization system are itemized in the following lists.

Cyber Risk Assessment

- There should be a formal and comprehensive assessment of risk exposure and tolerance levels.

- A risk impact evaluation rubric (see Table 4) should be developed to guide the risk assessment of initiatives and digital assets.

- Developing a risk probability matrix (see Figure 16) to display the probability of occurrence and extent of loss of the different types of cyber risks will help with threat prioritization.

- Consider adopting a cyber risk visualization platform to monitor and manage cyber risks in real time.

Asset Identification and Prioritization

- From a preparedness and cost optimization standpoint, it is imperative that a comprehensive inventory of digital assets and data types is maintained and used to classify application systems into different levels of criticality. Such categorization would help with the formulation and implementation of appropriate data protection strategies.

- A complete record of authorized and unauthorized hardware and software assets should be maintained and regularly updated. Such an inventory will help in the quick identification and removal of unauthorized devices and applications from the organization's information systems network.

- The digital assets catalog should include external systems and platforms that connect with the organization's internal systems for information sharing.

- Dynamic Host Configuration Protocol (DHCP) and IP address management tools should be used for hardware inventory identification and updates.

- Information flows between networks, applications, and systems should be mapped and regularly reviewed.

- Noncritical systems should be monitored and checked regularly for sensitive data.

8.2.2 Securing Sensitive Data and Related Digital Assets

A multilayer and multipronged defense mechanism should be in place to secure sensitive data. Following are itemized recommendations relating to some key elements of this protection strategy.

Access Management

- A mix of physical, technical, and administrative controls (see Appendix 5) should be used to identify, authenticate, and authorize access. Standard controls include use of strong passwords, multi-factor authentication, and biometric tools.

- Consider investing in a robust identity access management (IAM) system to continuously check user credentials, update permissions as roles change, and raise alerts and immediately revoke privileges when it detects unauthorized access.

- Access credentials of third-party service providers should be regularly reviewed and monitored.

- An IAM team should be in place to a) manage the access control process, b) regularly submit reports to senior management, and c) take prompt and proactive action to protect organizational assets.

- The principle of least privileged (PoLP) should be followed when setting access rights to data and systems.

- Separation of duties and job rotation are important control mechanisms to mitigate the risk of insider attacks.

- Robust screening and background checks during the hiring process are other effective ways of reducing the probability of insider threats and attacks.

- Virtual private network (VPN) tools should be used to secure and monitor remote access.

- Network segmentation is essential to protect critical data and systems from unauthorized access. Procedures should be in place to keep the production, development, and testing environments separate.

Configuration Management

- Appropriate automation tools should be used to manage configuration settings of systems, devices, and networks.

- Notification and quick response processes should be in place to effectively address unauthorized activities and changes.

- Industry standards for configuration settings of the different elements of IT infrastructure should be used as a guide to establish suitable benchmarks.

Securing Email Clients and Browsers

- The organization should implement domain-based message authentication, reporting, and conformance (DMARC) policy.

- Latest and fully supported versions of email clients and web browsers should be used.

- All inbound email attachments should be screened for malware.

- Domain Name System (DNS) filtering services should be used to block access to malicious sites.

- Network-based URL filters and URL categorization services should be used to prevent access to malicious sites.

Securing Networks, Ports, and Removable Media

- A review and approval system should be in place to effectively secure network ports, protocols, and service.

- Automated scanning tools should be used to detect unauthorized ports.

- A comprehensive inventory of removable media and portable devices should be maintained and regularly reviewed. Policies and procedures should be in place to secure removable media. For instance, auto-run features should be disabled on optical and USB drives.

Data Security

- Strongest encryption algorithms should be used to encrypt data-at-rest and data-in-motion.

- When selecting an encryption mechanism, ensure the tool is compatible and will easily integrate with third-party applications.

- Encrypted data should be frequently backed up, and such backed-up data should be regularly restored to ensure the backup system is working effectively.

- Tools such as a managed file transfer (MFT) platform should be in place to protect, track, and audit data-in-transit.

- Data loss protection solutions (DLP) should also be considered for adoption.

- Other methods of protecting data from unauthorized access, such as data masking and steganography, should be considered.

Mobile Device Usage

- A mobile device usage policy should be clearly communicated and enforced. This policy should address issues such as remote access, protecting data stored on the devices, remote monitoring and wipe-off capabilities, and the use of dual-factor authentication.

Data Backup and Retention

- Method and frequency of data backup should be carefully determined and closely followed.

- Data should be backed up in both online and offline storage space.

- The data restoration process should be tested frequently.

- Data storage and deletion policies should be determined based on careful review of regulatory guidelines.
- Service level agreements (SLAs) with managed service providers must clearly spell out data backup, storage, and purge provisions.

Asset Maintenance

- A routine maintenance plan for digital assets should be in place and executed consistently.
- Records of maintenance, update, and repair activities should be kept and reviewed regularly.

Awareness and Training

- Customized awareness and training programs should be developed and delivered regularly.
- Continuous training is encouraged to remind and reinforce information security knowledge domains and skillsets.
- Content and delivery of these training workshops should be engaging and interactive.
- Participation and performance in such training programs should be an important element of an employee's performance review.

Business Continuity Planning

- Business continuity planners must conduct a business impact assessment to identify and rank order the adversity scenarios.
- Both technical and administrative control measures should be in place to proactively deal with the potential crisis conditions.
- Technical measures would include implementing device redundancies such as disk mirroring and disk striping, load balancing, and use of multiple power sources to run data centers.
- Administrative control measures would include succession planning, job enrichment programs, rewards and incentives, and backup sites.

- Leadership roles and responsibilities should be clearly defined.

- Crisis management teams must be trained to work collaboratively.

- The Business Continuity Plan (BCP) plan should be regularly reviewed and tested.

8.2.3 Detecting Threats and Attacks

The ability to proactively detect potential threats and vulnerabilities is a competency that sets apart the highly prepared firms. The following are some recommendations:

- A comprehensive cyber intelligence gathering plan and process should be in place for threat detection purposes.

- The organization should consider deploying automated tools such as Security Information and Event Management (SIEM).

- A security operations center (SOC) and team should be in place to consistently and effectively execute the threat detection plan.

- The detection process should be regularly reviewed and tested to ensure conformance to expectations.

8.2.4 Responding and Recovering from Breach Incidents

Highly resilient organizations are able to quickly and effectively respond to and recover from cyberattacks. The following recommendations should help in the development of respond and recovery capabilities.

- A cross-functional incident response (IR) team should be in place with top management oversight.

- Response plans for different threat scenarios should be clearly documented.

- Roles, responsibilities, and reporting relationships of the IR team members should be clearly defined and articulated.

- Regular drills such as tabletop exercises should be conducted to assess readiness of the IR teams.

8.3 Discipline

A disciplined approach to cybersecurity governance is reflected in the organization's approach to planning and implementation activities. Recommendations relating to six such activities are summarized below.

8.3.1 Information Security Governance Policy

- A comprehensive information security governance policy should be crafted by a cross-functional team of senior leaders. There should be a strong legal presence on the team to ensure conformance with the various information security and privacy laws and guidelines.

- The policy document should be frequently reviewed and updated.

- Regular conformance tests and audits should be carried out to ensure the policy is in effect.

8.3.2 Communication and Enforcement of Policies

- There should be a customized plan for communication of the different components of the information security policy.

- Senior leadership should own and be held accountable for conformance to the different policy elements.

- Surprise tests and audits should be carried out to check on policy compliance.

8.3.3 Continuous Monitoring

- A monitoring (of vulnerabilities and defenses) schedule should be in place and followed meticulously.

- The organization should invest in automated tools to facilitate monitoring.

- Structural mechanisms should be in place to promptly act on findings and recommendations.

- Clearly defined measures and metrics should be used to assess the effectiveness of the continuous monitoring program.

8.3.4 Continuous Performance Assessment and Improvement

The state of information security preparedness should be assessed holistically, using multiple sets of performance indicators. Such measures come under the following categories:

- Business value impact measures

- Productivity impact measures

- Nature of incidence and frequency of occurrence measures

- Audit and compliance measures

- Vulnerability measures

Mechanisms and procedures should be in place to continuously gather and analyze performance data and take prompt action.

8.3.5 Security Audits and Drills

- The organization should undergo security audits to detect vulnerabilities and threats.

- Prior to entering into a contractual agreement with third-party service providers, an organization should ask for audit reports confirming compliance with relevant standards and regulations.

- Regular security drills, such as tabletop exercises, are also highly recommended to stress test the current state of cyber readiness.

- Formal procedures and mechanisms should be in place to share and promptly act on the findings.

8.3.6 Penetration Testing and Red Team Exercises

- The organization should regularly conduct penetration testing and Red Team exercises.

- Formal procedures and mechanisms should be in place to share and promptly act on the findings.

NOTES TO CHAPTER 8 ─────────────

1. Huy, Q. and Shipilov, A. (2012). The Key to Social Media Success within Organizations. *MIT Sloan Management Review,* 54(1), Fall 2012, 74–81.
2. Quick, J. C. (1992). Crafting an Organization Culture: Herb's Hand at Southwest Airlines. *Organizational Dynamics,* 21(2), 45–56.
3. Ward, M. and Subramanium, S. (2018). *States at risk: The cybersecurity imperative in uncertain times.* 2020 Deloitte-NASCIO Cybersecurity Study. Retrieved July 18, 2020 from https://www2.deloitte.com/content/dam/insights/us/articles/6899_nascio/DI_NASCIO_interactive.pdf
4. Leventhal, R. (2018, March 16). Cyber Attacks Increase as IT Security Budgeting Remains Static, Report Finds. *Healthcare Innovation.* Retrieved May 14, 2018 from https://www.hcinnovationgroup.com/cybersecurity/news/13030218/cyber-attacks-increase-as-it-security-budgeting-remains-static-report-finds

Appendix 1

Information Security Monitoring Controls

Organizations need to have an information security controls monitoring system and schedule in place. This is a representative guide, adapted from FedRAMP Continuous Monitoring Strategy Guide (April 4, 2018, http://www.fedramp.gov) that can be suitably customized for use.

Nature and Types of Control	Brief Description
Continuous and Ongoing	
Information System Monitoring	• Monitor and detect attacks and indicators of potential attacks. • Detect unauthorized local, network, and remote connections. • Identify unauthorized use of information systems. • Deploy monitoring devices at strategic locations to track sensitive data and specific types of transactions. • Protect information, gathered from intrusion-monitoring tools, from unauthorized access. • Seek and comply with legal opinion regarding monitoring activities. Especially, ensure compliance with applicable federal laws, executive orders, directives, policies, and regulations.
Auditable Events	Continuously monitor the following types of events: • Successful and unsuccessful account logon events • Account management events • Policy changes • Privilege functions • Process tracking • System events

(Continued)

(Continued)

Nature and Types of Control	Brief Description
Auditable Events	For Web applications, all • Administrator activities • Authentication checks • Authorization checks • Data deletions • Data access • Data changes • Permission changes
Information System Component Inventory	• Continuous detection of new assets using automated mechanisms with a maximum permissible delay of five minutes.
Incident Reporting	• Prompt reporting of security threat–related incidents in accordance with documented protocols and procedures.
Temperature and Humidity Controls	• Continuous monitoring of temperature and humidity controls and ensure they remain at the set level.
Vulnerability Scanning	• Run scans and update the list of vulnerabilities scanned. • Before running scans, signatures must be updated to the most recent version.
Wireless Intrusion Detection	• Deploy wireless intrusion detection system to identify rogue wireless devices and detect attack attempts.
10 Days	
Contingency Training	• Personnel must be trained in their contingency roles and responsibilities within 10 days of assuming that role and responsibility. • The date of training must be recorded in the security plan document.
Weekly	
Audit Review, Analysis, and Reporting	• Audit records must be reviewed to note comments, observations, and recommendations related to information system vulnerabilities and potential threat activities.

Nature and Types of Control	Brief Description
Monthly	
Vulnerability Scanning	• The organization must mitigate all discovered high-risk vulnerabilities within 30 days, mitigate moderate vulnerability risks in 90 days, and mitigate low vulnerability risks in 180 days. Action reports must be sent to appropriate authorities detailing steps taken to mitigate the high-risk vulnerabilities.
Continuous Monitoring Security State	• The security state of the system must be reported on a monthly basis to the appropriate organizational personnel/unit.
Access Record	• Visitor access records must be reviewed monthly.
Least Functionality	• Applications and devices must be checked to identify and eliminate unnecessary functions, ports, protocols, and/or services. The changes made must be consistent with the configuration management plan. The system security plan document must be suitably updated to reflect the changes.
Vulnerability Scanning	• Web applications, operating systems, and databases must be scanned on a monthly basis and the scan report must be promptly shared with the appropriate organizational personnel.
Flaw Remediation	• Security-relevant software and firmware updates must be installed within 30 days of the release of the updates. • Automated tools for identifying system flaws must be in place.
Software and Information Integrity	• Integrity scans must be performed monthly and the scan reports must be promptly shared with appropriate personnel.
Account Management	• Temporary and emergency accounts must be terminated within 30 days of creation.
Security Functionality Verification	• Automatic verification of system security functionalities must be conducted on a regular basis. Security verification reports must be promptly sent out to appropriate personnel.

(Continued)

(Continued)

Nature and Types of Control	Brief Description
Plan of Action & Milestones	• The information security plan of action and milestones document must be reviewed monthly and updated (as needed).
Monitoring Physical Access	• Physical access logs must be reviewed at least once a month. The dates of review must be recorded.
60 Days	
Authenticator Management	• Passwords and any other forms of authentications must be changed every 60 days.
90 Days	
Account Management	• User accounts must be disabled after 90 days of inactivity.
Identifier Management	• Disable user IDs after 90 days of inactivity.
Publicly Accessible Content	• Content on publicly accessible systems must be reviewed to identify and remove any nonpublic information
Access Restrictions for Change	• Information access privileges must be reviewed for all users and any discrepancies must be addressed and logged. Date of review must also be recorded.
Annually	
Information Security Policies	• Information security policies must be reviewed annually. Revisions and modifications should be made to fit the organizational and compliance needs.
Account Management	• Accounts must be reviewed and user accounts recertified for continued access. Account review and recertification date must be recorded.
Security Awareness	• All users must be provided with basic security awareness training and the date of last training must be recorded.
Auditable Events	• List of auditable events must be reviewed and updated annually, or whenever there is a change in the threat environment. The changes made must be recorded. Meeting notes with names of attendees must be archived.

Nature and Types of Control	Brief Description
Security Assessments	• A subset of the security controls must be assessed by a certified third-party assessor. The assessment report must be submitted to the appropriate organizational personnel and archived.
Penetration Testing	• Penetration testing must be conducted at least annually, and the report must be promptly sent to the appropriate organizational personnel for review and action. • Penetration testing must be performed by a certified and accredited third-party service provider.
Baseline Configuration	• Baseline configurations must be reviewed annually or during updates. • Changes to the baseline configuration must be made in accordance with the configuration management plan.
Configuration Management Plan	• The Configuration Management Plan must be reviewed and updated annually.
IT Contingency Plan	• The IT Contingency Plan must be reviewed and updated annually.
Contingency Training	• Personnel assigned to contingency roles and responsibilities must be trained at least once a year. The date of training must be recorded.
IT Contingency Plan Testing & Exercises	• The IT Contingency Plan must be tested annually by conducting exercises that simulate different threat incident scenarios.
Information System Backup	• Backups must be tested annually to verify integrity and reliability. The testing dates and who performed the tests need to be recorded.
Incident Response Training	• Incident response training must take place annually. Training details such as when it took place, where, who was involved, and training materials used must be documented.
Incident Response Testing	• Testing the effectiveness of the incident response plan must take place annually. Testing details such as when it took place, where, individuals involved, and training materials used must be documented.

(Continued)

(Continued)

Nature and Types of Control	Brief Description
Incident Response Plan	• The Incident Response Plan must be reviewed and updated annually.
Physical Access Authorizations	• Physical access authorization credentials must be reviewed annually to ensure appropriate access privileges. Necessary adjustments must be made and recorded to remove or modify access based on the current roles and responsibilities.
Physical Access Control	• Keys and combinations to locks must be changed annually and details of such change including the personnel responsible for making the changes should be recorded.
System Security Plan	• The System Security Plan must be reviewed annually and recorded.
Access Agreements	• Agreements allowing access to information and information systems must be reviewed and updated annually. Such access agreements must be re-signed.
Vulnerability Scans	• An accredited and certified third party must be hired to carry out scans of operating systems, applications, infrastructure, and databases annually.
Boundary Protection	• Changes and updates to traffic flow must be made based on evolving business needs. The Configuration Management Plan must be updated to reflect the changes.
Security Training	• Role-based security training must be provided annually and on an as-needed basis. Training details must be recorded.
Security Training Records	• Security training records must be archived annually. Details on how to access the archive and who archived the records must also be recorded.
Every Two Years	
Identifier Management	• User and device identifiers must be changed every two years.

Nature and Types of Control	Brief Description
Every Three Years	
Security Authorization	• Security authorization must be reevaluated and reauthorized every three years.
IT Contingency Plan Testing and Exercises (Low Systems)	• The IT Contingency Plan must be tested every three years using tabletop exercises.
Risk Assessment	• Information security risk assessments must be carried out every three years and details recorded.
Every Five Years	
Personnel Screening	• Screening of organizational personnel to gauge potential information security threat level must be carried out every five years. Details of screening and findings must be recorded.

Appendix 2

Cybersecurity Performance Measures

C ybersecurity performance can be measured along different dimensions. Here is a sample set of measures that can be suitably modified to meet an organization's needs.

Business Value Impact	• Dollar amount of damages and losses from security breaches • Dollar amount of savings from prevention of security attacks • Dollar amount spent on resolving security issues
Productivity Impact	• Number of worker hours spent on resolving security issues • Number of worker hours lost due to disruption of operations
Nature of Incidence and Frequency of Occurrence	• Number of security breaches • Types of security breaches
Extent of Preparedness	• Frequency of review of third-party accesses • Percentage of business partners with effective cybersecurity policies • Mean-Time-to-Detect and Mean-Time-to-Respond • Number of days to deactivate former employee credentials
Audit and Compliance	• Extent of compliance with ISO 27001 guidelines • Number of outstanding high-risk findings open from last audit

(Continued)

(Continued)

Vulnerability Assessment	• Number of systems with known vulnerabilities • Number of SSL certificates configured incorrectly • Volume of data transferred using the corporate network • Number of users with "super user" access level • Number of communication ports open during a period of time • Frequency of access to critical enterprise systems by third parties

Appendix 3A

Cybersecurity Readiness Scorecard: Commitment

This scorecard can be used to gauge an organization's state of cyber readiness from the standpoint of organizational commitment. The scores will reveal areas of strength and opportunities for improvement. The assessment template is meant to serve as a guide and can be suitably customized to meet an organization's unique needs.

Hands-on Top Management

1. To what extent is top management intimately familiar with the organization's security vulnerability points?

   0 = Not at all 1 = To a small extent 2 = To some extent
   3 = To a moderate extent 4 = To a great extent
   5 = To a very great extent

2. To what extent is top management intimately familiar with the organization's information security defense mechanisms?

   0 = Not at all 1 = To a small extent 2 = To some extent
   3 = To a moderate extent 4 = To a great extent
   5 = To a very great extent

3. To what extent is top management actively engaged in cybersecurity planning and strategizing?

   0 = Not at all 1 = To a small extent 2 = To some extent
   3 = To a moderate extent 4 = To a great extent
   5 = To a very great extent

4. Do members of the top management team serve on cybersecurity governance committees?

   0 = No 1 = Yes

5. To what extent does top management take the lead, ownership, or responsibility in ensuring strong cybersecurity governance?

   0 = Not at all 1 = To a small extent 2 = To some extent
   3 = To a moderate extent 4 = To a great extent
   5 = To a very great extent

(Continued)

(Continued)

6. To what extent does the senior leadership support the following aspects of cybersecurity governance:

   a. Strategic planning
   b. Education and training
   c. Hiring of talent
   d. Mobilizing organization-wide support
   e. Instituting appropriate roles and responsibilities
   f. Remediation of vulnerabilities

   0 = Not at all 1 = To a small extent 2 = To some extent
   3 = To a moderate extent 4 = To a great extent
   5 = To a very great extent

"We-Are-in-It-Together" Culture

1. To what extent are employees eager and motivated to participate in information security training and awareness programs?

   0 = Not at all 1 = To a small extent 2 = To some extent
   3 = To a moderate extent 4 = To a great extent
   5 = To a very great extent

2. To what extent are employees eager and motivated to join information security initiative teams?

   0 = Not at all 1 = To a small extent 2 = To some extent
   3 = To a moderate extent 4 = To a great extent
   5 = To a very great extent

3. To what extent do assessments indicate motivated employees who are striving hard to learn and apply the learned security awareness skills?

   0 = Not at all 1 = To a small extent 2 = To some extent
   3 = To a moderate extent 4 = To a great extent
   5 = To a very great extent

4. To what extent are supply chain partners and service providers eager and motivated to comply with the prescribed information security plans and protocols?

   0 = Not at all 1 = To a small extent 2 = To some extent
   3 = To a moderate extent 4 = To a great extent
   5 = To a very great extent

Cross-Functional Participation

1. Is there cross-functional involvement in cyber governance activities such as:

   a. risk assessment
   b. cybersecurity strategy formulation and alignment

    c. vulnerability evaluation

    d. implementation of controls

    e. data classification and governance

    f. software development

    g. training

    h. disaster recovery planning

    i. oversight committees

    0 = No 1 = Yes

2. To what extent are representatives from the following functions actively involved in cyber governance activities (stated above)?

    a. Operations/Manufacturing

    b. Human Resources

    c. Marketing and Sales

    d. Logistics

    e. Procurement

    f. Legal

    g. Accounting

    h. Others (please specify)

    0 = Not at all 1 = To a small extent 2 = To some extent 3 = To a moderate extent 4 = To a great extent 5 = To a very great extent

Sustainable Budget

1. To what extent is investment in cybersecurity initiatives considered strategic?

    0 = Not at all 1 = To a small extent 2 = To some extent 3 = To a moderate extent 4 = To a great extent 5 = To a very great extent

2. To what extent is top management committed to adequately funding cybersecurity initiatives?

    0 = Not at all 1 = To a small extent 2 = To some extent 3 = To a moderate extent 4 = To a great extent 5 = To a very great extent

3. During the last five years, has cybersecurity funding been on the rise or decline?

    0 = Decline 1 = Rise

(Continued)

(Continued)

4. During the last 12 months, how much has been invested on external resources (such as consultants and third-party service providers) to develop and implement cybersecurity initiatives?

   0 = Did not invest in external resources

   1 = Less than $50,000

   2 = Between $50,000 and $69,999

   3 = Between $70,000 and $89,999

   4 = Between $90,000 and $109,000

   5 = Above $109,000

5. During the last 12 months, how much has been invested in internal resources (such as new hires, training, etc.) to develop and implement cybersecurity initiatives?

   0 = Did not invest in internal resources

   1 = Less than $50,000

   2 = Between $50,000 and $69,999

   3 = Between $70,000 and $89,999

   4 = Between $90,000 and $109,000

   5 = Above $109,000

6. During the last 12 months, how much time has been invested in understanding or managing the implementation of policies and procedures related to cybersecurity?

   0 = None

   1 = Less than 10 hours

   2 = Between 10 and 19 hours

   3 = Between 20 and 29 hours

   4 = Between 30 and 39 hours

   5 = More than 40 hours

Strategic Alignment and Partnerships

1. Does senior leadership view cybersecurity as a strategic necessity and capability?

   0 = No 1 = Yes

2. Do information security leaders recognize that security controls should not become an impediment to realizing the organizational goals?

   0 = No 1 = Yes

3. Does the process for evaluation and selection of information security investments include making a business case with qualitative and quantitative justifications?

    0 = No 1 = Yes

4. Is there a representation from the information security function on the various organizational governance committees such as information governance committee, data governance committee, risk management committee, board of directors, and board of trustees?

    0 = No 1 = Yes

5. Is there a rigorous vendor evaluation and selection process in place?

    0 = No 1 = Yes

6. Is there a governance process in place to manage vendor relations?

    0 = No 1 = Yes

Joint Ownership and Accountability	1. To what extent are cybersecurity planning and implementation teams headed by senior business executives? 0 = Not at all 1 = To a small extent 2 = To some extent 3 = To a moderate extent 4 = To a great extent 5 = To a very great extent 2. To what extent are senior level business executives sponsoring and owning cyber governance initiatives? 0 = Not at all 1 = To a small extent 2 = To some extent 3 = To a moderate extent 4 = To a great extent 5 = To a very great extent 3. Is a tollgate approach in place to manage the implementation of cybersecurity programs? 0 = No 1 = Yes 4. Is senior leadership sign-off required before a cybersecurity project can move on to the next phase? 0 = No 1 = Yes 5. Do performance review systems include assessment of cybersecurity involvement and effectiveness? 0 = No 1 = Yes

(Continued)

(Continued)

6. Are relevant organizational members rewarded when there are no breaches in a particular year?

   0 = No 1 = Yes

7. To what extent do SLA agreements with business partners and vendors include explicit data protection expectations and consequences for noncompliance?

   0 = Not at all 1 = To a small extent 2 = To some extent
   3 = To a moderate extent 4 = To a great extent
   5 = To a very great extent

Empowerment

1. To what extent is the CISO involved in strategic decision-making processes?

   0 = Not at all 1 = To a small extent 2 = To some extent
   3 = To a moderate extent 4 = To a great extent
   5 = To a very great extent

2. Does the CISO report directly to the CEO?

   0 = No 1 = Yes

3. Does the CISO report directly to the audit committee?

   0 = No 1 = Yes

4. Does the CISO report directly to the risk management committee?

   0 = No 1 = Yes

5. Is the CISO part of the senior leadership team?

   0 = No 1 = Yes

6. Is the CISO provided an independent operating budget?

   0 = No 1 = Yes

Appendix 3B

Cybersecurity Readiness Scorecard: Preparedness

This scorecard can be used to gauge an organization's state of cyber readiness from the standpoint of identifying data protection needs to securing data, network, devices, storage locations, and people. The scores will reveal areas of strength and opportunities for improvement. The assessment tool is meant to serve as a guide and template and can be suitably customized to meet an organization's unique needs.

Identify—Organizational Role Recognition	1. Does the leadership recognize the organizational role and responsibility within its supply chain and beyond? Is such recognition explicitly documented in the cybersecurity strategic plan? 0 = No 1 = Yes
	2. Are the organizational goals, mission, and objectives explicitly documented in the cybersecurity strategic plan? 0 = No 1 = Yes
	3. Is it clearly stated (in the cybersecurity strategic plan) how the cybersecurity strategy is aligned with the overall organizational strategy? 0 = No 1 = Yes
	4. Is there a cross-functional team in place to assist with supply chain role recognition, risk assessment, cybersecurity strategy formulation and alignment, and identification of threat scenarios? 0 = No 1 = Yes
Identify—Cyber Risk Assessment	1. Does the organization engage in a comprehensive and periodic evaluation of its cyber risk tolerance levels and vulnerabilities? 0 = No 1 = Yes
	2. Are cross-functional teams with representation from senior leadership engaged in such risk evaluation? 0 = No 1 = Yes

(Continued)

183

(Continued)

3. Are tools such as a cyber risk matrix and dashboard in use to monitor and manage threat levels?

0 = No 1 = Yes

4. Are key risk indicators for each strategic initiative determined and monitored?

0 = No 1 = Yes

Identify—Asset Identification and Prioritization

1. Are hardware and software assets of the organization inventoried?

0 = Not at all 1 = To a small extent 2 = To some extent 3 = To a moderate extent 4 = To a great extent 5 = To a very great extent

2. Do the hardware inventory records capture comprehensive details such as network address, hardware address, machine name, owner and department name for each device, and whether the asset has received approval to be connected to the network?

0 = Not at all 1 = To a small extent 2 = To some extent 3 = To a moderate extent 4 = To a great extent 5 = To a very great extent

3. Do software records include comprehensive details such as: name, version, publisher, and install date?

0 = Not at all 1 = To a small extent 2 = To some extent 3 = To a moderate extent 4 = To a great extent 5 = To a very great extent

4. Are hardware devices that are not connected to the networks also recorded in the asset inventory?

0 = Not at all 1 = To a small extent 2 = To some extent 3 = To a moderate extent 4 = To a great extent 5 = To a very great extent

5. Is an authentication system in place to ensure only authorized devices are able to connect to the network?

0 = Not at all 1 = To a small extent 2 = To some extent 3 = To a moderate extent 4 = To a great extent 5 = To a very great extent

6. Are client certificates used to authenticate hardware devices on the network?

0 = Not at all 1 = To a small extent 2 = To some extent 3 = To a moderate extent 4 = To a great extent 5 = To a very great extent

7. Are active and passive discovery tools being used to identify hardware devices on the network and suitably update the hardware inventory list?

    0 = Not at all 1 = To a small extent 2 = To some extent 3 = To a moderate extent 4 = To a great extent 5 = To a very great extent

8. Are Dynamic Host Configuration Protocol and IP address management tools being used for hardware inventory identification and updates?

    0 = Not at all 1 = To a small extent 2 = To some extent 3 = To a moderate extent 4 = To a great extent 5 = To a very great extent

9. Is unauthorized and unsupported software identified, recorded, and removed on a regular basis?

    0 = Not at all 1 = To a small extent 2 = To some extent 3 = To a moderate extent 4 = To a great extent 5 = To a very great extent

10. Is application whitelisting technology used to ensure only authorized software executes and all unauthorized software is blocked?

    0 = Not at all 1 = To a small extent 2 = To some extent 3 = To a moderate extent 4 = To a great extent 5 = To a very great extent

11. Is software, used for running high-risk business operations, identified and run on segregated networks and systems?

    0 = Not at all 1 = To a small extent 2 = To some extent 3 = To a moderate extent 4 = To a great extent 5 = To a very great extent

12. Are hardware and software tools such as asset inventory recording and tracking systems in use? Are these systems integrated?

    0 = Not at all 1 = To a small extent 2 = To some extent 3 = To a moderate extent 4 = To a great extent 5 = To a very great extent

13. Are external systems and devices that reside outside an organization's managed domains but connect with internal systems included in the digital assets inventory?

    0 = Not at all 1 = To a small extent 2 = To some extent 3 = To a moderate extent 4 = To a great extent 5 = To a very great extent

(Continued)

	14.	Are organizational communication and data flows mapped?

14. Are organizational communication and data flows mapped?

0 = Not at all 1 = To a small extent 2 = To some extent 3 = To a moderate extent 4 = To a great extent 5 = To a very great extent

15. Are resources (e.g., hardware, devices, data, and software) prioritized based on their classification, criticality, and business value?

0 = Not at all 1 = To a small extent 2 = To some extent 3 = To a moderate extent 4 = To a great extent 5 = To a very great extent

16. Are suitable organizational criteria used to classify the level of data sensitivity?

0 = Not at all 1 = To a small extent 2 = To some extent 3 = To a moderate extent 4 = To a great extent 5 = To a very great extent

Protect—Access Control

1. Are policies and procedures in place to manage authorized access to devices and systems?

0 = No 1 = Yes

2. Is multifactor authentication (MFA) in place?

0 = No 1 = Yes

3. Are access logs maintained and periodically reviewed?

0 = No 1 = Yes

4. Are access permissions managed, incorporating the principles of least privilege and separation of duties?

0 = No 1 = Yes

5. Are access privileges regularly reviewed and updated?

0 = No 1 = Yes

6. Does the organization conduct thorough screening and background checks during the hiring and recruiting process?

0 = No 1 = Yes

7. Are employees continuously reminded (through education and training programs) of their roles and responsibilities in protecting sensitive data and complying with organizational access control policies?

0 = No 1 = Yes

	8.	Are access privileges promptly revoked at the time of voluntary or involuntary termination of jobs?
		0 = No 1 = Yes
	9.	Is network integrity protected, incorporating network segregation where appropriate?
		0 = No 1 = Yes
	10.	Are firewalls used to segregate and secure critical network segments?
		0 = No 1 = Yes
	11.	Is remote access secured and monitored by using tools such as virtual private networks?
		0 = No 1 = Yes
	12.	Is a Wi-Fi network with the strongest encryption (e.g., WPA2) in use?
		0 = No 1 = Yes
	13.	Are Identity and Access Management solutions in use to automate the access control monitoring process?
		0 = No 1 = Yes
	14.	Is access to server rooms and data centers physically secured with locked doors?
		0 = No 1 = Yes
	15.	Are closed-circuit surveillance cameras in place to monitor traffic in server rooms and data centers?
		0 = No 1 = Yes
	16.	Is multi-factor authentication system in use to ensure authorized access to server rooms and data centers?
		0 = No 1 = Yes
Protect—Configuration Management	1.	To what extent are configuration specifications in place for all systems, devices, and networks?
		0 = Not at all 1 = To a small extent 2 = To some extent 3 = To a moderate extent 4 = To a great extent 5 = To a very great extent
	2.	Has a baseline configuration been established?
		0 = No 1 = Yes
	3.	How frequently are configuration settings reviewed, monitored, and updated?
		0 = Almost Never 1 = Annually 2 = Quarterly 3 = Monthly 4 = Weekly 5 = Daily
	4.	Are automated tools/solutions in use to facilitate configuration management?
		0 = No 1 = Yes

(Continued)

(Continued)

Protect—Secure Email Clients and Web Browsers	1. To what extent is the organization using the latest and fully supported versions of email clients and web browsers? 0 = Not at all 1 = To a small extent 2 = To some extent 3 = To a moderate extent 4 = To a great extent 5 = To a very great extent
	2. To what extent are systems appropriately configured to prevent the deployment of unauthorized browsers and email client plugins? 0 = Not at all 1 = To a small extent 2 = To some extent 3 = To a moderate extent 4 = To a great extent 5 = To a very great extent
	3. Are only authorized scripting languages running in web browsers and email clients? 0 = No 1 = Yes
	4. Does the organization subscribe to URL categorization services? 0 = No 1 = Yes
	5. Are network-based URL filters used to prevent access to certain websites? 0 = No 1 = Yes
	6. Are Domain Name System (DNS) filtering services used to block access to malicious sites? 0 = No 1 = Yes
	7. Are inbound email attachments screened for malware? 0 = No 1 = Yes
	8. Has the organization implemented a Domain-based Message Authentication, Reporting and Conformance (DMARC) policy? 0 = No 1 = Yes
Protect—Securing Network Ports, Protocols, and Services	1. Is a defense-in-depth strategy followed to secure the data transmission and communication networks? 0 = No 1 = Yes
	2. Is there an approval system in place to ensure only a select set of network ports, protocols, and services are activated? 0 = No 1 = Yes

	3. How often are automated scans performed to detect unauthorized open ports?
	0 = Almost Never 1 = Annually 2 = Quarterly 3 = Monthly 4 = Weekly 5 = Daily
	4. Are host-based firewalls with a default/deny rule in place to block unauthorized traffic?
	0 = No 1 = Yes
	5. Are AI-driven next-generation firewalls being used to inspect and filter traffic without degrading user experience?
	0 = No 1 = Yes
	6. Are port-filtering tools in use to block unauthorized traffic?
	0 = No 1 = Yes
	7. Is a serial-layered approach used to secure access to organizational networks and systems?
	0 = No 1 = Yes
Protect— Managing Removable Media	1. Is an inventory of removal media and portable devices maintained and periodically reviewed and updated?
	0 = No 1 = Yes
	2. Are policies in place to govern usage of portable storage devices?
	0 = No 1 = Yes
	3. Are auto-run features disabled on optical and USB drives?
	0 = No 1 = Yes
Protect—Data Security	1. Are encryption tools in use to secure data-at-rest and data-in-transit?
	0 = No 1 = Yes
	2. How frequently is the performance of the encryption tools reviewed and are changes made as deemed necessary?
	0 = Almost Never 1 = Annually 2 = Quarterly 3 = Monthly 4 = Weekly 5 = Daily
	3. To what extent is data-in-transit protected?
	0 = Not at all 1 = To a small extent 2 = To some extent 3 = To a moderate extent 4 = To a great extent 5 = To a very great extent

(Continued)

4. Is a persistent file-level security policy in place when encrypting sensitive data?

   0 = No 1 = Yes

5. Are steganography tools used to hide the transmission of sensitive data?

   0 = No 1 = Yes

6. Are data loss protection technologies being used to secure data in use, in motion, and at rest?

   0 = No 1 = Yes

7. Is a policy of least privilege in place to restrict access to sensitive data?

   0 = No 1 = Yes

8. Are sensitive data masked using one of the recommended methods such as character scrambling, nulling out or deletion, substitution, and shuffling?

   0 = No 1 = Yes

9. How frequently is encrypted data backed-up?

   0 = Almost Never 1 = Annually 2 = Quarterly
   3 = Monthly 4 = Weekly 5 = Daily

10. How frequently are tests conducted to ensure the data backup method is satisfactory?

    0 = Almost Never 1 = Annually 2 = Quarterly
    3 = Monthly 4 = Weekly 5 = Daily

11. Is a policy in place to govern use of personal mobile devices?

    0 = No 1 = Yes

12. Are mechanisms such as creating dual personas, use of strong passwords, remote wipe-off capability, regular backups, and secure remote access in place to manage use of mobile devices?

    0 = No 1 = Yes

13. Are appropriate tools such as a managed file transfer (MFT) platform in place to provide complete visibility but also protect data in transit or at rest, provide tracking and audit capabilities, enable data wiping and sanitization, set and monitor security standard violation alerts, and generate compliance reports?

    0 = No 1 = Yes

14. Are integrity checking mechanisms used to verify software, firmware, and information integrity?

    0 = No 1 = Yes

15. Are the development and testing environments kept separate from the production environments?

    0 = No 1 = Yes

16. Does the organization have a well thought-through and clearly documented data disposal plan?

    0 = No 1 = Yes

17. Are users regularly made aware of the consequences of data leaks and trained on how to prevent such leakages?

    0 = No 1 = Yes

Protect—Data Backup and Retention

1. Is data being automatically backed up to multiple storage locations?

    0 = No 1 = Yes

2. Is data being automatically backed up to physical and virtual storage locations?

    0 = No 1 = Yes

3. Is a copy of the backed-up data maintained in an offline storage space?

    0 = No 1 = Yes

4. Is the frequency of data backup determined after thorough and careful deliberation?

    0 = No 1 = Yes

5. How often is the data restoration process tested for reliability?

    0 = Almost Never 1 = Annually 2 = Quarterly 3 = Monthly 4 = Weekly 5 = Daily

6. Did the organization implement an appropriate data retention and purge policy after thorough and careful deliberation?

    0 = No 1 = Yes

7. Is there an appropriate oversight mechanism, such as the role of the data controller, to ensure that the data retention and purge policies are being followed?

    0 = No 1 = Yes

(Continued)

(Continued)

	8.	Are data storage and purge expectations clearly documented in the SLAs? 0 = No 1 = Yes
Protect—Asset Maintenance	1.	Is the process for maintaining and updating hardware and software clearly documented? 0 = No 1 = Yes
	2.	Are logs maintained to track the maintenance, update, and repair activities? 0 = No 1 = Yes
	3.	Are automated tools in use to constantly monitor digital assets and detect unauthorized access or malware? 0 = No 1 = Yes
	4.	Is a software patch management system in place to automate the update process? 0 = No 1 = Yes
Protect— Awareness and Training	1.	Is cybersecurity training performance an important component of an employee's assessment? 0 = No 1 = Yes
	2.	Is the training customized to employee roles and needs? 0 = No 1 = Yes
	3.	Is the cybersecurity training continuous? 0 = No 1 = Yes
	4.	Are the content and delivery interactive and engaging? Are dramatic scenarios, games, and funny videos used to make the training program a fun and informative experience? 0 = No 1 = Yes
	5.	Are techniques such as role-playing, testing, and hacking contests used to make the training interactive and hands-on? 0 = No 1 = Yes
	6.	To what extent are all users informed and trained? 0 = Not at all 1 = To a small extent 2 = To some extent 3 = To a moderate extent 4 = To a great extent 5 = To a very great extent

7. To what extent do privileged users understand their roles and responsibilities?

   0 = Not at all 1 = To a small extent 2 = To some extent 3 = To a moderate extent 4 = To a great extent 5 = To a very great extent

8. To what extent do senior executives understand their roles and responsibilities?

   0 = Not at all 1 = To a small extent 2 = To some extent 3 = To a moderate extent 4 = To a great extent 5 = To a very great extent

9. To what extent do third-party stakeholders (e.g., suppliers, customers, partners) understand their roles and responsibilities?

   0 = Not at all 1 = To a small extent 2 = To some extent 3 = To a moderate extent 4 = To a great extent 5 = To a very great extent

10. To what extent do physical and information security personnel understand their roles and responsibilities?

   0 = Not at all 1 = To a small extent 2 = To some extent 3 = To a moderate extent 4 = To a great extent 5 = To a very great extent

Prepare—Business Continuity Planning

1. Is there a cross-functional team of business continuity planners?

   0 = No 1 = Yes

2. Is a business impact analysis (BIA) methodology in place to drive BCP efforts?

   0 = No 1 = Yes

3. To what extent are multiple systems and devices in use to protect against single points of failure?

   0 = Not at all 1 = To a small extent 2 = To some extent 3 = To a moderate extent 4 = To a great extent 5 = To a very great extent

4. To what extent is the company using RAID or similar technology to protect against storage device failures?

   0 = Not at all 1 = To a small extent 2 = To some extent 3 = To a moderate extent 4 = To a great extent 5 = To a very great extent

5. Do servers come with multiple power sources and are powered by two independent power providers?

   0 = No 1 = Yes

(Continued)

(Continued)

6. To what extent are server clustering and similar technologies in use to implement load balancing?

   0 = Not at all 1 = To a small extent 2 = To some extent 3 = To a moderate extent 4 = To a great extent 5 = To a very great extent

7. Are appropriate technologies in use to support and secure remote work?

   0 = Not at all 1 = To a small extent 2 = To some extent 3 = To a moderate extent 4 = To a great extent 5 = To a very great extent

8. Are training programs offered to enhance the remote work skill level of employees?

   0 = No 1 = Yes

9. Is there a succession plan, especially for the highly skilled information security personnel?

   0 = No 1 = Yes

10. Are job enrichment programs in place to motivate employees and help them realize their potential?

    0 = No 1 = Yes

11. To what extent has the company invested in backup sites that can ensure continuity of operations during crisis?

    0 = Not at all 1 = To a small extent 2 = To some extent 3 = To a moderate extent 4 = To a great extent 5 = To a very great extent

12. To what extent are leadership roles and responsibilities to guide business recovery efforts clearly identified and documented?

    0 = Not at all 1 = To a small extent 2 = To some extent 3 = To a moderate extent 4 = To a great extent 5 = To a very great extent

13. Are communication strategies formulated that specify the format and delivery of different types of crisis recovery messaging?

    0 = No 1 = Yes

14. To what extent are the business continuity plans of vendors in sync with those of the company?

    0 = Not at all 1 = To a small extent 2 = To some extent 3 = To a moderate extent 4 = To a great extent 5 = To a very great extent

15. How often is the business continuity plan tested?

    0 = Almost Never 1 = Annually 2 = Quarterly
    3 = Monthly 4 = Weekly 5 = Daily

16. How often is the business continuity plan subjected to a tabletop test?

    0 = Almost Never 1 = Annually 2 = Quarterly
    3 = Monthly 4 = Weekly 5 = Daily

Detect—Detecting Anomalies and Events

1. Is there a formal and well-documented cyber intelligence gathering process in place?

    0 = No 1 = Yes

2. To what extent is the cyber intelligence-gathering plan comprehensively written, addressing each of the four phases—planning, collection, processing and analysis, and dissemination?

    0 = Not at all 1 = To a small extent 2 = To some extent 3 = To a moderate extent 4 = To a great extent 5 = To a very great extent

3. To what extent are the various intelligence gathering sources clearly identified and a plan in place on how to leverage those resources?

    0 = Not at all 1 = To a small extent 2 = To some extent 3 = To a moderate extent 4 = To a great extent 5 = To a very great extent

4. Does the organization deploy a Security Information and Event Management (SIEM) platform for security monitoring, advanced threat detection, incident investigation and response, and other related services?

    0 = No 1 = Yes

5. Is a security operations center (SOC) and team in place to lead the threat intelligence-gathering initiatives?

    0 = No 1 = Yes

6. Is a formal and rigorous process in place to select external expertise to assist with intelligence-gathering and threat-detection activities?

    0 = No 1 = Yes

7. Considering the plethora of sophisticated detection tools, is a rigorous process in place to implement an integrated detection and response platform?

    0 = No 1 = Yes

(Continued)

(Continued)

	8.	Is a baseline of network operations and expected data flows for users and systems established and managed? 0 = No 1 = Yes
	9.	Are detected events analyzed to understand attack targets and methods? 0 = No 1 = Yes
	10.	Are event data aggregated and correlated from multiple sources and sensors? 0 = No 1 = Yes
	11.	Is there a process in place to determine the impact of events? 0 = No 1 = Yes
	12.	Are incident alert thresholds established? 0 = No 1 = Yes
	13.	To what extent are roles and responsibilities for detection well defined to ensure accountability? 0 = Not at all 1 = To a small extent 2 = To some extent 3 = To a moderate extent 4 = To a great extent 5 = To a very great extent
	14.	How often are detection processes tested? 0 = Almost Never 1 = Annually 2 = Semi-Annually 3 = Quarterly 4 = Monthly 5 = Weekly
	15.	Is event detection information promptly communicated to appropriate parties? 0 = No 1 = Yes
	16.	How often are detection processes reviewed and updated? 0 = Almost Never 1 = Annually 2 = Semi-Annually 3 = Quarterly 4 = Monthly 5 = Weekly
Respond and Recover—Incident Response Capability	1.	Is there an incident response team with cross-functional representation? 0 = No 1 = Yes
	2.	Do any of the senior leadership members have oversight responsibility for the incident response team? 0 = No 1 = Yes

3. To what extent are roles, responsibilities, and reporting relationships clearly defined for the team members?

0 = Not at all 1 = To a small extent 2 = To some extent 3 = To a moderate extent 4 = To a great extent 5 = To a very great extent

4. To what extent are steps associated with responding to different types of threat incidents clearly detailed and documented?

0 = Not at all 1 = To a small extent 2 = To some extent 3 = To a moderate extent 4 = To a great extent 5 = To a very great extent

5. Is the documented response plan tested periodically?

0 = Almost Never 1 = Annually 2 = Semi-Annually 3 = Quarterly 4 = Monthly 5 = Weekly

Respond and Recover—Disaster Recovery Planning

1. To what extent is a comprehensive asset inventory maintained to identify the various vulnerability points?

0 = Not at all 1 = To a small extent 2 = To some extent 3 = To a moderate extent 4 = To a great extent 5 = To a very great extent

2. To what extent are the various threat scenarios identified and rank ordered (based on risk and business impact analysis) prior to developing recovery strategies?

0 = Not at all 1 = To a small extent 2 = To some extent 3 = To a moderate extent 4 = To a great extent 5 = To a very great extent

3. To what extent are recovery performance measures (such as Recovery Point Objective and Recovery Time Objective) for mission-critical and noncritical applications and systems clearly defined?

0 = Not at all 1 = To a small extent 2 = To some extent 3 = To a moderate extent 4 = To a great extent 5 = To a very great extent

4. To what extent are the roles and responsibilities of the disaster recovery plan (DRP) team members clearly articulated and documented?

0 = Not at all 1 = To a small extent 2 = To some extent 3 = To a moderate extent 4 = To a great extent 5 = To a very great extent

(Continued)

(Continued)

5. To what extent are details on how individuals and teams will act, communicate, and report explicitly depicted in the plan document?

   0 = Not at all 1 = To a small extent 2 = To some extent 3 = To a moderate extent 4 = To a great extent 5 = To a very great extent

6. To what extent do the Incident Response and Disaster Recovery teams work in close cooperation and conduct joint training exercises?

   0 = Not at all 1 = To a small extent 2 = To some extent 3 = To a moderate extent 4 = To a great extent 5 = To a very great extent

7. To the extent applicable, are business partners (such as customers and vendors) kept informed of the recovery plan?

   0 = No 1 = Yes

8. Is there a written communication plan that details how the entire workforce, media, and the general public will be kept informed and updated during the disaster recovery process?

   0 = No 1 = Yes

9. Are backup sites, whether hot, warm, or cold, in place?

   0 = No 1 = Yes

10. Do service level agreements (SLAs) with vendors explicitly detail the expected level of service and support during disasters?

    0 = No 1 = Yes

11. Is the Disaster Recovery Plan (DRP) regularly tested and updated as needed?

    0 = No 1 = Yes

Appendix 3C

Cybersecurity Readiness Scorecard: Discipline

This scorecard can be used to gauge an organization's state of cyber readiness from the standpoint of planning and execution discipline. The scores will reveal areas of strength and opportunities for improvement. The assessment tool is meant to serve as a guide and template and can be suitably customized to meet an organization's unique needs.

Information Security Governance Policy	1. Is the organizational policy on information security governance documented? 0 = No 1 = Yes 2. Is the security policy document comprehensive and does it comprise of the following representative elements? • Purpose • Scope • Objectives • Risk Tolerance Levels and Posture • Asset and Data Identification and Classification Criteria • Authority and Access Control • Roles and Responsibilities • Vendor Selection Criteria • Service Level Agreement Guidelines • Incident Response Plan • Disaster Recovery Plan • Training Guidelines • Performance Measures • Rewards and Penalties 0 = No 1 = Yes

(Continued)

(Continued)

3. Are roles and responsibilities of information security personnel and information security responsibilities of other personnel clearly identified and documented?

   0 = Not at all 1 = To a small extent 2 = To some extent 3 = To a moderate extent 4 = To a great extent 5 = To a very great extent

4. Are security standards, baselines, guidelines, and procedures in place for effective implementation of the policies?

   0 = Not at all 1 = To a small extent 2 = To some extent 3 = To a moderate extent 4 = To a great extent 5 = To a very great extent

5. How frequently is the policy document reviewed and updated?

   0 = Almost Never 1 = Annually 2 = Semi-Annually 3 = Quarterly 4 = Monthly 5 = Weekly

6. How frequently are the policy document elements tested to ensure they are actually in use?

   0 = Almost Never 1 = Annually 2 = Semi-Annually 3 = Quarterly 4 = Monthly 5 = Weekly

7. Is a cross-functional team of senior leaders and experts involved in crafting the policy document and providing oversight?

   0 = No 1 = Yes

Communication and Enforcement Policies

1. Is there a communication plan in place for each type of information security policy?

   0 = No 1 = Yes

2. Does the plan document clearly state how each type of policy communication will happen? For instance, who will be communicating the policy and to whom; what will be the scope of the messaging content; what will be the delivery style and content; and what media/platforms will be used to communicate?

   0 = No 1 = Yes

3. For each information security policy type, is ownership and accountability assigned to one or more senior leaders?

   0 = No 1 = Yes

	4.	How often are surprise tests and audits carried out to ensure appropriate use of the policies?
		0 = Almost Never 1 = Annually 2 = Semi-Annually 3 = Quarterly 4 = Monthly 5 = Weekly
Continuous Monitoring	1.	Is there a documented strategy that clearly articulates the goals and scope of continuous monitoring?
		0 = No 1 = Yes
	2.	Is a monitoring schedule in place (refer to Appendix 1 for a sample schedule) and being followed meticulously?
		0 = No 1 = Yes
	3.	Are mechanisms in place to ensure conformance with the scheduled set of monitoring activities?
		0 = No 1 = Yes
	4.	Are automated vulnerability scanning tools in use to facilitate continuous monitoring?
		0 = No 1 = Yes
	5.	Are clearly defined measures and metrics in place to assess the effectiveness of the continuous monitoring program?
		0 = No 1 = Yes
	6.	Are there efficient and effective methods in place to collect and analyze relevant data?
		0 = No 1 = Yes
	7.	Are mechanisms in place to promptly act on the findings and recommendations?
		0 = No 1 = Yes
Continuous Performance Assessment and Improvement	1.	To what extent are Business Value Impact measures (such as the ones listed below) in place to holistically assess cybersecurity preparedness and performance?
		a) Dollar amount of damages and losses from security breaches
		b) Dollar amount of savings from prevention of security attacks
		c) Dollar amount spent on resolving security issues
		0 = Not at all 1 = To a small extent 2 = To some extent 3 = To a moderate extent 4 = To a great extent 5 = To a very great extent

(Continued)

(Continued)

2. To what extent are Productivity Impact measures (such as the ones listed below) in place to holistically assess cybersecurity preparedness and performance?

    a) Number of worker hours spent on resolving security issues

    b) Number of worker hours lost due to disruption of operations

    0 = Not at all 1 = To a small extent 2 = To some extent
    3 = To a moderate extent 4 = To a great extent
    5 = To a very great extent

3. To what extent are Nature of Incidence and Frequency of Occurrence type measures (such as the ones listed below) in place to holistically assess cybersecurity preparedness and performance?

    a) Number of security breaches

    b) Types of security breaches

    0 = Not at all 1 = To a small extent 2 = To some extent
    3 = To a moderate extent 4 = To a great extent
    5 = To a very great extent

4. To what extent are Extent of Preparedness type measures (such as the ones listed below) in place to holistically assess cybersecurity preparedness and performance?

    a) Frequency of review of third-party accesses

    b) Percentage of business partners with effective cybersecurity policies

    c) Mean-Time-to-Detect and Mean-Time-to-Respond

    d) Number of days to deactivate former employee credentials

    0 = Not at all 1 = To a small extent 2 = To some extent
    3 = To a moderate extent 4 = To a great extent
    5 = To a very great extent

5. To what extent are audit and compliance-related measures (such as the ones listed below) in place to holistically assess cybersecurity preparedness and performance?

    a) Extent of compliance with ISO 27001 guidelines

    b) Number of outstanding high-risk findings open from last audit

c) Extent of compliance with ISO 27001

d) Extent of implementation and use of a vendor risk management program

0 = Not at all 1 = To a small extent 2 = To some extent 3 = To a moderate extent 4 = To a great extent 5 = To a very great extent

6. To what extent are Vulnerability Assessment measures (such as the ones listed below) in place to holistically assess cybersecurity preparedness and performance?

a) Number of systems with known vulnerabilities

b) Number of SSL certificates configured incorrectly

c) Volume of data transferred using the corporate network

d) Number of users with "super user" access level

e) Number of communication ports open during a period of time

f) Frequency of access to critical enterprise systems by third parties

0 = Not at all 1 = To a small extent 2 = To some extent 3 = To a moderate extent 4 = To a great extent 5 = To a very great extent

7. Is there a mechanism in place to regularly review the results and take necessary action?

0 = No 1 = Yes

Security Audits and Drills

1. Does the organization conduct real-time security audits to detect vulnerabilities and threats?

0 = No 1 = Yes

2. Is there a formal process in place to guide the submission and review of the security audit report?

0 = No 1 = Yes

3. Is there documentation to record actions taken in response to security audit findings?

0 = No 1 = Yes

4. Does the organization conduct real-time security drills to assess preparedness for different types of attacks?

0 = No 1 = Yes

(Continued)

(Continued)

	5. Is there a formal process in place to guide the submission and review of the security drill report? 0 = No 1 = Yes
	6. Is there documentation to record actions taken in response to security drill findings? 0 = No 1 = Yes
	7. Are tabletop exercises conducted regularly to test incident response plans? 0 = No 1 = Yes
Penetration Testing and Red Team Exercises	1. How often does the organization conduct (with or without the help of external agencies) penetration testing exercises? 0 = Almost Never 1 = Annually 2 = Semi-Annually 3 = Quarterly 4 = Monthly 5 = Weekly
	2. Is there a formal process in place to guide the submission and review of the penetration testing report? 0 = No 1 = Yes
	3. Is there documentation to record actions taken in response to penetration testing findings? 0 = No 1 = Yes
	4. How often does the organization conduct (with or without the help of external agencies) Red Team exercises? 0 = Almost Never 1 = Annually 2 = Semi-Annually 3 = Quarterly 4 = Monthly 5 = Weekly
	5. Is there a formal process in place to guide the submission and review of the Red Team exercise report? 0 = No 1 = Yes
	6. Is there documentation to record actions taken in response to Red Team exercise report findings? 0 = No 1 = Yes

Appendix 4

Cybersecurity and Privacy Laws and Regulations

C ompiled and summarized in the following table are the various laws and regulations that govern cybersecurity and information privacy practices. This overview is meant to serve as a starting point to delve deeper into the legal ramifications and consequences of an organization's cybersecurity and information privacy responsibilities.

Laws & Regulations	Applicability	Compliance Guidelines	Penalties and Enforcements
California Consumer Privacy Act (CCPA)	On June 28, 2018, California passed the CCPA. CCPA became effective on January 1, 2020. This law is likely to affect clients whose websites collect data from California residents regardless of whether the client has a brick-and-mortar location in the State of California. CCPA largely parallels the General Data Protection Regulation (GDPR), and affects companies that collect data of individuals in the European Union (EU).	Specific provisions include that consumers may demand that a business disclose the personal information it collects on that consumer, the categories of sources for that information, its business purposes for collecting the information or selling it, and who it shares it with. To comply with the CCPA, businesses will need to understand the details of the data they collect, how they collect, and where they store it.	Intentional violations of the CCPA can bring civil penalties of up to $7500 for each violation in a lawsuit brought by the California Attorney General on behalf of the people of the State of California. The maximum fine for other violations is $2500 per violation.
Children's Online Privacy Protection Act (COPPA)	Enacted in 1998, COPPA is a privacy and cybersecurity law to protect the safety and privacy of children under the age of 13.	Must provide reasonable means for parents to review the personal information collected from a child, and enable them to refuse permission for further use or maintenance.	Violators are fined. The largest amount fined to date is $5.7 million.

Laws & Regulations	Applicability	Compliance Guidelines	Penalties and Enforcements
	COPPA applies to websites and online services that are directed at children under the age of 13 years. It also applies if the operator of the site has actual knowledge that children under the age of 13 years are using a website. The purpose of the Act is to regulate how these websites collect, use, and/or disclose personal information from and about children.	Cannot make the child's participation in a game, the offering of a prize, or any other activity, a condition for a child to provide information. Provide reasonable procedures to protect the confidentiality, security, and integrity of personal information collected from children.	
Commodity Futures Trading Commission (CFTC) Derivatives Clearing Organizations Regulation **17 CFR Part 39, Subpart B, 17 CFR 39.18—System safeguards**	The CFTC Regulation applies to derivatives-clearing organizations. These entities act as a medium for clearing transactions in commodities for future delivery or commodity option transactions. There are about 27 worldwide. These markets are at the heart of the global financial system.	To protect themselves, derivatives-clearing organizations must develop an extensive and robust information security program that includes the following: An annual compliance report that must be sent to the board and CFTC Vulnerability testing of independent contractors twice every quarter	Civil fines for violating this regulation can be up to $1,098,190 or triple the monetary gain. This rule can be enforced by a Securities Exchange Commission (SEC) action or by the Financial Industry Regulatory Authority (FINRA).

(Continued)

(Continued)

Laws & Regulations	Applicability	Compliance Guidelines	Penalties and Enforcements
		Internal and external penetration testing at least annually Control testing once every three years Annual security incident response plan testing Annual enterprise technology risk assessment	
Consumer Privacy Protection Act of 2017	Designed to ensure the privacy and security of sensitive personal information, to prevent and mitigate identity theft, to provide notice of security breaches involving sensitive personal information, and to enhance law enforcement assistance and other protections against security breaches, fraudulent access, and misuse of personal information. It will apply to organizations that collect, use, access, transmit, store, or dispose of sensitive personally identifiable information of 10,000 or more U.S. citizens during any 12-month period.		Civil penalty fines will not exceed $5 million unless the violation is found to be willful or intentional, in which an additional $5 million can be imposed.

Laws & Regulations	Applicability	Compliance Guidelines	Penalties and Enforcements
Defense Federal Acquisition Regulation (DFAR)	DFAR is a cybersecurity regulation that applies to the U.S. Department of Defense (DoD) contractors.	Department of Defense (DoD) contractors and subcontractors that possess, store, or transmit "covered defense information" are required to provide adequate security to safeguard the covered defense information on unclassified information system.

Regulation mandates compliance with a specific cybersecurity standard: the National Institute of Standards and Technology (NIST) Special Publication (SP) 800-171, "Protecting Controlled Unclassified Information in Nonfederal Information Systems and Organizations" (see Appendix D of NIST 800-171 for reference to other cybersecurity frameworks, including ISO 27001).

The Regulation provides a detailed process for investigating cyber incidents and reporting them to the DoD and the prime contractor (or next higher-tier subcontractor), including protecting and preserving evidence that includes malware for possible forensic analysis. | Failure to comply may result in debarment. |

Laws & Regulations	Applicability	Compliance Guidelines	Penalties and Enforcements
Electronic Communications Privacy Act (ECPA) and Stored Communications Act (SCA)	The ECPA together with the SCA, also known as the Wiretap Act, are privacy statutes. Originally designed to limit warrantless surveillance, these acts forbid the intentional use, disclosure, or access to any wire, oral, or electronic communication without authorization.	Policies should prohibit recording or disclosing any oral or electronic communications without obtaining consent from both parties. Policies should prohibit surveillance of nonemployees unless there is consent. Policies allow surveillance, including video and email interception of employees, if there is a valid business reason for doing so.	The acts provide criminal penalties that could be used to jail malicious hackers.
EU-US Privacy Shield	The European Commission adopted the EU-US Privacy Shield framework on July 12, 2016, and it came into effect the same day. The Privacy Shield was developed to protect EU residents' data held and processed by organizations in the U.S. The protection of an individual's data in the U.S. does not come anywhere near what the EU considers adequate.	To self-certify to the Privacy Shield, a company must undertake the following: Confirm that it is eligible. Most companies outside of the financial sector are eligible. Develop a Privacy Shield–compliant privacy policy statement and make sure that the organization's privacy policy conforms to the Privacy Shield principles.	For companies that fail to comply with certain GDPR requirements, fines may be up to 2% or 4% of total global annual turnover or €10 m or €20 m, whichever is greater.

Laws & Regulations	Applicability	Compliance Guidelines	Penalties and Enforcements
		Identify the organization's independent recourse mechanism to enforce the privacy policy.	
		Make sure that the privacy policy is publicly available.	
		Make sure the organization has a compliance verification mechanism.	
		Designate a contact within the organization regarding the Privacy Shield.	
		Submit the organization's self-certification to the Department of Commerce.	
Federal Privacy Act of 1974	The FPA applies only to agencies of the U.S. federal government. It governs the collection, maintenance, use, and dissemination of personally identifiable information about individuals that is maintained in systems of records by federal agencies.	All U.S. federal agencies must: Not disclose any record that is contained in a system of records by any means of communication to any person, or to another agency, without a written request from, or the prior written consent of, the individual to whom the record pertains.	Covered persons, which include lawful residents of the U.S. and citizens of certain foreign countries designated by the U.S. Secretary of State, may sue in a U.S. federal district court for actual damages or $1,000 (whichever is greater), attorney fees, and court costs.

(Continued)

Laws & Regulations	Applicability	Compliance Guidelines	Penalties and Enforcements
	It prohibits the disclosure of information from a system of records controlled by the federal agency without the written consent of the subject individual, unless the disclosure is permitted under one of twelve statutory exceptions. Until recently, it only applied to lawful residents of the United States. Amended by the Judicial Redress Act, which allows citizens of "covered countries" as determined by the Attorney General, with the agreement of the Secretary of State, the Secretary of the Treasury, and the Secretary of Homeland Security, to sue in a federal court for willful disclosures of personally identifiable information by a federal agency.	Allow any individual to gain access to their record or to any information pertaining to them that is contained in the system, and permit them and, if they request, a person of their own choosing to accompany them, to review the record and have a copy made. Maintain any record concerning any individual, making reasonable efforts to ensure such records are accurate, relevant, timely, and complete. Assure fairness in any determination relating to the qualifications, character, rights, or opportunities of, or benefits to, the individual.	The court may also require the federal agency to amend or correct any information on file concerning the covered person.
Federal Trade Commission (FTC) Act	This Act was enacted in 1914 to outlaw unfair trade and business practices.	Organizations are expected to engage in all "reasonable and necessary" security practices.	The FTC can and has imposed civil liabilities. Recently, Facebook was fined $5 billion.

Laws & Regulations	Applicability	Compliance Guidelines	Penalties and Enforcements
	Section 5 of the FTC Act is an information security regulation and a privacy law. The law applies to almost every organization in the United States with the exception of banks and common carriers.	Organizations should not deceive or mislead consumers by making material and false statements about their data security practices. Organizations should have in place robust data security practices to protect sensitive customer information.	
Food and Drug Administration (FDA) Regulations for the Use of Electronic Records in Clinical Investigations	The Food and Drug Administration (FDA) regulations for the Use of Electronic Records in Clinical Investigations is a cybersecurity law. It applies to organizations involved in clinical investigations of medical products, including sponsors, clinical investigators, institutional review boards (IRBs), and contract research organizations (CROs). The regulation is concerned with the IT systems of applicable organizations, including any electronic systems used to create, modify, maintain, archive, retrieve, or transmit records used in clinical investigations.	The regulations require the following: The IT systems ensure accuracy, reliability, and consistent performance. Only authorized individuals should have access to the IT systems. Audit trails must be maintained. Organizations must establish and adhere to written policies that hold individuals accountable. Organizations must provide adequate training.	The regulations are enforced by the FDA, which will conduct investigations and audits.

Laws & Regulations	Applicability	Compliance Guidelines	Penalties and Enforcements
	Since these records are to be used for validating the research by the FDA, the Regulations are geared more toward the integrity part of the confidentiality, integrity, availability triad.		
General Data Protection Regulation (GDPR)	The **GDPR**, agreed upon by the European Parliament and Council in April 2016, went into effect in Spring 2018 as the primary law regulating how companies protect EU citizens' personal data. GDPR requirements apply to each member state of the EU, aiming to create more consistent protection of consumer and personal data across EU nations. It is important to note that any company that markets goods or services to EU residents, regardless of its location, is subject to the regulation.	Some of the key privacy and data protection requirements of the GDPR include: Requiring the consent of subjects for data processing. Anonymizing collected data to protect privacy. Providing data breach notifications. Safely handling the transfer of data across borders. Requiring certain companies to appoint a data protection officer to oversee GDPR compliance.	For companies that fail to comply with certain GDPR requirements, fines may be up to 2% or 4% of total global annual turnover or €10m or €20m, whichever is greater.

Laws & Regulations	Applicability	Compliance Guidelines	Penalties and Enforcements
Gramm-Leach-Bliley Act	Passed in 1999, this regulation is both an information security and privacy law. The law applies to financial institutions, and that includes banks, insurance companies, securities firms, nonbank mortgage lenders, auto dealers, and tax preparers.	Employees must be subjected to background checks, especially those who are going to have access to customer information. New employees must sign a confidentiality pledge. Access to private information should be limited on a "Need to Know" basis. Strong passwords must be used, and they should be changed frequently. Computer screens should lock after a certain specified period of inactivity. Security policies must be in place for devices and data encryption. Employees should go through security training when they join the company and on a periodic basis. They should be regularly reminded of the company's security policies.	Violators could be fined in excess of $1 million. The Federal Deposit Insurance Corporation (FDIC) insurance could be terminated.

(Continued)

Laws & Regulations	Applicability	Compliance Guidelines	Penalties and Enforcements
		Information security policies for remote work must be in place.	
		There should be policies in place for security violations and there should be a disciplined enforcement of the policies.	
		Data at rest and data in transit must be secured. Controls should be in place to protect unauthorized access of data.	
		Information should be disposed in a secure manner.	
Health Insurance Portability and Accountability Act (HIPAA)	Passed in 1996 HIPAA is a privacy and security regulation that applies to healthcare providers, health plans, healthcare clearing houses, and certain types of businesses called "covered entities." The Act covers organizations as diverse as health insurance and pharmaceutical companies.	Electronic protected health information (ePHI), that is compromised of individually identifiable health care information, must be protected with administrative, physical, and technical safeguards. ePHI should only be used or disclosed under the following circumstances:	Violators are subjected to significant penalties in the range of millions of dollars. The largest reported penalty exceeded $16 million. In 2018, the total penalty amount was a record $28 million.

Laws & Regulations	Applicability	Compliance Guidelines	Penalties and Enforcements
		When individuals gives their consent. For treatment, payment, and healthcare operations purposes.	
		When disclosure is permitted for certain specific incidents.	
		When the disclosure is warranted for public interest.	
		HIPAA also has very specific breach notification rules:	
		Individuals must be notified within 60 days of the discovery of a breach.	
		The notification letter must include the type of information compromised, actions the individual needs to take to protect themselves, steps being taken by the organization to investigate and mitigate the breach, and the contact information of the organization.	

(Continued)

Laws & Regulations	Applicability	Compliance Guidelines	Penalties and Enforcements
		The media and the Secretary of Health and Human Services must be notified when the number of individuals breached exceeds 500. If the number of individuals breached is less than 500, the incident must be logged and reported to the Secretary of Health and Human Services.	
Payment Card Industry (PCI) Data Security Standards (DSS)	PCI-DSS is the data security standard for the payment card industry and is maintained by the PCI Security Standards Council (PCI-SSC).	There are six major principles of PCI-DSS: Build and maintain a secure network. Protect cardholder data. Maintain a vulnerability management program. Implement strong access control measures. Regularly monitor and test networks. Maintain an information security policy.	PCI noncompliance can result in penalties ranging from $5,000 to $100,000 per month by the credit card companies. These penalties depend on the volume of clients, the volume of transactions, the level of PCI-DSS that the company should be on, and the time that it has been noncompliant. For example, for Level 1-companies that have not met the requirements for more than 7 months, the penalties can reach up to $100,000 monthly.

Laws & Regulations	Applicability	Compliance Guidelines	Penalties and Enforcements
		There are 12 PCI-DSS requirements: Install and maintain a firewall configuration to protect cardholder data. Do not use vendor-supplied defaults for system passwords and other security parameters. Protect stored cardholder data. Encrypt transmission of cardholder data across open, public networks. Use and regularly update anti-virus software or programs. Develop and maintain secure systems and applications. Restrict access to cardholder data. Assign a unique ID to each person with computer access. Restrict physical access to cardholder data.	

(Continued)

Laws & Regulations	Applicability	Compliance Guidelines	Penalties and Enforcements
		Track and monitor all access to network resources and cardholder data Regularly test security systems and processes Maintain a policy that addresses information security for all personnel	
Sarbanes-Oxley (SOX) Act	Enacted in July 2002, the SOX Act requires publicly traded organizations to prove their cybersecurity credentials.	A SOX compliance audit of a company's internal controls must be conducted once a year. To avoid a conflict of interest, an independent auditor must be hired to conduct the SOX compliance audit and report the findings to a high-level governance committee, often referred to as the Audit Committee. The SOX audit must be conducted separately from other internal audits. **Guiding Questions** Is the organization following any one or more of the internal controls framework, such as the ones offered	Unlike many other cybersecurity or privacy statutes, SOX has criminal penalties. A CEO or CFO can be liable for maximum penalties of: $1 million and 10 years of imprisonment for false certification; and $5 million and 20 years for a willful false filing.

Laws & Regulations	Applicability	Compliance Guidelines	Penalties and Enforcements
		by COSO (Committee of Sponsoring Organizations of the Treadway Commission), COBIT (Control Objectives for Information and Related Technology), and ITGI (IT Governance Institute)?	
		Are policies in place to create, modify and maintain accounting systems, including computer programs handling financial data?	
		Are safeguards in place to prevent data tampering? Have they been tested and found operational?	
		Is there a protocol for dealing with security breaches?	
		Is access to sensitive data being monitored and recorded?	
		Have previous breaches and failures of security safeguards been disclosed to auditors?	
		Has the organization collected valid, recent SAS (Statement on Auditing Standards) 70 reports from all applicable service organizations?	

Laws & Regulations	Applicability	Compliance Guidelines	Penalties and Enforcements
		Access Control Measures	
		Whether adequate physical and electronic controls are in place to prevent unauthorized users from accessing sensitive information. Such access control measures include keeping servers and data centers in secure locations, making sure strong password controls are in place, the principle of least privilege (PoLP) is guiding the administration of access privileges, and automatic locking of computer screens after a certain duration of inactivity.	
		Prevention and Remediation	
		Whether appropriate controls are in place to prevent breaches and having tools to remediate incidents as they occur.	
		Monitoring and Protection	
		Whether the company has invested in appropriate tools, services, or appliances that will monitor and protect the financial database.	

Laws & Regulations	Applicability	Compliance Guidelines	Penalties and Enforcements
		Record Keeping Maintaining a record of changes to the Active Directory databases and other information architecture components. Maintaining an updated record of hardware and software. The records should indicate when the changes were made and who made them. **Backups** Backup systems should be in place to protect sensitive data. Data centers containing backed-up data including those stored off site or by a third party are subject to the same SOX compliance requirements as those hosted on premises.	

(Continued)

(Continued)

Laws & Regulations	Applicability	Compliance Guidelines	Penalties and Enforcements
United States Securities and Exchange Commission (SEC) Regulation S-P: Privacy of Consumer Financial Information (CFR) and Safeguarding Personal Information	SEC rule 30, which is part of Regulation S-P (17 CFR 248.30), is an information security regulation that requires appropriate cybersecurity measures. SEC rule 30 applies to United States and foreign brokers, dealers, investment companies, and investment advisers that are registered with the SEC.	Organizations must adopt appropriate written policies to: Ensure the security and confidentiality of customer records and information. Protect the security and integrity of customer information against any anticipated threats or hazards. Protect against unauthorized access to or use of customer records or information that could result in substantial harm or inconvenience to any customer. Organizations must provide initial and annual privacy notices to customers describing information-sharing policies and informing customers of their rights. Organizations must limit reuse of customer information and disclosure to third parties.	Civil fines for violating this regulation can be up to $1,098,190 or triple the monetary gain.

Laws & Regulations	Applicability	Compliance Guidelines	Penalties and Enforcements
		Organizations must properly dispose of the sensitive customer information by taking reasonable measures to protect against unauthorized access to or use of the information in connection with its disposal.	

Sources:

https://cyberexperts.com/cybersecurity-laws/

https://www.itgovernanceusa.com/federal-cybersecurity-and-privacy-laws

https://www.blackstratus.com/sox-compliance-requirements/

https://digitalguardian.com/blog/what-gdpr-general-data-protection-regulation-understanding-and-complying-gdpr-data-protection

https://www.globalpaymentsintegrated.com/en-us/blog/2019/11/12/the-twelve-requirements-of-pci-dss-compliance

https://www.americanbar.org/groups/litigation/committees/intellectual-property/practice/2018/how-will-california-cybersecurity-laws-affect-us-business/

https://www.clarip.com/data-privacy/california-consumer-privacy-act-fines/

https://www.blackstratus.com/compliance/iso-27001/

https://www.mymoid.com/pci-non-compliance-consequences/#:~:text=PCI%20non%2Dcompliance%20can%20result,it%20has%20been%20non%2Dcompliant.

Appendix 5

Physical, Technical, and Administrative Controls: A Representative List

Appendix 5 presents a summary list of administrative, technical, and physical controls to secure data, devices, networks, storage locations, and people. These controls reflect one or more of the three dimensions of a high-performance information security culture—commitment, preparedness, and discipline. Effectively implementing these controls is key to achieving a high level of cybersecurity readiness.

Securing Data	Physical Controls	Technical Controls	Administrative Controls
	Biometric authentication	Data Backup and Retention	Hands-on Top Management
		Encryption	"We-Are-in-It-Together" Culture
		Digital Signatures	Cross-Functional Participation
		Digital Certificates	Sustainable Budget
		Data Masking	Strategic Alignment and Partnerships
		Steganography	Joint Ownership and Accountability
		Data Loss Prevention Tools and Technologies	The Chief Information Security Officer (CISO) Function Empowerment
		Email Domain Restrictions	Organizational Role Recognition
		Remote wipe-off (data on mobile devices)	Cyber Risk Assessment
		Virtual Private Network	Asset Identification and Prioritization
		Multifactor Authentication	Business continuity planning
		Regular backups	Policy of Least Privilege
		Managed File Transfer Platform	Separation of Duties
		Network segmentation	Security screening and background checks
		Separating production, development, and testing environment	Job rotations
		Creating dual personas (mobile devices)	Awareness and Training
		Secure data wipe-off	Data retention and disposal policy

	Physical Controls	Technical Controls	Administrative Controls
		Username and password	Service Level Agreements with Vendors
		Identity and Access Management System	Rigorous vendor selection process
		Configuration management	Disaster recovery planning
		Domain Name System (DNS) Filtering	Security audits
		DMARC Protocol Implementation	Tabletop exercises and security drills
		Disk mirroring (RAID—Level 1)	
		Disk striping (RAID—Level 5)	
		Component redundancy	
		Load balancing	
Securing Devices	Biometric authentication	Monitoring for vulnerabilities	Hands-on Top Management
	Smart cards	Software patches and updates	"We-Are-in-It-Together" Culture
	Closed-circuit surveillance cameras	Device discovery and management tool	Cross-Functional Participation
	Security guards	Asset inventory recording and tracking systems	Sustainable Budget
	Identification cards	Username and password	Strategic Alignment and Partnerships
	Locked and dead-bolted steel doors	Identity and Access Management System	Joint Ownership and Accountability
		Configuration management	CISO Function Empowerment
		DNS Filtering	Organizational Role Recognition
			Cyber Risk Assessment

(Continued)

	Physical Controls	Technical Controls	Administrative Controls
		Disabling auto-run features on optical and USB drives	Asset Identification and Prioritization Policy of Least Privilege Separation of Duties Security screening and background checks Job rotations Business Continuity Planning Regular system maintenance and review Portable device management policies Disaster recovery planning Security audits Tabletop exercises and security drills
Securing Networks	Biometric authentication	Monitoring for vulnerabilities Intrusion detection and protection systems Firewalls Network segmentation Software patches and updates	Hands-on Top Management "We-Are-in-It-Together" Culture Cross-Functional Participation Sustainable Budget Strategic Alignment and Partnerships

	Physical Controls	Technical Controls	Administrative Controls
		Device discovery and management tool	Joint Ownership and Accountability
		Asset inventory recording and tracking systems	CISO Function Empowerment
			Organizational Role Recognition
		Username and password	Cyber Risk Assessment
		Identity and Access Management System	Asset Identification and Prioritization
		Configuration management	Policy of Least Privilege
		DNS Filtering	Separation of Duties
		Virtual Private Networks	Security screening and background checks
		Secure Wi-Fi Networks	Job rotations
		Automated scanning of ports	Business Continuity Planning
		Penetration testing	Threat intelligence gathering
			Disaster recovery planning
			Security audits
			Tabletop exercises and security drills
Securing Storage Locations (e.g., server rooms and data centers)	Biometric authentication Smart cards	Username and password	Hands-on Top Management "We-Are-in-It-Together" Culture Cross-Functional Participation

(Continued)

231

Physical Controls	Technical Controls	Administrative Controls
Closed-circuit surveillance cameras		Sustainable Budget
		Strategic Alignment and Partnerships
		Joint Ownership and Accountability
Security guards		CISO Function Empowerment
Identification cards		Organizational Role Recognition
		Cyber Risk Assessment
Locked and dead-bolted steel doors		Asset Identification and Prioritization
		Policy of Least Privilege
		Separation of Duties
		Security screening and background checks
		Job rotations
		Business Continuity Planning
		Disaster recovery planning
		Security audits
		Tabletop exercises and security drills

Securing People	Physical Controls	Technical Controls	Administrative Controls
	Biometric authentication		Hands-on Top Management
	Smart cards		"We-Are-in-It-Together" Culture
	Closed-circuit surveillance cameras		Cross-Functional Participation
	Security guards		Sustainable Budget
	Identification cards		Strategic Alignment and Partnerships
	Locked and dead-bolted steel doors		Joint Ownership and Accountability
			CISO Function Empowerment
			Organizational Role Recognition
			Cyber Risk Assessment
			Asset Identification and Prioritization
			Policy of Least Privilege
			Separation of Duties
			Screening and background checks
			Job rotation
			Awareness and Training
			Disaster recovery planning
			Security audits
			Tabletop exercises and security drills

APPENDIX 6

Case Studies

Case Study 1

Target's Debit/Credit Card Data Breach

Introduction

In an increasingly digitized business world where companies leverage the power of electronic networks to partner, transact, and collaborate, securing the digital assets of an organization is becoming a bigger challenge. An organization not only has to shore up its defense, but also make sure its business partners and service providers are maintaining similar or better security standards. Otherwise, the attack surface area grows exponentially, and hackers are able to exploit the vulnerabilities of a vendor network and use it as a gateway to breach the client's systems and databases. That is precisely what happened when Target experienced an external extrusion attack in November 2013. An employee of Target's HVAC vendor fell victim to a phishing attack and that resulted in a malware getting installed on one of Target's servers. The Citadel malware that was installed should have been detected by the anti-malware software available then. However, the vendor was using a free version of Malwarebytes, an anti-malware solution, and that was not powerful enough to detect the malware. The vendor also didn't have a multi-factor authentication (MFA) system in place. From the compromised vendor machine, the hackers were able to launch a Trojan attack on Target's systems and gain access to customer credentials.

As highlighted in the summary table at the end of Chapter 3, Target's management of vendor security is a potential area for improvement. It is a good practice to check the security credentials of vendors prior to doing business with them and establish an oversight mechanism to ensure they are living up to the agreed-upon security expectations.

Hands-on commitment from the senior leadership could go a long way in ensuring the company did its due diligence in establishing a strong security system and took due care in protecting confidential data. The importance of top management commitment is highlighted in Chapter 5.

From a preparedness standpoint, a potential weakness was lack of (or inadequate) network segmentation. Chapter 6 discusses a defense-in-depth approach that could benefit Target. This layered security strategy would include implementation of robust firewalls, use of powerful encryption methods to secure data, multi-factor authentication, and strong password controls. Use of intrusion detection systems and other sophisticated artificial intelligence–enabled technologies to proactively detect and thwart attacks are also important components of a thorough preparedness plan.

Finally, organizations such as Target can benefit from a disciplined approach to protecting sensitive data. Chapter 7 highlights some of the best practices associated with cybersecurity discipline. These include continuous monitoring of networks, maintaining intelligence logs, promptly acting on threat alerts, regular penetration testing, and conducting real-time security audits and drills.

—*Dave Chatterjee*

Target's Debit/Credit Card Data Breach
A Business Case by Kudzai Muku, PhD

Abstract

America's second-largest retailer, Target, was the victim of a data breach during the busiest shopping period in the United States, between November and December 2013. The data thieves gained access to Target's computer network, stole the financial and personal information of 110 million Target customers, and moved the data to a server in Eastern Europe. As a result of the data breach, Target faced many challenges, including damage to its corporate reputation, and the need to take steps to strengthen data security in the future. This case examines Target's efforts to restore its corporate reputation and increase digital security.

Case

Learning Outcomes

The purpose of this case study is to enable students to:

- understand the factors that led to Target's debit/credit card data breach;

- understand the impact on the company and its customers; and

- critically evaluate how Target handled the data breach.

Overview

Target first opened shop in 1962 in Roseville, Minnesota, with a focus on convenient shopping at competitive discount prices. Target is the second-largest general merchandise retailer in the United States, with 1,801 stores in the United States, 133 stores in Canada, and 366,000 employees worldwide. Target.com is consistently ranked as one of the most visited retail websites. Target's mission is to make Target the customer's preferred shopping destination in all channels by delivering outstanding value, continuous innovation, and exceptional guest experiences by consistently fulfilling Target's Expect More, Pay Less brand promise.

During the busiest shopping period of the year in the United States, data thieves stole the debit and credit card information of customers who shopped in Target between November 27 and December 15, 2013. At first, it was estimated that the data thieves got away with the personal information of 40 million customers. However, in 2014 Target announced that an additional 70 million customers had been affected by the data breach, a number equivalent to about one-third of the U.S. population.

The Retail Industry and Information Security

According to Verizon's Data Breach Investigations Report (DBIR) for 2014, the industries that are most commonly affected by point-of-sale (POS) intrusions are restaurants, hotels, grocery stores, and other brick-and-mortar retailers. In Verizon's DBIR, an analysis of security incidents with confirmed data loss by victim industry showed that the retail industry was among the top four industries with a high level of security incidents. Eleven percent of security incidents occur in the retail industry, and 31 percent of these security incidents are attributable to POS intrusions in the retail industry (Verizon Enterprise Solutions, 2014). In a POS intrusion, an attacker compromises a POS device, installs malware to gather card data, and then uses the card to access funds. According to Verizon's 2014 DBIR, the most popular POS attack involves RAM-scraping malware, which grabs payment card data while it's being processed in memory but before it's encrypted.

Following the Target data breach in 2013, other retailers were also victims of cybercrime the following year, including Neiman Marcus, Michael's, P. F. Chang's, Kmart, Sally Beauty, Bebe, Godiva, Staples,

Goodwill, Shutterfly, and Home Depot. These additional cyberattacks used similar techniques as in the Target data breach attack. According to the Retail Industry Leaders Association, data breach crimes are one of the biggest challenges facing retailers today. The cyber thieves take advantage of the holiday shopping season to get information from millions of credit and debit cards at once.

Security experts dubbed 2014 the year of the data breach, with data breaches becoming more common and not simply isolated incidents. Security experts have noted that the volume, scope, and frequency of third-party vendors as the source of the breaches have risen each year. In addition to the 110 million customers affected in the Target incident, data breaches in 2013–2014 included the following.

- In the Sally Beauty data breach (February 2014), credit card information for 25,000 customers was stolen.

- The Neiman Marcus data breach (July 2013 to January 2014) affected 1.2 million debit and credit card users.

- In the Home Depot data breach (April to September 2014), data thieves got away with information for 56 million debit and credit cards and also 53 million customer e-mail addresses.

- The Michaels data breach (May 2013 to January 2014) affected three million debit and credit card users.

- In the Dairy Queen data breach (October 2014), credit card numbers were stolen from 395 Dairy Queen locations, with the total number of customers affected still under investigation.

- The impact of the Kmart data breach (September to October, 2014) is still under investigation.

- In the Staples data breach (April to September 2014), debit and credit card information from 1.1 million customers was stolen.

The impact of the Bebe data breach (November 8–26, 2014), the impact of the Jewel-Osco (June 22 to July 17, 2014) and the impact of the P.F. Chang's breach (October 2013 to June 2014) is still under investigation.

In 2014, the Retail Industry Leaders Association, together with top retailers such as Gap, Target, Walgreen, Nike, and Lowes, launched the Retail Cyber Intelligence Sharing Center, which specializes in the prevention of cybercrimes against retailers. The intelligence sharing center would enable retailers to share information about data breaches and potential threats.

Implementation of the Target Data Theft

Target had given network access to a third-party vendor, Fazio Mechanical Services, a Pennsylvania-based heating, ventilation, and air conditioning (HVAC) contractor. As part of its subcontractor work, Target provided Fazio with limited network credentials for electronic billing, contract submission, and project management. The network access enabled Fazio to access parts of Target's computer network. The vendor's weak security allowed the attackers to gain a foothold in Target's network.

The data thieves installed malware on POS terminals at U.S.-based Target stores, enabling the theft of financial information from 40 million debit and credit cards. The malware allowed for the collection of unencrypted, plain text data as it passed through the infected POS machine's memory before the data was transferred to Target's payment processing provider. Hackers tampered with the POS systems used at check-out registers and gained access to the data that is stored on the cards. According to Target, only 25 cash registers were hacked but information for 110 million Target customers was compromised. The data thieves later sold the information they had stolen online. According to Target, the data breach included information such as customer names, credit or debit card numbers, expiration dates, and card verification security codes. Once the data thieves had obtained the data, they could use the data to encode that information on counterfeit cards, sell the cloned cards in batches online, or use the cloned cards at retailers to purchase goods. According to security blogger Brian Krebs, the data stolen from Target flooded the underground online black markets or "card shops," selling in batches of one million cards at prices ranging from $20 to more than $100 per card. Newer cards are sold at higher prices before the banks have identified and canceled the cards. By August 2014, the expenses in connection to the data breach had reached $235 million.

Timeline of the Target's Debit/Credit Card Data Breach

The following timeline is based on a combination of information from the Target website, *International Business Times* timeline (Clark, 2014), and the *FierceRetail* timeline (Heller, 2014). Only key information relevant to this case study was incorporated in this timeline.

- Sept. 2013: Attackers steal Fazio credentials. Target certified as Payment Card Industry Data Security Standards (PCI-DSS) compliant.

- Nov. 12, 2013: Attackers gain access to Target's internal network.

- Nov. 15–28, 2013: Attackers test malware on Target POS.

- Nov. 30, 2013: POS malware fully installed. Attackers install data exfiltration malware. Symantec software identifies malicious activity. First FireEye alerts triggered. However, Target does not respond to the multiple warnings of the attack.

- Nov. 27–Dec. 15, 2013: A data hack at U.S. Target stores exposes approximately 40 million credit and debit card customers to fraud through a compromised POS system.

- Dec. 2, 2013: More FireEye alerts triggered. Attackers begin exfiltrating data.

- Dec. 12, 2013: Department of Justice notifies Target of data breach.

- Dec. 14, 2013: Target hires a third-party forensics team to investigate the hack.

- Dec. 15, 2013: Target removes the malware. Attackers lose foothold in Target network.

- Dec. 18, 2013: Computer security expert and investigator Brian Krebs reports on the data breach.

- Dec. 19, 2013: Target officially acknowledges that it has been the victim of a data breach. The stolen information includes customer names, credit or debit card numbers used, their expiration dates, and encrypted security codes.

- Dec. 21, 2013: JP Morgan Chase places daily limits on spending and withdrawals of its debit card customers as it works to reissue cards in the following two weeks.

- Jan. 10, 2014: Target announces that an additional 70 million customers had their personal nonfinancial information stolen during the Thanksgiving and Christmas holiday data breach. The stolen information included names, addresses, phone numbers, and e-mail addresses.

- Jan. 2014: Target announces it will provide one year of credit screening services for free to affected customers.

- Jan. 15, 2014: Target invests $5 million to support a new cybersecurity coalition to educate consumers and announces it will pay for one year of credit-monitoring services and identity theft protection by Experian.

- Jan. 20, 2014: The *Wall Street Journal* (Ziobro & Sidel, 2014) reports that Target had the more secure chip and PIN cards in 2004 but abandoned the program after less than three years when shoppers failed to adopt the cards.

- Feb. 4, 2014: Target says it will roll out chip and PIN card readers at a cost of $100 million.

- Feb. 6, 2014: Fazio Mechanical Services acknowledges it had access to Target's network for electronic billing and project management purposes. It is suspected that thieves used Fazio's vendor credentials to access Target's network and upload their malware to cash registers. Only 25 registers were hacked, but up to 110 million cards were compromised during the attack, according to Target.

- March 5, 2014: Target's chief information officer (CIO) Beth Jacob resigns.

- March 6, 2014: Target's bank joins the Financial Services Information Sharing and Analysis Center (FS-ISAC), a private-sector initiative that facilitates detection, prevention, and response to cyberattacks and fraud.

- April 29, 2014: Bob DeRodes, a former tech adviser in several federal government agencies (including the Center for CIO Leadership, the U.S. Department of Homeland Security, the U.S. Secretary of Defense, and the U.S. Department of Justice), appointed as the new CIO, effective May 5.

- May 5, 2014: Target CEO Gregg Steinhafel resigns. Target CFO John Mulligan will serve as interim president and CEO.

- May 2014: Target announces that it will update all its REDcards to chip and PIN technology in early 2015. These cards encode information differently with each transaction, making it harder for thieves to clone the cards and use the stolen data.

- June 10, 2014: Brad Maiorino appointed as senior vice president, chief information security officer. Brad is General Motors' former chief information security and information technology risk officer.

- Dec. 18, 2014: U.S. District Court for the District of Minnesota rules that a group of consumers could proceed with a majority of their claims against Target.

Target's Vulnerabilities

According to an analysis of the Target breach by the United States Senate Committee on Commerce, Science, and Transportation, the data thieves were able to steal the data because (1) they took advantage of weak security at a Target vendor, gaining a foothold in Target's inner network; (2) Target missed warnings from its anti-intrusion software that attackers were installing malware in its network; (3) attackers took advantage of weak controls within Target's network to maneuver into sensitive areas of the network; and (4) Target missed information provided by its anti-intrusion software about the attackers' escape plan, allowing them to steal 110 million customer records. It was only after the U.S. Department of Justice notified Target of the data breach that Target began to investigate what had happened.

Costs of the Data Breach

As a result of the data breach, Target faced many challenges. As of August 2014, the expenses in connection with the data breach had reached $235 million, with $90 million being paid from insurance. In the face of network security failure, Target had to identify ways to address future data security. It faced damage to its corporate reputation, a threat to stock prices, and, ultimately, reduced profits.

Corporate Reputation

Reputational damage may occur after a data breach because customers may not feel safe continuing to do business with a retailer. In response to the data breach crisis, Target used several tools to reach out to its customers, including full-page newspaper ads, an e-mail from the CEO Gregg Steinhafel apologizing about the breach and offering free credit monitoring, and an appearance by the CEO on CNBC on January 13, 2014. In order to regain customer trust and reassure customers that it was safe to shop at Target, the retailer developed a public relations campaign that included the building of a microsite specifically for addressing the breach. Customers criticized Target for not responding immediately to the data breach. Target offered one year of free credit monitoring by Experian to affected customers. These services are meant to monitor customers' credit and personal information and inform customers if any new accounts are opened in their name or if their information appears in the list of stolen information in a data breach.

Increasing Cybersecurity through Technology and Personnel Changes

After the data breach Target announced that it would introduce REDcards (Target store-brand credit cards) with chip and PIN technology in early 2015 to improve security. These smart cards with chip and PIN technology use microchips to encrypt transactions. Target also invested in updating technology for increased security, in new infrastructure, customer service, and data centers to protect it from future data breaches. Target also gave $5 million to support a new cybersecurity coalition to educate consumers.

The data breach led to the resignation of the CEO and the CIO. After the data breach Target announced that it would overhaul its information security and compliance systems and personnel. Furthermore, two new positions were created—chief information security officer and chief compliance officer—to improve Target's data security. At first, Target named Bob DeRodes, a former technology advisor to U.S. government departments, as its interim CIO to guide Target's security efforts after the data breach. According to *A BullsEye View*, Target's online magazine, Bob DeRodes would be responsible for enhancing Target's data security and technology infrastructure and hiring Brad Maiorino as the chief information security officer. Brad Maiorino is one of the top leaders in information security and risk in the United States. His main responsibility involved ensuring that Target and its customers are protected from information security threats through an information security and technology risk strategy. On February 3, 2015, Target appointed Mike McNamara, a technology innovation expert with experience as a CIO at a UK-based retailer, as the new CIO. The role of the new CIO included overseeing the technology team and operations, and information security. Target also appointed Jacqueline Hourigan Rice (a global expert in ethics, compliance, and corporate security) as its first chief risk and compliance officer. Some of the duties of Target's chief risk and compliance officer included oversight of enterprise risk management, vendor management, compliance, and corporate security.

Summary of Costs

According to the Ponemon Institute's Cost of Data Breach Study (2013), the average cost of a breached record for the United States is $188 per stolen record. This cost is so high because breaches can spur multiple lawsuits and ongoing expenses as firms work to prevent their customers from suffering full-fledged identity theft. Target's incurred costs included free credit monitoring for customers, new technologies to strengthen data security and issuing new cards, hiring new staff, legal expenses, and fines. Other expenses Target incurred as a result of the data breach included expenses for protecting the company from future attacks by investing in new infrastructure, security features, customer service, and data centers.

As of December 2014, investigation into the Target data breach is ongoing and no arrests have yet been made related to the data breach.

DISCUSSION QUESTIONS

1. If you had been hired as a public relations consultant by Target to handle the data breach crisis, what would you have done differently and why?

2. In your opinion, could the Target data breach have been prevented? Why or why not?

3. You are hired as the next CIO of Target. What strategies would you implement to prevent another data breach?

4. Identify the challenges that Target faced as a result of the data breach.

5. Develop a policy document for the retail industry regarding information security and data breaches. Outline some areas that need to be addressed by the retail industry to prevent future data breaches.

6. What are the pros and cons of delaying to notify customers of a data breach?

FURTHER READING

A Bullseye View. (2013, December 20). (Target online magazine) Message from CEO Gregg Steinhafel about Target's payment card issues. Retrieved from https://corporate .target.com/discover/article/Important-Notice-Unauthorized-access-to-payment-ca

A Bullseye View. (2015, February 3). Target names global tech and innovation leader Mike McNamara as new CIO. Retrieved from http://pressroom.target.com/news/ target-names-global-tech-and-innovation-leader-mike-mcnamara-as-new-cio

A Bullseye View. (2014, June 10). Target names Brad Maiorino Senior Vice president, Chief Information Security Officer. Retrieved from http://pressroom.target.com/news/ target-names-brad-maiorino-senior-vice-president-chief-information-security-officer

A Bullseye View. (2014, November 6). Target names Jacqueline Hourigan Rice as Senior Vice President, Chief Risk and Compliance Officer. Retrieved from http://pressroom .target.com/news/target-names-jacque-line-hourigan-rice-as-senior-vice-president-chief-risk-and-compliance-officer.

A Bullseye View. (n.d.). Data breach FAQ. Retrieved from https://corporate.target.com/ about/shopping-experience/payment-card-issue-FAQ

A Bullseye View. (2014, February 18). Target invests $5 in cybersecurity coalition. Retrieved from https://corporate.target.com/discover/article/Target-to-invest-5-million-in-cybersecurity-coalit

Greenwald, J. (2014, August 6). Target maxes out insurance coverage for 2013 data breach. Business Insurance. Retrieved from http://www.businessinsurance.com/article/ 20140806/NEWS07/140809889 http://dx.doi.org/10.4135/9781473953369

REFERENCES

Clark, M. (2014, May 5). Timeline of Target's data breach and aftermath: How cyber-theft snowballed for the giant retailer. International Business Times. Retrieved from http:// www.ibtimes.com/timeline-targets-data-breach-aftermath-how-cybertheft-snowballed-giant-retailer-1580056

Heller, L. (2014, February 16). Target: Timeline of a data breach. FierceRetail. Retrieved from http://www.fierceretail.com/story/target-timeline-data-breach/2014-02-16

Ponemon Institute. (2013). 2013 Cost of data breach study: global analysis. Retrieved from https://www4.symantec.com/mktginfo/whitepaper/053013_GL_NA_WP_Ponemon-2013-Cost-of-a-Data- Breach-Report_daiNA_cta72382.pdf

Verizon Enterprise Solutions. (2014). 2014 Data breach investigations report. Retrieved from http://www.verizonenterprise.com/DBIR/2014/

Ziobro, P., & R. Sidel. (2014, January 20). Target tried antitheft cards. *Wall Street Journal*. Retrieved from http://www.wsj.com/articles/SB10001424052702304027204579332990728181278

Case Study 2

Bangladesh Bank's Cyber Heist

Introduction

In February 2016, Bangladesh Bank's computer systems were compromised by hackers who successfully stole SWIFT (Society for Worldwide Interbank Financial Telecommunication) platform credentials of some of the bank's employees and ordered the execution of fund transfers to the tune of $951 million. Thirty-five payment requests were sent via the SWIFT platform to the Federal Reserve Bank of New York (Fed) on a Friday (February 4) to take advantage of the weekend and thereby further delay the detection of the cyber heist. Fortunately, several of the fund transfer requests were blocked but the hackers were still able to successfully siphon off $81 million.

Neither SWIFT nor the Fed was willing to take any responsibility for the attack and placed the blame squarely on the lax access controls at Bangladesh Bank. In the absence of joint ownership and accountability, business partners have very little incentive in working collaboratively to create as bullet-proof a system as possible. As discussed in Chapter 5, one of the cybersecurity success factors is a high level of commitment on the part of both internal and external stakeholders.

What is also concerning is that the malware installed on the bank's systems went undetected for weeks as the perpetrators observed the fund transfer process. Avoiding detection for that long a period reflects poorly on the level of preparedness of the organization. One of the key dimensions of cybersecurity preparedness is detection and Chapter 6 recommends strengthening detection capabilities. From investing in tools (such as Intrusion Detection Systems) and platforms (Security Information and Event Management) to establishing a Security Operations Center (SOC), there are several ways to proactively detect threats. Establishing multiple layers of access controls is another preparedness recommendation highlighted in Chapter 6.

Finally, as reviewed in Chapter 7, the discipline of continuously monitoring systems and networks, reviewing intelligence, and promptly acting on them are other recommended best practices to mitigate the risk of delayed detection of malware. Hopefully, readers will recognize the importance

and applicability of all three key readiness traits—commitment, preparedness, and discipline—in preventing the recurrence of the attack suffered by
Bangladesh Bank.

—Dave Chatterjee

The Soft Threat: The Story of the Bangladesh Bank Reserve Heist

A Business Case by Tanisha Bukth, MBA, and Sadrul Huda, PhD

Abstract

In February 2016, Bangladesh Bank, the Central Bank of Bangladesh,
became the victim of an unprecedented cyber heist, in which unknown
hackers attempted to steal a mammoth $951 million from its reserves. In
their scheme, which involved the introduction of malware into Bangladesh
Bank's systems and manipulation of the SWIFT system to send seemingly
authentic payment requests, the hackers succeeded in siphoning off as
much as $81 million, making this the first known case of fund theft from
a Central Bank. This case strives to develop an understanding of the manner in which the heist was accomplished, with a key focus on how vulnerabilities within the relevant stakeholders could have facilitated the event. In
addition, it has been developed against the backdrop of a growing number
of cyberattacks on banks across the world and thus encourages students to
come up with strategic measures that could allow targets like Bangladesh
Bank and the global financial system as a whole to reduce their vulnerability
to future threats.

Case

Learning Outcomes

By the end of this case study, students should be able to:

- gain an understanding of the manner in which funds were stolen
  from Bangladesh Bank's reserve in one of the largest cyber thefts
  in history;

- gain a perspective on the key stakeholders affected directly and indirectly by the heist, namely Bangladesh Bank, the Federal Reserve Bank of New York, SWIFT, and the Philippines;

- analyze the weaknesses and/or vulnerabilities of the concerned stakeholders that catalyzed the fund theft;

- identify the growing susceptibility of the global financial system to cyberattacks; and

- come up with strategies that can allow the Central Banks in developing countries like Bangladesh Bank and players in the global financial system to insulate themselves against future attacks.

Introduction

Shockwaves were sent across the global financial system in February 2016 as news of one of the biggest cyber heists in history made the headlines. In a brazen attempt to embezzle $951 million, cyber criminals had attacked the information system of Bangladesh Bank, the Central Bank of Bangladesh, and succeeded in stealing a staggering $81 million from its account at the Federal Reserve Bank of New York. To accomplish this massive heist, hackers had introduced malware into Bangladesh Bank's computer systems and used it to learn about the correct protocol for transferring funds from its New York account through the SWIFT code–based money transfer system. Their strategy, although technically complex, can perhaps be labeled as intuitively simple, and it is this very simplicity that is shocking in its ramifications for the security of the global financial system (Quadir, 2016a).

About three months into the heist, in May 2016, key stakeholders including Bangladesh Bank, the Federal Reserve Bank of New York, and the SWIFT were still "passing the buck" and pointing fingers at each other. But with the Chief Executive of SWIFT commenting on May 12, "I don't think it was the first, I don't think it will be the last," one thing was clear: the global financial system lay vulnerable and such attacks were more likely than not to happen again. The essential question is: What were the loopholes in the system that had permitted such an act? And what should the relevant stakeholders do to address these loopholes (Canepa, 2016)?

The Soft Theft

It was not until the morning of February 8, 2016 that officials at Bangladesh Bank realized that it had become the unsuspecting target of an unprecedented cyberattack. The first sign that something was amiss had appeared on February 5, when officials noticed that the printer set up to automatically print all SWIFT wire transfers had failed to record the previous day's transactions. The problem was initially dismissed as a regular glitch, but after being unable to access the SWIFT system and activate it using alternate methods, Bangladesh Bank discovered a number of confirmation messages which had come from the Federal Reserve Bank of New York. Struck by the realization that these confirmation messages had been sent in response to unauthorized fund transfer requests sent from its network, Bangladesh Bank sent messages to six banks, including the Fed, to immediately stop payment. But it was all too late for by then, Bangladesh Bank had already been robbed of $81 million of its reserve (Islam, 2016a; Quadir, 2016b).

In order to accomplish this act of stealth, unknown hackers had introduced malware into Bangladesh Bank's computer systems and surreptitiously observed the inner workings of the bank for weeks to gain knowledge of its fund transfer process. On February 4, 2016, they finally made their move, and sent 35 requests to the Federal Reserve Bank of New York over the SWIFT network to transfer $951 million from Bangladesh Bank's reserve account. Given that the hackers used the correct protocols, the requests seemed authentic at the time and the Fed effected five payments, routing $81 million to the Rizal Commercial Banking Corporation (RCBC) of the Philippines and $20 million to the Pan Asia Banking Corporation of Sri Lanka, as shown in Figure 1 (Spicer & Finkle, 2016). As suspicion brewed at the Fed over the nature of these transactions, the remaining 30 orders were blocked and so was the transfer to Sri Lanka owing to a spelling mistake by the hackers. However, when it came to siphoning away the $81 million routed to the Philippines, the hackers made no mistake, leaving the global financial system stunned by the craftiness of their planning (Finkle, 2016; Wagstaff & Finkle, 2016).

Figure 1 shows how the stolen funds disappeared from Bangladesh Bank's reserve account at the Federal Reserve Bank of New York and ended up in the Philippines. At first, the hackers sent 35 payment requests to the Fed totaling $951 million, of which 30 were blocked and the remaining five were affected. One of these, targeted Sri Lanka, was later blocked owing to a spelling mistake. But the remaining four were affected, resulting in $81 million being routed to four individuals in the Philippines through

Figure 1   The money trail

Bangladesh Bank heist

In one of the largest cyber heists in history, hackers ordered the Federal Reserve Bank of New York to transfer $81 million from Bangladesh Bank to accounts in the Philippines.

THE MONEY TRAIL

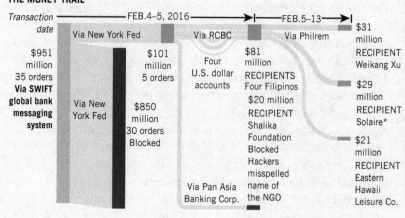

the RCBC. The money was eventually funneled out very craftily from the Philippines banking system and into the country's casinos, thus causing the trail to run cold.

That February 4 had been picked as the day for the heist was hardly a matter of chance. Rather, the hackers had carefully chosen this date knowing that February 4 and 5 (Friday and Saturday) would fall over the weekend in Bangladesh, with the following day being a weekend in the United States and the day after, a holiday in the Philippines, owing to celebration of the Chinese New Year. This, along with their manipulation of Bangladesh Bank's computer and printer system delayed the discovery of the theft and allowed the hackers to quickly channel $81 million out of the banking system without leaving a trail. Interestingly, the four accounts into which the $81 million was initially transferred had been opened in May 2015 with an initial deposit of only $500 and remained inactive till the day of the heist. On February 9, all but $68,305 of the stolen money was withdrawn from these accounts and transferred within the next four days to two casino resorts based in the Philippines and a Chinese individual named William Xu, through the remittance firm Philrem. It is here that the money trail ran cold, leaving the stakeholders with little recourse as to how to recover the stolen funds (Lema & Marshall, 2016; Mahajan, 2016).

A "Wake-Up Call" for Bangladesh

While the heist took place in early February, it was not until March 7 that Bangladesh Bank came out in the open regarding the stolen funds, fueling severe backlash from the government and civil society alike. From a meager $1 billion in 2001, Bangladesh's foreign exchange reserve had crossed the $25 billion mark in 2015, making sound reserve management a feather in Bangladesh Bank's cap. The soft theft, therefore, came as a major blow to the country's confidence in its Central Bank. Faith was further disturbed as it became clear that not only the general public, but also the Ministry of Finance had been kept in the dark for almost a month regarding the incident. As the Finance Minister Abul Maal Abdul Muhith declared to the media that he had known nothing of the theft, severe questions were raised about Bangladesh Bank's professionalism, resulting in the resignation of much acclaimed governor Dr. Atiur Rahman and the removal of seven others, including two deputy governors ("Forex reserve crosses $25b," 2015; "Most of the stolen funds has not been recovered," 2016; "The Governor had to step aside," 2016).

In the aftermath of the event, Bangladesh Bank came under fire when observers questioned whether the stolen funds could have been recovered by promptly announcing news of the heist to the international media. While the departing Governor maintained that publicizing the heist would serve to create distrust in the country's financial system, many experts believe that suppressing the matter only helped the hackers hide their footprint. In the words of Executive Director of Transparency International Bangladesh (TIB) Dr. Iftekharuzzaman: "Strict administrative measures and assistance from the international media could have helped us trap the funds within the Philippines' banking system. Unfortunately, we failed to take advantage of either. Now the recovery process will be much more elongated and complex" ("Could the funds have been blocked by publicizing the matter sooner?," 2016).

However, all debates aside, the heist had clearly been a "wake-up call" for Bangladesh, as stated by Dr. Mohammed Farashuddin, former Governor of Bangladesh Bank and head of the three-member committee formed by the government of Bangladesh to investigate the theft. As later investigations revealed, Bangladesh Bank's systems had lacked a proper firewall, and the use of second-hand $10 switches to connect network computers to SWIFT made it even easier for hackers to break into the system. The issue of insider involvement, suspected by the Federal Bureau of Investigation (FBI), was unconfirmed by Bangladesh police; but investigations clearly showed that three months into the heist, hackers were still lurking in Bangladesh Bank's system, leaving residual risks that needed to be addressed. Investigators believed that although such risks may not involve further fraudulent fund transfers, the hacker groups could engage in other "malicious acts" such as seeking to monitor ongoing cyber investigations or cause other damage, the nature of which they refused to clarify in the interest of secrecy. However, the need for building a "cyber fortress" a term used by Governor Atiur, was clearly evident and Bangladesh had learnt it the hard way, by becoming the victim of the first ever incident of fund theft from a Central Bank (Miglani & Quadir, 2016; Quadir, 2016c,d).

The Philippines—A "Black-Hole" for the Money Transfer

All but one of the 35 fund transfer requests had been directed to the Philippines, making the country a vital link in the grand scheme of the hackers. The four fake accounts into which the stolen funds had been transferred had all been opened a year before at the Jupiter branch of the RCBC, and investigations by the bank and the Philippines Anti-Money Laundering Council (AMLC) both highlighted the role of the branch manager, Maia Santos Deguito, in facilitating the heist. Upon discovering that its systems had been breached, Bangladesh Bank had sent a special message to RCBC on February 9 to "stop payment," which was reiterated by the bank's head office and conveyed to the concerned branch before the afternoon. However, these requests were completely overlooked and the bulk of the stolen funds was withdrawn on the same day, leading to the allegation that Deguito had deliberately ignored the messages to aid the theft. She was also accused of sanctioning the withdrawals without going through the proper authentication protocols, but Deguito maintained that she was merely a pawn in a high-stakes game that involved bigger players with far greater reach over the financial system ("Could the funds have been blocked by publicizing the matter sooner?," 2016; "The branch manager was waiting for Bangladesh Bank funds," 2016).

In addition, the loopholes that had allowed the Philippines to become a black hole for the money transfer went far beyond the actions of any individual or bank. As the Philippine Secretary of Finance, Cesar Purisima, said in a statement: "The exclusion of casinos from the current scope of the anti-money laundering laws and a strict bank secrecy law have made it difficult for authorities to track the Bangladeshi money trail and identify the perpetrators." Since 2013, the Philippines had been trying to amend its anti-money laundering law to bring casinos under legislation. But intense lobbying by the gaming industry had thwarted these efforts, making the Philippines a soft target for money launderers. In addition, banking secrecy law in the Philippines mandates that all deposits with banks or banking institutions should be considered as absolutely confidential and should not be examined by any person, government official or office, except upon written permission of the depositor. The combination of these factors meant that once the stolen money had entered the fake accounts in the Philippines, few questions were raised. Furthermore, after the funds had been withdrawn, the casinos, owing to their non-accountability, were an obvious destination, causing the money trail to run cold (Chalmers & Lema, 2016; "Law on secrecy of bank deposits," n.d.).

SWIFT under the Spotlight

Since its inception in 1974, SWIFT has established itself as the dominant platform for global processing of transactional messages, causing it to be labeled the "linchpin" of the global financial system. SWIFT is used by 11,000 financial institutions across 200 countries and as of April 2016, the average number of messages transferred by SWIFT per day stood at over 25 million, 47% of which constituted payment instructions. The SWIFT network itself does not handle any funds. Rather, it works by assigning each member institution a unique code, which is then used to send payment orders between institution's accounts, thus completing transactions in a timely and secure manner ("SWIFT in figures April 2016," 2016).

In the wake of the cyberattack on Bangladesh Bank's reserve, SWIFT came into the spotlight as it became apparent that the hackers had not only used the correct SWIFT codes to send the fund transfer requests, but had also hidden their tracks by manipulating the SWIFT Alliance Access server software, which banks use to interface with the SWIFT messaging platform. Dr. Mohammed Farashuddin, head of the probe panel formed by the government of Bangladesh, also criticized SWIFT sharply, saying: "SWIFT cannot rule out its responsibility." According to the primary findings of his panel, SWIFT had failed to implement 13 security measures when connecting its network to Bangladesh's real-time gross settlement system in October 2015, thus exposing the Central Bank's systems to potential malware. He also accused SWIFT of not providing any necessary technical assistance for protecting Bangladesh Bank's systems from external attacks, thus making the former even more liable for the subsequent security breach (Finkle, 2016a; "SWIFT to bear brunt of blame," 2016).

SWIFT's initial stance on the issue was a defensive one as it maintained that the heist was an "internal operational issue" of Bangladesh Bank and that its network had not been compromised. "It was, from our perspective, a customer fraud," the Chief Executive of SWIFT, Leibbrandt, commented. However, as it came under increasing scrutiny, SWIFT eventually acknowledged that the Bangladesh Bank fund heist was one of two incidents in which miscreants had used valid operator credentials to submit fraudulent messages through the SWIFT network and then covered their trail by tampering with the confirmations that banks rely on to spot suspicious activity. At the same time, SWIFT issued a security alert to its customers, reportedly for the first time in its four decades of existence, warning them of the need to protect their systems and review security protocols. "SWIFT is not, and cannot, be responsible for your decision to select, implement (and maintain) firewalls, nor the proper segregation of your internal networks. We urge you to take all necessary precautions," the letter said ("Financial messaging service SWIFT says banks responsible for own cyber security," 2016; Grande, 2016).

While SWIFT's contention that customers are liable for their own security is not unfounded, the fact that the SWIFT network had been instrumental in accomplishing the soft theft raised questions about whether the system itself was as impenetrable as once believed. From a legal standpoint, SWIFT could escape unscathed; but perhaps, the same could not be said of its image and of the faith placed in it by the global financial system.

A "Lucky Coincidence" for the Fed

Since the soft theft had been targeted at Bangladesh Bank's account at the Federal Reserve Bank of New York, it naturally raised questions about the accountability of the Fed, which holds trillions of dollars in funds for central banks all over the world. The immediate response from Bangladesh's end was a claim for the stolen funds and the Finance Minister, Abul Maal

Abdul Muhith, even mentioned the possibility of filing a lawsuit against the Fed. The Fed, however, maintained from the start that it had "acted properly" in releasing the funds and that it had no legal liability on the matter. In the words of general counsel and executive vice president at the Fed, Thomas Baxter, the Fed's systems "are designed to flag transfers to people and jurisdictions subject to sanctions but not to block a transfer if it had passed the authentication process on the SWIFT messaging network."

On a regular day, the Fed processes about 2,000 fund transfer requests, most of which are approved automatically after computer screening. These automatic scanners are effective for preventing money laundering and enforcing economic sanctions, along with blocking requests containing typographical errors. However, in addition to maintaining security, the Fed also has to ensure timely settlement of orders in the interest of its customers, meaning that authentic messages like the ones sent by the hackers end up getting approved without any scope for manual review. Originally, experts believed that this need to ensure rapid fulfillment of instructions along with the fact that all Fed customers give it the legal mandate to rely on the SWIFT system for authentication purposes could act as strong points for the Fed in any lawsuit.

However, a later investigation by Reuters revealed that the Fed had clearly missed some early warning signals and its inertia could have played a rather significant role in catalyzing the heist. The payment requests sent by the hackers were exceptional in many ways. First, all 35 requests were incorrectly formatted to begin with and they were mostly directed to individuals rather than institutions, which is rather unusual for such large payments from a Central Bank's account. Second, the flood of requests was another rare phenomenon and this becomes more apparent when one considers the fact that over the eight months to January 2016, the number of payment instructions sent by Bangladesh Bank to the Fed averaged less than two per working day.

However, it was not all these red flags, but rather a hacker's spelling mistake in typing the name of the Sri Lankan beneficiary and the appearance of the word "Jupiter" in one of the requests that first alerted the Fed. Coincidentally, Jupiter was also the name of a shipping company and an oil tanker under United States' sanctions against Iran and it was this chance occurrence, rather than any deliberate measure on the part of the Fed, that prevented the hackers from stealing the entire $951 million as originally intended. The Fed did eventually realize that the transactions were of an unusual nature, particularly with respect to the beneficiary accounts, and proceeded to inform Bangladesh Bank; but its initial oversight, coupled with the fact that it was too slow to react, could well tilt the balance in favor of Bangladesh in a potential lawsuit (Das & Spicer, 2016; Layne, 2016; Spicer & Finkle, 2016).

Not an Isolated Incident

Although the Bangladesh Bank heist was arguably the first reported incident of cyberattack on a Central Bank on such a massive scale, it clearly is not one of a kind as far as the global financial system is concerned. According to the leading cybersecurity firm, Fire Eye, there have been at least four instances of cyberattacks on banks using fraudulent SWIFT messages, one of which dates back to 2013. In 2015, for instance, Ecuador's Banco del Austro (BDA) lost $12 million from its account at San Francisco–based Wells Fargo as unknown hackers ordered 12 transfer requests through the SWIFT network stretching over a span of 10 days. In addition, as SWIFT eventually disclosed, labeling the Bangladesh incident as "part of a wider campaign targeting banks," a Vietnamese bank, later discovered to be the Tien Phong Bank, had been assailed similarly. Tien Phong Bank is ironically considered one of Vietnam's most technologically savvy banks and cyber experts including Europe's BAE Systems believe that the malware targeted at it was very similar to the one used in the Bangladesh Bank heist as well as in the much publicized 2014 attack on Sony Pictures Entertainment that caused the conglomerate to suffer massive losses (Pham, Nguyen & Finkle, 2016; Volz & Wagstaff, 2016).

Furthermore, while the heist encouraged key stakeholders all over the world to take note of the risks to which their systems might be exposed, it has been followed by repeated attacks on banks around the world by cybercriminals who seem to be getting ever more audacious. In April 2016, for instance, Ukraine's central bank issued a warning, stating that one of the country's banks had been subject to a cyberattack that sought to steal money using fraudulent SWIFT messages. In the following month, the websites of as many as four central banks, namely those in South Korea, Indonesia, Greece, and Cyprus, were attacked by hackers who had openly declared a 30-day campaign targeting Central Banks worldwide. While none of these four incidents had resulted in financial losses for the targets, their sheer frequency is dizzying, highlighting that the hackers are spreading their footprint everywhere. As stated by SWIFT Chief Executive Leibbrandt, "there will be a before and an after Bangladesh. This is a big deal and it gets to the heart of banking"

(Jones & Bergin, 2016; Setiaji, 2016; "Ukraine central bank flagged cyberattack in April: memo," 2016).

The Road to Recovery

After the heist, several recovery initiatives were adopted by Bangladesh Bank and the Government of Bangladesh. The newly appointed Governor of Bangladesh Bank, Dr. Fazle Kabir, issued letters to the U.S. Federal Reserve, the Philippines Central Bank and the Philippines AMLC, requesting an "all-out initiative to recover the stolen money." Following this, a tripartite meeting attended by the highest level officials of Bangladesh Bank, the Fed and SWIFT was held on May 10, in which the three stakeholders issued a joint statement expressing their "continued commitment to work together to normalize operations" and "to recover the entire proceeds of the fraud." The government of Bangladesh also launched multipronged investigations and recovery efforts, involving the formation of a three-member probe committee headed by Dr. Mohammed Farashuddin and the creation of a separate seven-member interagency taskforce, assigned specifically with reviewing legal aspects and securing the assistance of relevant stakeholders for return of the stolen funds. Help was also requested from the U.S. FBI, and several local and international law enforcement agencies, IT security companies, and forensic experts have been engaged in a concerted effort to recover the money. As of July 24, 2016, investigations were still underway and the government of Bangladesh was waiting for the full report of the probe committee to be published before deciding what, if any, legal action should be taken against the parties involved ("Government forms taskforce to bring back stolen money," 2016; Sharma, 2016).

From its end, the Philippines took the heist with much seriousness and the country's Blue Ribbon Senate Committee, after several hearings, identified a total of eleven perpetrators, including junket operator Kim Wong, four bankers of RCBC, the owner couple and an employee of Philrem, and two Chinese individuals associated with Kim Wong. As a result of these efforts, $15 million was recovered from junket operator Kim Wong and in September 2016, the Philippines trial court ordered the Central Bank of Philippines to return these funds to Bangladesh, declaring the latter as the rightful owner. However, as of October 8, 2016, Bangladesh had yet to receive those funds as due procedures for repatriating the money were still underway (Abdullah, 2016; "BB likely to recover part of $81m hacked from its FRBNY account," 2016; "Philippine central bank ordered to return recovered money to Bangladesh," 2016).

Fear that the lion's share of the funds may not be recovered has been rife in Bangladesh from the start and even the Finance Minister, Abul Maal Abdul Muhith, expressed his concern over the matter, stating that the manner in which the money had been stolen made it difficult to trace. He labeled the event as an unusual one and "a signal to the world to take proper security measures in respect to money transfers" (Choudhury & Devnath, 2016).

Conclusion

Long before the Bangladesh Bank heist actually took place, the Federal Reserve Bank of New York had mulled over the possibility that "lax security procedures and outdated technology" at some foreign Central Banks and overall loose controls over points of access to the SWIFT network could make them vulnerable to cybercriminals. The attack on Bangladesh Bank's reserve had proved that the Fed's fear was not misplaced and most experts believe that technological limitations on the part of Bangladesh Bank were largely responsible for the event. As pointed out by the former Governor of Bangladesh Bank, Dr. Salehuddin Ahmed, there is an overall lack of appreciation within the country's financial system regarding the adverse impacts of technology and an absence of measures for safeguarding concerned systems from such impacts. There is a huge gap in supply where qualified information technology (IT) professionals are concerned and this leads to an overwhelming dependence on foreign resources for maintaining critical IT systems. The latter, according to Anis A. Khan, Chairman of the Association of Bankers Bangladesh (ABB), must be reduced if the country wishes to strengthen itself against future attacks ("Punishment for financial anomalies should be fast and significant," 2016; Spicer & Finkle, 2016; "The issue of IT security was neglected till date," 2016).

Also, the general apathy of the country's banking system toward investment in IT security was revealed in a 2016 study by Bangladesh Institute of Bank Management (BIBM), which found that 4% of commercial banks' total IT budget is dedicated to security measures, while only 2% is spent for training purposes. Currently, 52% of commercial banks are at high risk with regards to information security and even more worrying, perhaps, is the myopic attitude of bank management in this regard. This is evidenced by the fact that about 85% of high officials who participated in the BIBM study viewed IT investment as an "extra expense" and only 8% believed that such investment would yield returns in the future. Furthermore, there is a lack of uniform structure when it comes to implementing IT security; it has been suggested that such uniformity needs to be established by Bangladesh Bank through a strong IT governance framework based on international standards (Islam, 2016; "More than half the banks at risk of information security," 2016).

While Bangladesh Bank was the main victim of the theft, the heist has undoubtedly served to shed light on major areas of concern for other stakeholders as well. The Philippines, for one, seemingly needs to pay careful attention to its anti-money laundering laws in order to avoid becoming a safe haven for unauthentic fund transfers. The sluggishness of the Fed is another issue that deserves attention, with some experts pointing out that the absence of a real-time system for spotting potential fraud and a system of checking payments after they have already been made are weaknesses that must be overcome (Das & Spicer, 2016).

Serious questions can also be raised about the accountability of SWIFT on the matter and perhaps more importantly, about the wisdom of relying so overwhelmingly on SWIFT for ensuring the security of the international payment system, at a time when its protective mechanisms seem to be getting increasingly vulnerable. Some experts believe that SWIFT should review what they consider to be an "outdated security system" and also explore the possibility of imposing a minimum standard of security that all customers must meet before availing the services of the SWIFT network. SWIFT's reputation stands severely dented and the cooperative itself has clearly taken note of the issue as evidenced by its decision to introduce a set of 16 mandatory security controls, which customers will be required to show each year (Bergin, 2016; Grande, 2016; Jones & Bergin, 2016).

The existing legal procedures for indicting cybercriminals are probably an area that also deserves more attention. Punishment for cybercrime in the U.S. can range up to 10 years for first time offences and 20 years for repeat offences and it has often been criticized for being way too harsh. However, with the growing challenges to financial and information security posed by cybercrime, there is perhaps a need to create a finer distinction between different types of offences, their potential impact and the punishment deserved by offenders. Complicating matters further is the cross-border nature of cybercrime and its constantly evolving nature, which requires judgment on a case-by-case basis. However, given that cybercrime is a relatively new form of offence, there is limited precedence to fall back on in punishing the criminals, making definitive legislation even more important (Williams, 2016).

Finally, as the growing proliferation of cyberattacks on banks across the world indicates, Bangladesh is not the only victim and definitely not the only possible target of future attacks. As revealed in a research study titled "State of Information Security 2016" by PricewaterhouseCoopers, hackers have stolen $1 billion across 25 countries in the past year and the incidence of cyberattacks on the financial sector has increased by as much as 34% over the same period. According to Shane Shook, an independent security consultant, "substantial bank hacks" are more lucrative than customer-targeted attacks since it takes "less effort to get more money." The average number of attacks on financial institutions is four times higher compared to other companies, but most of these security breaches do not get reported owing to fear of reputational damage. This inclination toward secrecy is compounded by the fact that many jurisdictions do not require banks and financial service companies to report a breach unless there is "material impact"—a term that leaves too much room for interpretation. The resulting lack of transparency has historically enabled the perpetrators to escape unscathed. However, after the Bangladesh Bank heist, Central Banks all over the world are waking up to the emerging threat of cybercrime and the committee of central banks, which is a part of the Bank for International Settlements (BIS), has set up a task force to consider setting broad rules for protecting the global banking network from such incidents. Cybercriminals are becoming increasingly more sophisticated in their attempts and could become a "game changer" for the global financial system, thus making a concerted effort, underpinned by greater teamwork and information sharing, the call of the day (Korolov, 2015; "Need for investigation regarding reserve theft," 2016; Spicer & Bergin, 2016; Wagstaff & Finkle, 2016).

DISCUSSION QUESTIONS

1. What were the key strategies used by the hackers in stealing from Bangladesh Bank's reserve without leaving a trail?

2. What internal weaknesses within Bangladesh Bank could have prompted the heist? Is the financial system of the Bangladesh Bank capable of handling the dynamics and challenges of present-day international financial environments? Explain why or why not.

3. What factors made the Philippines a soft target for the hackers?

4. In what ways are SWIFT and the Fed accountable for the heist? Assume the role of a representative of Bangladesh Bank and discuss what factors you would bring to the negotiation table in your talks with the Fed and SWIFT.

5. Recommend some strategies that might enable the global financial system to address the growing challenge posed by cybercrime.

6. How might a new legal system be developed to protect the cyber financial crime, recover the money in case of any theft, and punish the offenders? Develop your answer based on researching existing legal systems.

FURTHER READING

Ahmed, F. (2016, July 24). BB ready to file case against US Fed after green signal. *The Daily Observer*. Retrieved from http://www.eobserverbd.com/2016/07/24/index.php

Bangladesh Bank heist exposes Philippines as dirty money destination. (2016, March 21). *The Japan Times*. Retrieved from http://www.japantimes.co.jp/news/2016/03/21/asia-pacific/bangladesh-bank-heist-exposes-philippines-as-dirty-money-destination/#.V5Zr-2h97IU

Hurst, S. (2016, May 13). Blockchain teamwork could help banks fight hackers. *Reuters*. Retrieved from http://blogs.reuters.com/breakingviews/2016/05/13/blockchain-teamwork-could-help-banks-fight-hackers/

Volz, D. (2016, June 1). Congress probes NY Fed's handling of Bangladesh Bank heist: letter. *Reuters*. Retrieved from http://www.reuters.com/article/us-cyber-heist-congress-idUSKCN0YN59X

REFERENCES

Abdullah, M. (2016, April 26). Senate identifies 11. *The Independent*. Retrieved from http://www.theindepen-dentbd.com/home/printnews/41979

BB likely to recover part of $81m hacked from its FRBNY account. (2016, July 22). *The Daily Observer*, pp. 17.

Bergin, T. (2016, September 26). SWIFT says bank hacks set to increase. *Reuters*. Retrieved from http://www.reuters.com/article/us-cyber-heist-swift-idUSKCN11W1XY

Canepa, F. (2016, May 12). SWIFT network wasn't hacked in $81 million Bangladesh heist: CEO. *Reuters*. Retrieved from http://www.reuters.com/article/us-bangladesh-heist-swift-idUSKCN0Y320K

Chalmers, J., & Lema, K. (2016, March 21). For bank heist hackers, the Philippines was a handy black hole. *Reuters*. Retrieved from http://www.reuters.com/article/us-usa-fed-bangladesh-philippines-idUSKCN0WM13B

Choudhury, A., & Devnath, A. (2016, April 29). Hackers may pocket about $70 million in Bangladesh cyber heist. *Bloomberg Technology*. Retrieved from http://www.bloomberg.com/news/articles/2016-04-29/hackers-may-pocket-about-70-million-in-bangladesh-cyber-heist

Could the funds have been blocked by publicizing the matter sooner? (ঘটনাদরুতপর্কা শহেলঅথর্আটিকাোনাোযত?). (2016, March 17). *ProthomAlo*.

Das, K. N., & Spicer, J. (2016, July 21). How the New York Fed fumbled over the Bangladesh Bank cyber-heist. *Reuters*. Retrieved from http://www.reuters.com/investigates/special-report/cyber-heist-federal/

Financial messaging service SWIFT says banks responsible for own cybersecurity. (2016, May 12). *Reuters*. Retrieved from http://www.reuters.com/article/us-bangladesh-heist-swift-fed-idUSKCN0Y22O8

Finkle, J. (2016, March 9). Criminals in Bangladesh heist likely studied bank's inner workings. *Reuters*. Retrieved from http://www.reuters.com/article/us-usa-fed-bangladesh-idUSKCN0WB2PI

Finkle, J. (2016a, April 26). Exclusive: SWIFT warns customers of multiple cyber fraud cases. *Reuters*. Retrieved from http://www.reuters.com/article/us-cyber-banking-swift-exclusive-idUSKCN0XM2DI

Forex reserve crosses $25b. (2015, June 26). *Star Business Report*. Retrieved from http://www.thedailystar.net/business/forex-reserves-cross-25b-103024

Government forms task force to bring back stolen money. (2016, April 14). *The Financial Express*. Retrieved from http://www.thefinancialexpress-bd.com/2016/04/14/26070/Govt-forms-taskforce-to-bring-back-stolen-money

Grande, A. (2016, May 17). SWIFT hack leaves little room for banks to feign ignorance. *Law360*. Retrieved from http://www.law360.com/articles/796232/swift-hack-leaves-little-room-for-banks-to-feign-ignorance

Islam, A. (2016, March 25). Most expenditure on purchases, little on security (োকনাকাটায়বায়েবিশিনরাপত্তায়সামান্). *ProthomAlo*.

Islam, A. (2016a, March 26). Chronology of Bangladesh Bank reserve theft (োদনপিঞ্জেতবাংলাোদশবয়োাোংক–এরিরসাভর্ চু োির). *ProthomAlo*.

Jones, H., & Bergin, T. (2016, May 23). SWIFT to unveil new security plan after hackers' heists. *Reuters*. Retrieved from http://www.reuters.com/article/us-cyber-banks-swift-idUSKCN0YE2S6

Korolov, M. (2015, June 23). Banks get attacked four times more than other industries. *CSO*. Retrieved from http://www.csoonline.com/article/2938767/advanced-persistent-threats/report-banks-get-attacked-four-times-more-than-other-industries.html

Law on secrecy of bank deposits. (n.d.). *Philippines Deposit Insurance Corporation*. Retrieved from http://www.pdic.gov.ph/index.php?nid1=10&nid2=3

Layne, N. (2016, May 13). New York Fed defends fund transfer after Bangladesh heist. *Reuters*. Retrieved from http://www.reuters.com/article/us-bangladesh-heist-fed-idUSKCN0Y42NB

Lema, K., & Marshall, A. R. C. (2016, March 29). Casino agent in Philippines says high-rollers brought in heist money. *Reuters*. Retrieved from http://www.reuters.com/article/us-usa-fed-bangladesh-philippines-idUSKCN0WV1N7

Mahajan, S. (2016, March 9). Fund stolen using central bank code (কেন্দ্রীয়বয্যাংক-এরেকাডিদেয়ইটাকাচুরি). *ProthomAlo*.

Miglani, S., & Quadir, S. (2016, May 13). *Exclusive: Bangladesh Bank remains compromised months after heist—forensics report. Reuters*. Retrieved from http://www.reuters.com/article/us-usa-fed-bangladesh-investigation-idUSKCN0Y40SM

More than half the banks at risk of information security (অধর্েকরেবিশবয্যাংকত থয্যিনরাপত্তারঝুঁিকেত). (2016, May 8). *ProthomAlo*.

Most of the stolen funds has not been recovered (িরসাভর্ েথেকচু িরকরােঅথ র্বড়অংশইউদ্ধারহয়িন). (2016, March 8). *ProthomAlo*.

Need for investigation regarding reserve theft (িরসাভর্-এরঅথর্চু িরিনেয়িনরীক্ষাতদ ন্তপর্েয়াজন). (2016, March 13). *ProthomAlo*.

Pham, M., Nguyen, M., & Finkle, J. (2016, May 15). Vietnam bank says interrupted cyber heist using SWIFT messaging. *Reuters*. Retrieved from http://www.reuters.com/article/us-vietnam-cybercrime-idUSKCN0Y60EN

Philippine central bank ordered to return recovered money to Bangladesh. (2016, September 19). *Reuters*. Retrieved from http://www.reuters.com/article/us-cyber-heist-philippines-idUSKCN11P0TL

Punishment for financial anomalies should be fast and significant (আিথর্কিজিনয়ে মরশ ািতদ্রুততওদৃ্যান্তমলকহওয়াউিচত). (2016, April 2) *ProthomAlo*.

Quadir, S. (2016a, March 13). Bangladesh bank says hackers tried to steal $951 million. *Reuters*. Retrieved from http://www.reuters.com/article/us-bangladesh-bank-idUSKCN0WF0IL

Quadir, S. (2016b, March 16). Software, printer problems delayed discovery of Bangladesh heist. *Reuters*. Retrieved from http://www.reuters.com/article/usa-fed-bangladesh-idUSL2N16O1JO

Quadir, S. (2016c, March 20). Bangladesh bank gets FBI help on bank heist, cyber expert missing. *Reuters*. Retrieved from http://www.reuters.com/article/us-usa-fed-bangladesh-idUSKCN0WM0KA

Quadir, S. (2016d, April 21). Bangladesh Bank exposed to hackers by cheap switches, no firewall: police. *Reuters*. Retrieved from http://www.reuters.com/article/usa-fed-bangladesh-idUSL2N17N0FZ

Setiaji, H. (2016, June 21). Indonesia, South Korea central bank websites hit by cyber-attacks; no losses. *Reuters*. Retrieved from http://www.reuters.com/article/us-asia-banks-cyber-idUSKCN0Z70KI

Sharma, K. (2016, March 28). Bangladesh central bank expects to recover stolen money. *Nikkei Asian Review*. Retrieved from http://asia.nikkei.com/Politics-Economy/Economy/Bangladesh-central-bank-expects-to-recover-stolen-money?page=1

Spicer, J., & Bergin, T. (2016, September 15). Exclusive: Central banks seek global standards in wake of Bangladesh heist. *Reuters*. Retrieved from http://www.reuters.com/article/us-cyber-heist-basel-taskforce-idUSKCN11L269

Spicer, J., & Finkle, J. (2016, May 9). INSIGHT – Before massive Bangladesh heist, New York Fed feared such cyber-attacks. *Reuters*. Retrieved from http://www.reuters.com/article/bangladesh-heist-fed-insight-pix-tv-grap-idUSL2N18320D

SWIFT in figures April 2016. (2016). In *SWIFT FIN Traffic document center*. Retrieved from https://www.swift.com/about-us/swift-fin-traffic-figures/monthly-figures#topic-tabs-menu

SWIFT to bear brunt of blame. (2016, May 16). *The Financial Express*. Retrieved from http://www.thefinancial-express-bd.com/2016/05/16/30391/SWIFT-to-bear-brunt-of-blame

The branch manager was waiting for Bangladesh Bank funds (বাংলাদেশরঅেথর্অে পক্ষায়িছেলনশাখাবাবস্থাপক). (2016, March 17). *ProthomAlo*.

The Governor had to step aside (সেরেজেতহলগভনর্-েেক). (2016, March 16). *ProthomAlo*.

The issue of IT security was neglected till date (এতিদনাে িনরাপত্তারিবষয়টাউেপি ক্ষতিছল). (2016, March 26). *ProthomAlo*.

Ukraine central bank flagged cyber-attack in April: memo. (2016, June 30). *Reuters*. Retrieved from http://www.reuters.com/article/cyber-heist-ukraine-idUSL8N19M5TU

Volz, D., & Wagstaff, J. (2016, May 27). Cyber firms say Bangladesh hackers have attacked other Asian banks. *Reuters*. Retrieved from http://www.reuters.com/article/us-cyber-heist-swift-symantec-idUSKCN0YH29J

Wagstaff, J., & Finkle, J. (2016, March 31). When mobsters meet hackers—the new, improved bank heist. *Reuters*. Retrieved from http://www.reuters.com/article/us-usa-fed-bangladesh-alliance-idUSKCN0WW2QP

Williams, K. B. (2016, September 1). Judges struggle with cyber-crime punishment. *The Hill*. Retrieved from http://thehill.com/policy/cybersecurity/265285-judges-struggle-with-cyber-crime-punishment and http://dx.doi.org/10.4135/9781526411228

Originally Published as: Bukth, T. & Huda, S., (2017). The soft threat: The story of the Bangladesh bank reserve heist. In SAGE Business Cases. 2020. 10.4135/9781526411228. © Tanisha Bukth & Sadrul Huda 2017.

Note: This case was prepared for inclusion in SAGE Business Cases primarily as a basis for classroom discussion or self-study and is not meant to illustrate either effective or ineffective management styles. Nothing herein shall be deemed to be an endorsement of any kind.

Case Study 3

Ashley Madison Security Breach

Introduction

Ashley Madison, an adult dating site, was breached in July 2015 by a team of hackers. It published 10 GB of the stolen customer data within a month of the attack. Personally identifiable and embarrassing customer information were released to the public—from contact information to credit card details and sexual fantasies. Not surprisingly, Ashley Madison was sued by the 39 million users who were victims of the breach. A $578 million class-action lawsuit was filed against the company. Could such an attack have been prevented? Even if a company were to diligently adopt the information security best practices recommended in this book, immunity from attacks cannot be guaranteed. But that cannot be an excuse for negligence in not properly securing sensitive information.

As discussed in Chapter 3, companies should follow the Generally Accepted Privacy Principles (GAPP). According to the minimization principle, organizations should collect and store the bare minimum customer information needed to provide the necessary services. They should purge the sensitive data as soon as the purpose has been served. Ashley Madison showed scant regard for their customers by duping them with female "bots" and not deleting customer information even after they had paid for the deletion service. With data privacy and security laws getting stronger such as the General Data Protection Regulation (GDPR), it is imperative that companies such as Ashley Madison not only ramp up their data privacy and security methods but also think of innovative ways of protecting customer data. For instance, they should consider deleting credit card details as soon as the payment transaction is complete.

Yet another important Generally Accepted Privacy Principle (GAPP) is to protect the information from unauthorized access. As part of information security preparedness initiatives, numerous access control measures are discussed in Chapter 6. Ashley Madison failed to effectively implement strong access controls such as a) powerful hashing algorithms to encrypt the data, b) robust password controls, c) multi-factor authentication, and d) network segmentation. In addition to strong access control measures, organizations should consider investing in proactive monitoring and detection tools and mechanisms. It is critical for any organization to have in place a well-rehearsed breach incident response protocol and procedure and that includes a SWAT team ready to spring into action.

From a discipline standpoint, the breach at Ashley Madison highlights the need to document policies for purging customer data, clearly communicate such policies with customers, and consistently execute them. Organizations should also consider hiring specialized services for regular penetration testing of the various vulnerability points.

Thus, the Ashley Madison case reveals shortcomings in all the three key dimensions of cybersecurity readiness—commitment, preparedness, and discipline. It might be a good exercise for the reader to conduct a comprehensive assessment of Ashley Madison's state of cybersecurity readiness by using the scorecards in Appendices 3A, 3B, and 3C.

—*Dave Chatterjee*

Internet Vigilantism and Ashley Madison: Rebranding after a Cyberattack

A Business Case by Karen Robson and Leyland Pitt, PhD

Abstract

Avid Life Media was the parent company of a number of dating websites, including Ashley Madison, a dating website for married people seeking affairs. In July 2015, the dating website suffered a massive cyberattack by a group of hackers that resulted in the user data and personal information of nearly 37 million users being publicized. In the aftermath of the attack, Avid Life Media and Ashley Madison have undergone a number of changes in an effort to rebuild and rebrand. This case explores the Ashley Madison brand and the crisis that ensued after the cyberattack. The case encourages students to consider how to approach a complicated business situation involving ethics, customer privacy, cybersecurity, public relations, and rebranding.

Case

Learning Outcomes

By the end of this case study, students will be able to:

- analyze the role of information and cybersecurity in a business context;

- grasp the ethical complexities of the offerings provided through the dating service Ashley Madison;

- delve into the ethical complexities of internet vigilantism as demonstrated by hackers who exposed the Ashley Madison data; and

- evaluate the steps Avid Life Media, the parent company of Ashley Madison, has taken to regain trust and repair the Ashley Madison brand.

Rebranding after a Cyberattack

After a massive cyberattack, the website Ashley Madison needed to regain trust with its consumers—many of whom had been exposed as adulterers, resulting in divorces and, in some cases, suicides. In the year and a half since the attack, Ashley Madison's parent company, Avid Life Media, had undergone a change in leadership and was in the midst of rebuilding itself.

As Avid Life Media and the Ashley Madison brand moved forward, a number of questions about the company remained. Was Ashley Madison an ethical brand? What could they learn from their past that would strengthen the company in the future? How serious was the impact of the cyberattack, and was it even possible to recover from the devastating loss of customer privacy? Moving forward, how should the brand regain public trust and grow?

Ashley Madison

Ashley Madison was founded in 2001 as a dating website for adults—specifically married adults who were seeking romantic encounters with people other than their spouses. The idea behind Ashley Madison was to be open and honest about what the dating service was all about—a place for married people to cheat on their spouses without judgment.

The Ashley Madison brand reinforced its positioning through brand imagery and its motto—"Life is Short. Have an Affair." The brand logo was a wedding ring, and often paired with this logo was an image of a brunette woman making a "hush" gesture, her finger over her lips, signaling the company's focus on secrecy and privacy.

The business model for Ashley Madison was unlike those of other dating websites like eHarmony or Match.com. Rather than pay a monthly subscription for the service, Ashley Madison users purchased credits and then used these to pay per interaction. That is, to initiate contact with another member, an Ashley Madison user had to pay five credits, after which point further communication would be free.

Ashley Madison understood the need for secrecy and privacy of their users. The company especially understood that when a user no longer wished to pursue an extramarital affair, they likely wanted all trace of their Ashley Madison membership erased. To that end, when a user no longer wished to be a member of the Ashley Madison community, the site provided a paid option for a "full delete." This option, which was priced at $19, ostensibly ensured that all messages, site use history, personal information, photographs, and other information in a user profile would be completely erased.

Avid Life Media

Avid Life Media was a social entertainment company that ran a number of dating websites and social networking websites. In addition to Ashley Madison, Avid Life Media's dating site portfolio included: Cougar Life, a dating website for older women interested in younger men; Man Crunch, a dating website for gay men; Established Men, a dating website for wealthy men to connect with young, beautiful women; Big and Beautiful, a dating website for connecting people to curvy women; as well as other dating sites.

Within the Avid Life Media portfolio, Ashley Madison and Established Men received the most public criticism. Many believed that the idea behind Ashley Madison was harmful to society as it could be seen as encouraging and enabling extramarital affairs. In addition, Established Men was seen by some as a front for prostitution—specifically for wealthy men to pay young women for sex (Bashir & Yiu, 2009).

Although Established Men received criticism for preying on women, a series of television interviews and other publicity revealed that the idea behind it—and also behind the sites Cougar Life, and Big and Beautiful—all came from women. An ABC *Nightline* Profile reported that Simone Dadoun-Cohen, an attractive college drop-out who became a stripper, first came up with the idea for Established Men. As a stripper, Dadoun-Cohen learned that there were many generous, successful men who wanted the attention of attractive women. EstablishedMen.com was created by Avid Life Media shortly thereafter in 2009. The woman behind Cougar Life was Claudia Opdenkelder, whose experiences of being discriminated against simply because she was an older woman who was interested in younger men led her to the idea behind Cougar Life. Weary of discrimination, Opdenkelder came to the idea of Cougar Life and, with the help of Avid Life Media, saw the website launched in 2009. Whitney Thompson, the first plus-sized winner of the reality TV series *American's Next Top Model*, revealed that the dating website for large women seeking men—launched by Avid Life Media as Big and Beautiful—had been her idea.

Ashley Madison itself was an international brand. However, it was clear that the brand was not welcome everywhere. When the brand announced its plans to expand to Singapore, the Singapore Media Development Authority announced that Ashley Madison would not be permitted to operate in the country as it "aggressively promotes and facilitates extramarital affairs" and demonstrated a "flagrant disregard of family values and public morality" (IMDA, 2013).

In addition to criticism regarding the premise behind the website's offering, Ashley Madison had been accused of scamming its users by using female "bots" in place of actual female users (Edwards, 2013). In 2012, a former employee sued the company, stating that she developed a stress injury from creating thousands of fake member profiles of women. The employee stated that these fake profiles were intended to lure men to the site. However, this lawsuit was dismissed by the Ontario Superior Court in 2015 (Loriggio, 2015).

The Attack

On July 15th, 2015, the Impact Team, a consortium of hackers, executed a cyberattack on Ashley Madison in which they stole the user data and personal information of Ashley Madison customers. Rather than release the data, the Impact Team demanded that Avid Life Media shut down the websites AshleyMadison.com and EstablishedMen.com, and indicated that failure to do so would result in the Impact Team publicizing the stolen information.

Prior to the cyberattack on Ashley Madison, there were no known hacks performed by the Impact Team, and little was known about the group other than what they shared about themselves. One statement from the hackers related to the security of the information—the Impact Team stated that "nobody was watching. No security. . . . You could use Pass1234 from the internet to VPN to root on all servers" (Basu, 2015). The Impact Team published their manifesto (http://pastebin.com/3SepJr8Q) in which they expressed that they intended to expose the fraud committed by Avid Life Media—including that the company's promises of secrecy were without basis and that the paid "full delete" option was a scam as the hackers had the user information for individuals who had paid for this service. The hackers revealed that they had information including the real names, addresses, and credit card information of users, as well as photographs, and lists of sexual fantasies.

On July 20th, Avid Life Media released a statement (Avid Life Media, 2015a) indicating that they had been able to secure their sites and prevent further data breaches and were working with the authorities to uncover the hackers behind the attack. By July 22nd, the websites were still in operation, and the Impact Team released the names of two Ashley Madison users. Nearly one month later, on August 18th, Avid Life Media still operated their Ashley Madison and Established Men dating services, and the Impact Team released a data dump entitled "Time's Up" that contained roughly 10GB of user email addresses and other information.

In response to the August 18th data dump, Avid Life Media vilified the hackers, saying in a statement that "this event is not an act of hacktivism, it is an act of criminality. It is an illegal action against the individual members of AshleyMadison.com, as well as any freethinking people who choose to engage in fully lawful online activities" (Avid Life Media, 2015b).

Between August 20th and 28th, the hackers released a series of other data dumps—including more information on users, as well as internal company information. On August 24th, the company was served with a $578 million class-action lawsuit on behalf of the 39 million users whose information was exposed in the data breach (Perez, 2015).

The Data

The hacked information revealed not only information about user data and customer personal information, but also brought to light new questions around the use of female "bots" in place of actual women, and phony back-stories regarding some of the Avid Life Media Brands.

The user information leaked by the Impact Team included e-mails—many of which were government, military, and corporate e-mail addresses—as well as mailing addresses, signup dates, total amounts of money spent on the website, and more. Many reporters and analysts were quick to point out that the e-mail addresses could be fake, and that the information was not necessarily accurate or reliable. However, cybersecurity experts suggested that although the volume of data made it impossible to immediately determine if all of the information was verifiable, that overall the data appeared to be genuine (Victor, 2015). Regardless of the veracity of the information, people whose identities were found within the Ashley Madison data leak suffered real consequences—including extortion and blackmail attempts, identity theft risk, and some cases of suicides (Baraniuk, 2015). Families were also impacted, with Ashley Madison customer service representatives receiving phone calls from crying spouses and angry clients (Brownell, 2015a).

The cyberattack not only revealed information about Ashley Madison and Established Men users, but also information about the internal activities of Avid Life Media. Company emails from the hack revealed that Opdenkelder, Dadoun-Cohen, and Thompson were all hired to pose as founders of the dating websites and did not actually create the websites themselves (Brownell, 2015b). They also revealed that the ABC *Nightline* Profile about Simone Dadoun-Cohen was simply a made-up story regarding the background of the Established Men dating website.

Further, the data provided confirmation of the existence of the female "bots," revealing that the number of female users of Ashley Madison was indeed artificially inflated by these "fembots" (Morris, 2016).

Throughout the data leaks and ensuing analysis of the information, Avid Life Media did not confirm the veracity of the information on its users.

Ashley Madison after the Attack

Noel Biderman's tenure as Chief Executive Officer (CEO) of the company ended in April of 2016, and Ashley Madison transitioned to new leadership under CEO Rob Segal and President James Millership. Under this new leadership, cybersecurity and rebranding became priorities for the company.

In a July 2016 company statement, Millership and Segal revealed that the ultimate goal was to "rebuild Ashley Madison as the world's most open-minded dating community" (Avid Life Media, 2016). As part of the rebuilding process, the parent company dropped the name Avid Life Media in place of Ruby Corporation, a move that Segal stated was "an important step in our journey to completely rebuild the company as a relevant, digital dating innovator that truly cares for our customers" (Ruby Corporation, 2016).

As Ruby Corporation, the company maintained its brand portfolio, including the Ashley Madison, Cougar Life, Big and Beautiful, Man Crunch, and Established Men brand lines.

Another change was in dropping the longstanding Ashley Madison tagline of "Life is Short. Have an Affair." Segal said of this move: "it was a limiting label that's outdated and doesn't speak to the wide variety of connections people find on Ashley Madison," noting also that about 45% of Ashley Madison users were single, and that the brand needed to "evolve, grow, and attune to modern sexuality in 2016" (Ruby Corporation, 2016). In its place, Ruby Corporation chose the tagline "Find Your Moment." In addition, the brand dumped their wedding ring logo and "hush" imagery.

In over a year since the massive data leak and cyberattack, Ashley Madison, and parent company Ruby, had undergone a number of changes—reframing Ashley Madison as a dating site for extramarital affairs to one that was at the forefront of sexual encounters in 2016. However, the people responsible for the cyberattack had still not been held accountable for their illegal actions, the outcome of the class-action lawsuit against the company remained in litigation, and the scandal remained fresh in many people's minds. What did the future hold for Ruby and the Ashley Madison brand? Were these changes sufficient to rebuild the brand? Was there anything else that Ruby should do? Beyond any future steps, the question remained as to whether Ashley Madison or the Impact Team was the real villain.

DISCUSSION QUESTIONS

1. Are Avid Life Media and the Impact Team ethical organizations?

2. Who was to blame for the devastating events in the aftermath of the data leak—Ashley Madison customers, Avid Life Media, or the Impact Team?

3. Had you been in a leadership position at Avid Life Media during this situation, what would you have done differently or the same from the real-life executives?

4. What could Ashley Madison have done to better protect its customers' privacy?

5. How serious was the impact of the cyberattack and data leak on the Ashley Madison business?

FURTHER READING

Morey, T. Forbath, T. T., & Schoop, A. (2015). Customer data: Designing for transparency and trust. *Harvard Business Review*, 93(5), 96–105.

Shackelford, S. J. (2016). Business and cyber peace: We need you! *Business Horizons*, 59(5), 539–548.

REFERENCES

Avid Life Media. (July 20, 2015a). Statement from Avid Life Media, Inc. July 20—12:25 pm. *Avid Life Media*. Retrieved from http://www.prnewswire.com/news-releases/statement-from-avid-life-media-inc-300115394.html

Avid Life Media. (August 18, 2015b). Statement from Avid Life Media, Inc. August 18, 2015. *Avid Life Media*. Retrieved from https://article.wn.com/view/2015/08/31/Statement_from_Avid_Life_Media_Inc_August_18_2015_Ashley_Mad/

Avid Life Media. (July 4, 2016). Avid Life Media Breaks Its Silence—Announces New CEO & President. *Avid Life Media*. Retrieved from http://www.prnewswire.com/news-releases/avid-life-media-breaks-its-silence---announces-new-ceo--president---new-leadership-and-vision-set-to-transform-ashley-madison-300293808.html

Baraniuk, C. (August 24, 2015). Ashley Madison: "Suicides" over website hack. *BBC News*. Retrieved from http://www.bbc.com/news/technology-34044506

Bashir, M., & Yiu, K. (May 19, 2009). Impoverished Woman, Early 20s, Seeks "Established Man." *ABC News*. Retrieved from http://abcnews.go.com/Business/story?id=7614347

Basu, E. (October 26, 2015). Cybersecurity Lessons Learned from the Ashley Madison Hack. *Forbes*. Retrieved July 11, 2017 from https://www.forbes.com/sites/ericbasu/2015/10/26/cybersecurity-lessons-learned-from-the-ashley-madison-hack/#2d8a941d4c82

Brownell, C. (September 11, 2015a). Inside Ashley Madison: Calls from crying spouses, fake profiles and the hack that changed everything. *Financial Post*. Retrieved from http://business.financialpost.com/technology/inside-ashley-madison-calls-from-crying-spouses-fake-profiles-and-the-hack-that-changed-everything/wcm/452efb18-f1b9-4fc4-9f4e-eaee7a35d4f0

Brownell, C. (October 2, 2015b). The women who fooled everyone by pretending to be executives at Ashley Madison's sister websites. *Financial Post*. Retrieved from http://business.financialpost.com/technology/from-cougar-life-to-established-men-the-real-backstory-behind-ashley-madisons-fake-founders-for-its-spinoff-sites/wcm/736c9066-f185-4d11-a7b3-6dde844f45ca

Edwards, J. (November 11, 2013). Women Alleges She Hurt Her Wrists Writing Up Fake Profiles for Ashley Madison. *Business Insider*. Retrieved from www.businessinsider.com/ashley-madison-fake-profile-lawsuit-2013-11

IMDA1. (November 8, 2013). Ashley Madison website not allowed to operate in Singapore. *Infocomm Media Development Authority*. Retrieved from https://www.imda.gov.sg/about/newsroom/archived/mda/media-releases/2013/ashley-madison-website-not-allowed-to-operate-in-singapore

Loriggio, P. (January 18, 2015). Lawsuit against dating site for married people seeking affairs dismissed. *The Globe and Mail*. Retrieved from http://www.theglobeandmail.com/news/national/lawsuit-against-dating-site-for-married-people-seeking-affairs-dismissed/article22511386/

Morris, D. (July 10, 2016). Ashley Madison Used Chatbots to Lure Cheaters, Then Threatened to Expose Them When They Complained. *Fortune*. Retrieved from http://fortune.com/2016/07/10/ashley-madison-chat-bots/

Perez, C. (August 24, 2015). Ashley Madison facing massive lawsuit "on behalf of all Canadians." *New York Post*. Retrieved from http://nypost.com/2015/08/24/ashley-madison-facing-578m-class-action-lawsuit/

Ruby Corporation. (July 12, 2016). Avid Life Media Rebrands as Ruby—Officially Drops Ashley Madison Life is Short. Have an Affair. Tagline. *Ruby Media Room*. Retrieved from http://media.ashleymadison.com/avid-life-media-rebrands-as-ruby/

Victor, D. (August 19, 2015). The Ashley Madison Data Dump, Explained. *The New York Times*. Retrieved from https://www.nytimes.com/2015/08/20/technology/the-ashley-madison-data-dump-explained.html http://dx.doi.org/10.4135/9781526438348

Originally published as: Robson, K. & Pitt, L. (2018). Internet vigilantism and Ashley Madison: Rebranding after a cyberattack. In SAGE Business Cases. 2020. 10.4135/9781526438348. © Karen Robson and Leyland Pitt 2018.

Note: This case was prepared for inclusion in SAGE Business Cases primarily as a basis for classroom discussion or self-study and is not meant to illustrate either effective or ineffective management styles. Nothing herein shall be deemed to be an endorsement of any kind.

Case Study 4

Yoti and Responsible Cybersecurity Innovation

Introduction

The Yoti case highlights the importance of acting carefully and responsibly when engaging in cybersecurity innovation activities. These organizational values and traits are centric to cybersecurity preparedness. As discussed in Chapter 5, in the section on Joint Ownership and Responsibility, information security professionals are expected to abide by the principles of Due Care and Due Diligence. They must do everything within their power and authority to protect confidential data and that includes complying with security regulations, adhering to privacy principles, and following information security best practices.

As a provider of a digital identity platform to authenticate individuals and businesses, Yoti gathers a lot of personally identifiable information. The company must honor the trust of their users and clients by taking every possible precautionary measure to secure the sensitive data. Chapter 3 discusses some of the Generally Accepted Privacy Principles (GAPP) that are extremely important for organizations such as Yoti. For instance, the minimization principle suggests that companies gather the minimum amount of information needed to conduct their business activities.

Another of the GAPP guidelines is to take every possible step to secure the collected data from unauthorized access. Chapter 6 provides guidance on the various methods of data security, from encryption to strong access controls, multifactor authentication, and adhering to the policy of Least Privilege. In addition, organizations should comply with the industry and legislation guidelines on data retention and purge.

Organizations such as Yoti can also benefit from following the information security discipline guidelines laid out in Chapter 7. Continuous monitoring of threats, conducting penetration testing, and real-time security audits are representative of a meticulous and disciplined approach to mitigating cyber risks.

—*Dave Chatterjee*

Yoti: Responsible Innovation in Cyber Security

A Business Case by Katharina Jarmai, PhD and Barbara Stacherl

Abstract

This case demonstrates how the concept of responsible innovation is practically applied in a cyber security company. It first outlines the work and context of cybersecurity companies and provides an introduction to the concept of responsible innovation. It then describes how Yoti Ltd. was founded with ethics and security considerations at the heart of the company, and how it puts an emphasis on data responsibility, transparency, consumer trust, and stakeholder collaboration. The case provides students with a real-world example of how elements of responsible innovation can be integrated into core business activities. Readers are challenged to find ways in which Yoti could deal with the danger of criminal misuse and the risks of future data privacy legislation that could undermine their business model.

Case

Learning Outcomes

By the end of this case study, students should be able to:

1. analyze the characterizing features of the cybersecurity sector and understand how these are connected to the concept of responsible innovation;

2. understand how the concept of responsible innovation is practically applied in the context of small and medium-sized enterprises (SMEs);

3. illustrate the value of integrating ethical considerations into innovations in the information and communication technology (ICT) sector; and

4. assess whether a cybersecurity company's practices that particularly target doing business responsibly foster profitability, and if so in what way.

Introduction

In the past decades, a vast amount of technological advancement and digital innovation has come about in ICT industry, connecting people in different places of the world and facilitating everyday life. The storing and further usage of large amounts of data have enabled the development of sophisticated software, programs, and networks. These changes have been accompanied by the emergence of, and an increase in, cyber threats and digital innovations that counteract privacy and security principles.

The concept of responsible innovation aims at aligning innovation processes and outcomes with societal values, needs, and expectations, while at the same time minimizing potential negative impacts on society and the natural environment. To achieve responsible innovation, it is considered crucial to involve a diverse set of stakeholders in idea generation and development processes, and implement ethical standards that exceed compliance with existing laws and regulations. Yoti is a cybersecurity company that has developed its business model integrating those principles into its core operations. Thus, it can be argued that Yoti is an example of how the concept of responsible innovation can be applied in an SME context in order to anticipate consequences, minimize risks, and maximize beneficial outcomes of innovations.

Cybersecurity

Cybersecurity is a crucial branch of the ICT sector. It is concerned with various kinds of security challenges that arise from innovations, and their application and possible misuse within the ICT industry. Challenges such as the right to be forgotten, cybercrime and cyber threats, the vast amount of data produced and used as part of the digitalization process, and, last but not least, privacy and trust issues that result from all of these factors render cybersecurity companies vital to other businesses.

In that context, cybersecurity companies guard digital identities and user privacy, and defend against cyber crime. They cover a variety of focus areas: traditional cybersecurity (protection, penetration testing, security, etc.), education provision, digital identity provision, and cybersecurity infrastructure. Given that they often store sensitive data, a considerable amount of attention must be paid to privacy and trust concerns, which are a characterizing feature of the cybersecurity sector. Robust measures that ensure a secure handling of data and protection against hackers and fraudsters are of particular importance for cybersecurity companies.

Resulting from these special features of the cybersecurity sector, there are three major challenges that cybersecurity companies face:

- privacy dilemma;

- expectation to "do good"; and

- fast and numerous innovations.

Privacy Dilemma

One of the distinctive features of cybersecurity companies is that they hold personal information, which their clients expect to remain personal—that is, private and inaccessible to third parties. This means that cybersecurity companies have particular contractual commitments toward their clients that function at a high level of trust. It is possible, however, that circumstances arise in which a cybersecurity company is under legal or moral obligation to provide access to their stored customer data to authorities, creating a dilemma for a company that is contractually bound to ensure privacy. This challenge becomes pressing especially with regard to countries or situations where governments' interference into personal privacy is disconcerting. Cybersecurity companies are working on solutions that allow them to guarantee privacy, but not under all circumstances.

Expectation to "Do Good"

Cybersecurity companies are closely connected to the ICT industry, and the associations and promises that this sector holds. In addition to protecting individual and corporate rights, cybersecurity firms may aspire to transform the lives of their clients through connecting them and enabling virtual interaction. In this way, they face the challenge of running a business while at the same time providing social benefits.

Fast and Numerous Innovations

The third major challenge for the cybersecurity sector arises from the nature of the ICT sector itself, being fundamentally different from other industries with respect to change within the sector. Frequent innovations, constant change, and rapid developments within the ICT sector are interrelated with a continuous occurrence of cyber threats. This industry characteristic requires cybersecurity companies to be highly flexible, responsive, and reactive, and makes the speed of innovation a crucial determinant for success. As well as fighting for customers and market shares, these firms simultaneously engage in a constant fight against cyber threats.

In this context, ethics are an integral concern in the cybersecurity sector. When it comes to innovation in the industry, acting carefully and responsibly is not only desirable, but also necessary.

Responsible Innovation

The concept of responsible innovation originates in discourses on potential undesired effects of (technological) innovations on their social and natural environments (Owen, Macnaghten, & Stilgoe, 2012). It was introduced into discourses on research ethics and innovation in 2010 by the European Commission under the term "Responsible Research and Innovation" (RRI). The five principles of RRI—ethics, gender equality, public engagement, science education, and open access—have been promoted through the European Commission's seventh and eighth Framework Programmes for Research and Innovation.[1] In the business context, the term "responsible innovation" is most often used to communicate contents of the RRI concept. Responsible innovation practices aim to ensure that corporate innovation activities and outputs are aligned with the values, needs, and expectations of society, and that potential negative impacts on society and the natural environment are minimized. Notwithstanding the European Commission's efforts, some companies in Europe still operate unaware of the responsible innovation concept (Blok & Lemmens, 2015; Davies & Horst, 2015; Khan et al., 2016). As recent studies have found, however, it is possible to recognize the principles of responsible innovation in extant company practices, processes, and purposes (Asante, Owen, & Williamson, 2014; Auer & Jarmai, 2018; Gurzawska, Mäkinen, & Brey, 2017; Chatfield, Iatridis, Stahl, & Paspallis, 2017).

In a nutshell, we can describe responsible innovation as a company's efforts to create a positive impact on society and minimize potential negative impacts of their research, development, and innovation processes, as well as their innovative products or services. Because innovations are, by definition, something that has not been on the market before, companies cannot rely on experience when assessing potential (future) impacts. First good practice examples of companies that have implemented responsible innovation show that the concept can be made operational through a diverse set of company practices. This includes a general orientation of company research and innovation toward tackling societal challenges to targeted activities that, for example, aim to increase diversity in innovation or to support science education endeavors (Schroeder, 2014, 2017).

Yoti Ltd.

Responsible Innovation as Decision Support System

Yoti (https://www.yoti.com/) is a medium-sized information technology company with 230 employees. The company is based in London, and has offices in India, the United States, and Canada. The business was established in 2014 when the three soon-to-be founders observed the simultaneous rapid developments in biometric technologies and smartphone capacities, and decided that what was missing was a digital solution that would allow users to prove who they are online without compromising their privacy. The Yoti solution was to combine biometric information with validation of a government-issued identity document in a smartphone application (app). These documents include passport, driving license, and certain national identity and proof of age cards.

The main company product, the Yoti app, was launched in November 2017 and was downloaded over 1.5 million times within the first six months. The app allows organizations to verify who people are, both online and in person. Individuals can use the app to prove their age or identity to businesses, verify other individuals' identities, and to log in to websites without passwords. By using their "Yoti," users are able to show only the piece or pieces of information that are relevant in a certain situation without revealing other information about themselves. They can, for example, verify their age without sharing their name or address. The app can be downloaded and set up within the few minutes that are needed to link the user's facial biometrics to his or her phone and validate them against their driving license or passport.

Responsible Innovation Practices and Processes

Yoti has been certified as a B Corporation[2] since 2015, and is thus legally required to consider the impact of its decisions on its workers, customers, suppliers, community, and the environment. As a cybersecurity B Corporation based in the United Kingdom, Yoti was invited to participate in the European Commission–funded COMPASS[3] project in 2017. Yoti was highly active in cocreating a roadmap toward responsible innovation in cybersecurity.

Yoti considers data responsibility to be a core strategy of its business model. Users of the app are asked to provide as little data as possible in the first place and, after a seven-day anti-fraud window, only the user can see the data they provided. This is made possible by a system in which all personal data—for example, name, gender, date of birth—are encrypted and stored separately. Only the individual user can tie them all together. It is also part of Yoti's business strategy to encourage other businesses that use its services to ask only for the minimum amount of data from individuals that they can work with.

Transparency and consumer trust are among the main goals of the company. The management team has established a set of seven core principles (https://www.yoti.com/about/principles/) to orient company development toward these goals. These principles include considering the impact of company decisions on users, employees, suppliers, partners, and the environment, being transparent about applied terms and conditions, and providing a digital identity to any individual free of charge. The company has installed an independent advisory body, which it calls a "Guardian Council," that fulfills a combination of functions relating to the company's responsibility toward its users and society in general (Yoti, 2016). The mission of the Guardian Council includes ensuring that the company stays consistent with its mission to give the user control of their personal data, reporting any breaches of trust, and representing concerns voiced by the user community. Yoti representatives meet with the Guardian Council on a quarterly basis. Meeting minutes are made public on the company website. The council is made up of influential individuals, including a prominent human rights lawyer and a serial entrepreneur with expertise on ownership of personal data.

Yoti has been pursuing collaboration with different stakeholder groups to ensure that both company and product development are in line with company principles. Yoti has participated in creating the "Responsible 100"[4] development tool in areas such as cybersecurity and data responsibility, and has engaged with its users through focus groups to find out what product features would be most valuable to them. The company has also organized two charity hack events at which representatives of nonprofit organizations were supported by teams of software developers to develop designs for apps that would solve a specific challenge they were facing at the time. The most promising idea at each event won a dedicated development team for one month to create and test a working prototype solution. In its call for expressions of interest to take part in these charity hack events, Yoti emphasized its commitment to ensuring the valuable time of charity staff would be well spent at the event.

The company has been part of the UK Digital Policy Alliance Steering Group to create a British standard of regulatory compliance needs for businesses conducting online age checks. Yoti is also industry chair of the Digital Policy Alliance Age Verification & Internet Safety Steering Group, and a member of the newly formed Association of Document Validation Professionals, and the newly installed Age Verification Providers Association. Yoti serves on TechUK boards for Justice & Emergency Services, Data

Protection, and Digital Identity. It is a key partner of the London Digital Security Centre, which helps businesses innovate, grow, and prosper through operating in a secure digital environment, and is accredited by "Met Police Secure by Design," recognizing the high standards of security that the Yoti app provides when an individual uses it to prove their identity.

Yoti follows a diversity and gender balance policy in product design in order to expand its market to as many different user groups as possible. In 2018, the company created the position "head of social impact," to increase understanding of the needs of those people worldwide who are denied access to essential services because they are not able to prove their identity.

Challenges

Yoti is facing a combination of challenges inherent to the collection and storage of data. This includes, first and foremost, the identity privacy of individual users. Data privacy and safe storage of user data are at the core of the company's business model. Consequently, the company has taken a range of measures to ensure that user data will remain private and data storage will remain safe. Beyond these issues, however, the company has recognized the dilemma that comes with perfect privacy of user data; namely, the possible implication of facilitating illegal activity. Yoti has engaged in extensive consultation with international human rights and consumer rights groups to minimize the risk of criminal misuse while maintaining maximum data privacy and safety procedures.

Another challenge specific to the collection and safety of user data comes with changing regulatory environments. With its 2018 General Data Protection Regulation (GDPR), the European Union has recently increased legal requirements for data protection and privacy. However, if laws or regulations were to be configured to provide authorities with easier access to personal data held by companies, such legislation would come into conflict with Yoti's company values and would undermine a core aspect of its business model. While companies that collect and store personal data will always need to obey the respective laws which are in place, they can reserve their right to challenge them in order to maintain consumer trust.

Conclusions

An examination of Yoti Ltd. offers a real-world example of how elements of responsible innovation can be integrated into core business activities.

The company aims at implementing ethics and security considerations into its core operations by working toward high degrees of transparency, data responsibility, and stakeholder collaboration. Yoti has put several responsible innovation practices in place, but questions remain about how the company can maintain its business model in the face of the danger of criminal misuse and the risks of future data privacy legislation that could undermine its business model.

DISCUSSION QUESTIONS

1. Which of the five principles of responsible innovation (ethics, gender equality and diversity, open access, science education, and stakeholder engagement) do you think are of special importance in the cybersecurity sector as opposed to other sectors, and why? What are your thoughts on the principle of open access in the case of the cybersecurity industry?

2. What responsible innovation practices has Yoti put into place? What else could the company do to make a positive impact on society?

3. If you became a partner at Yoti with the task to develop a business strategy to increase revenues over the next three years, would you argue to keep the Guardian Council in place or try to get rid of it? How would you argue for/against keeping the council?

4. How could Yoti solve the dilemma of perfect privacy of user data in light of the possible implications of facilitating illegal activity?

5. How can Yoti decrease the risk of future legislation undermining core aspects of its business model?

NOTES

1. The Seventh Framework Programme for Research and Innovation (FP7) ran from 2007 until 2013 with a total budget of over EUR 50 billion. The Eighth Framework Programme for Research and Innovation (Horizon 2020) runs from 2014 until 2020 and has a total budget of almost EUR 80 billion. Further information can be found at http://ec.europa.eu/programmes/horizon2020/.
2. Certified B Corporations ("B Corps") are businesses that have verified that they meet the B Corps community's standards of social and environmental performance, public transparency, and legal accountability to balance profit and purpose. B Corps are accelerating a global culture shift to redefine success in business and build a more inclusive

and sustainable economy. Further information can be found at https://bcorporation.net/about-b-corps.

3. The Horizon 2020 project "COMPASS—Evidence and Opportunities for Responsible Innovation in SMEs" (https://innovation-compass.eu/; https://cordis.europa.eu/project/rcn/203168/factsheet/en) ran from 2016 until 2019 and developed tools to implement responsible innovation practices in SMEs.

4. Responsible 100 is a platform delivered by the social business Profit Through Ethics Ltd. Responsible 100 provides tools to help businesses to determine which responsibility issues they should tackle most urgently, to measure and benchmark their performance, and to improve. Further information can be found at https://www.responsible100.com/about/.

FURTHER READING

ACM Code of Ethics and Professional Conduct. Retrieved from https://ethics.acm.org/

Fisk, M., Flick, C., & Ogoh, G. (2018). *Responsible Innovation Lab Report & Roadmaps*. D 2.2. Report 1: Cybersecurity (UK). Retrieved from https://innovation-compass.eu/wp-content/uploads/2018/10/D2.2-Responsible-Innovation-Lab-Report-and-Roadmap-1-UK_FINAL.pdf

Samandari, M. (2017). How to implement responsible research and innovation in SMEs. Retrieved from https://innovation-compass.eu/wp-content/uploads/2017/07/Mahmud-Samandari_How-to-implement-Responsible-Research-and-Innovation-in-SMEs.pdf

Yoti YouTube channel. Retrieved from https://www.youtube.com/channel/UCFM8EC MDGFhamlczBagtGuw

REFERENCES

Asante, K., Owen, R., & Williamson, G. (2014). Governance of new product development and perceptions of responsible innovation in the financial sector: Insights from an ethnographic case study. *Journal of Responsible Innovation*, 1(1), 9–30.

Auer, A., & Jarmai, K. (2017). Implementing responsible research and innovation practices in SMEs: Insights into drivers and barriers from the Austrian medical device sector. *Sustainability*, 10(1), 17.

Blok, V., & Lemmens, P. (2015). The emerging concept of responsible innovation. Three reasons why it is questionable and calls for a radical transformation of the concept of innovation. In Koops, B.-J., Oosterlaken, I., Romijn, H., Swierstra, T., & van den Hoven, J. (Eds.), *Responsible innovation 2: Concepts, approaches, and applications* (pp. 19–35). Cham, Switzerland: Springer International Publishing.

Chatfield, K., Iatridis, K., Stahl, B. C., & Paspallis, N. (2017). Innovating responsibly in ICT for ageing: Drivers, obstacles and implementation. *Sustainability*, 9(6), 971.

Davies, S. R., & Horst, M. (2015). Responsible innovation in the US, UK and Denmark: Governance landscapes. In Koops, B.-J., Oosterlaken, I., Romijn, H., Swierstra, T., & van den Hoven, J. (Eds.), *Responsible innovation 2: Concepts, approaches, and applications* (pp. 37–56). Cham, Switzerland: Springer International Publishing.

Gurzawska, A., Mäkinen, M., & Brey, P. (2017). Implementation of responsible research and innovation (RRI) practices in industry: Providing the right incentives. *Sustainability*, 9, 1759.

Khan, S. S., Timotijevic, L., Newton, R., Coutinho, D., Llerena, J. L., Ortega, S., Benighaus, L., Hofmaier, C., Xhaferri, Z., de Boer, A., Urban, C., Strähle, M., Da Pos, L., Neresini, F., Raats, M.M., & Hadwiger, K. (2016) The framing of innovation among European research funding actors: Assessing the potential for "responsible research and innovation" in the food and health domain. *Food Policy*, 62, 78–87.

Owen, R., Macnaghten, P., & Stilgoe, J. (2012). Responsible research and innovation: From science in society to science for society, with society. *Science and Public Policy*, 39(6), 751–760.

Schroeder, D. (2014). D1.2 Case study descriptions. Deliverable of the FP7 project Responsible-Industry. Retrieved from http://docs.google.com/viewer?a=v&pid=sites&srcid=ZGVmYXVsdGRvbWFpbnxyZXNwb25za-WJsZWluZHVzdHJ5d2Vic2l0ZXxne DoyZjdkYmZkNWJmMzVhYzkx

Schroeder, D. (2017). D1.2 Case study descriptions. Deliverable of the Horizon 2020 project COMPASS. Retrieved from https://innovation-compass.eu/wp-content/uploads/2017/07/Deliverable-1_3-Compass-Case-Study-Descriptions.pdf

Yoti. (2016). Yoti guardian role description and code of conduct. Retrieved from https://www.yoti.com/downloads/docs/Yoti%20Guardian%20Role%20Description%20and %20Code%20of%20Conduct.pdf http://dx.doi.org/10.4135/9781529704303

Originally Published as: Jarmai, K. & Stacherl, B., (2020). Yoti: Responsible innovation in cyber security. In SAGE Business Cases. 2020. 10.4135/9781529704303. © Katharina Jarmai and Barbara Stacherl 2020.

Cybersecurity Resources

I. Articles

Chapter 1. Introduction

1. Abraham, C., Chatterjee, D., and Sims, R. (2019) "Muddling through Cybersecurity: Insights from the U.S. Healthcare Industry," *Business Horizons*. Available at https://doi .org/10.1016/j.bushor.2019.03.010

Chapter 2. The Cyberattack Epidemic

1. Boehm, J., Kaplan, J., Sorel, M., Sportsman, N., and Steen, T. (2020, March). "Cybersecurity Tactics for the Coronavirus Pandemic," New York: McKinsey & Company, https://www.mckinsey.com/business-functions/risk/our-insights/cybersecurity-tactics-for-the-coronavirus-pandemic, accessed on September 29, 2020.

2. B. Dobran (2019). "17 Types of Cyber Attacks To Secure Your Company From in 2019," https://phoenixnap.com/blog/cyber-security-attack-types, February 21, 2019, accessed on September 26, 2019.

Chapter 3. Breach Incidents and Lessons Learned

1. Radichel, T. (2014, September). Case Study: Critical Controls That Could Have Prevented Target Breach. SANS Institute. https://www.sans.org/reading-room/white papers/casestudies/paper/35412, accessed on August 26, 2019.

Chapter 4. Foundations of the High-Performance Information Security Culture Framework

1. "Building a Culture of Cybersecurity: A Guide for Corporate Executives and Board Members." April 2018, CompTIA White Paper. Available at https://www.comptia.org/ content/whitepapers/building-a-culture-of-cybersecurity-a-guide-for-corporate-execu tives-and-board-members

2. Schein, E. (1983). "The Role of the Founder in Creating Organizational Culture." *Organizational Dynamics*, Summer, pp. 13–28.

3. Barney, J. B. (1986). "Organizational Culture: Can It Be a Source of Sustained Competitive Advantage?" *Academy of Management Review*, 11, pp. 656–665.

4. Sorensen, J. B. (2002). "The Strength of Corporate Culture and the Reliability of Firm Performance." *Administrative Science Quarterly*, 47(1), pp. 70–91.

5. Gcaza, N., von Solms, R., Grobler, M. M., and van Vuuren, J. J. (2017). "A General Morphological Analysis: Delineating a Cyber-Security Culture." *Information and Computer Security*, 25(3), pp. 259–278.

6. Chen, B. (2018). "Fostering a Culture of Cybersecurity." *Forbes*, October 21, 2018.

7. Chang, S. E. and Lin, C. (2007). "Exploring Organizational Culture for Information Security Management." *Industrial Management and Data Systems*, 107(3), pp. 438–458.

8. Harnish, R. (2017). "What It Means to Have a Culture of Cybersecurity." *Forbes*, September 21, 2017.

9. Zadelhoff, M. V. (2016). "The Biggest Cybersecurity Threats Are Inside Your Company." *Harvard Business Review*, September 19, 2016.

10. Veiga, A. D. (2016). "Comparing the Information Security Culture of Employees Who Had Read the Information Security Policy and Those Who Had Not." *Information and Computer Security*, 24(2), pp. 139–151.

11. Sager, T. (2018). "Developing a Culture of Cybersecurity with the CIS Controls." Available at https://www.cisecurity.org/blog/developing-a-culture-of-cybersecurity-with-the-cis-controls/ accessed on April 2, 2020.

12. Winnefeld Jr., J. A., Kirchhoff, C., and Upton, D. M. (2015). "Cybersecurity's Human Factor: Lessons from the Pentagon." *Harvard Business Review*, September, pp. 3–11.

Chapter 5. Commitment

1. McKinty, C. (2017). "The C-Suite and IT—Need to Get on the Same Page on Cybersecurity." *Harvard Business Review*, April 26, 2017.

2. Sweeney, B. (2016, September 13). "Cybersecurity Is Every Executive's Job." *Harvard Business Review*, pp. 2–4.

3. Visner, C. (2016, November 15). "Cybersecurity is Everyone's Responsibility—And It Starts at the Top." Available at www.csoonline.com.

4. Chatterjee, D. (2019). "Should Executives Go To Jail Over Cybersecurity Breaches," *Journal of Organizational Computing and Electronic Commerce*, February 17, 2019. pp. 1–3.

5. Rothrock, R. A., Kaplan, J., and Van der Oord, F. (2018). "The Board's Role in Managing Cybersecurity Risks," *Frontiers,* Winter 2018.

6. Bailey, T., Kaplan, J. and Rezek, C. (2014). "Why Senior Leaders Are the Front Line against Cyberattacks," McKinsey & Company, June 2014. Available at https://www.mckinsey.com/business-functions/mckinsey-digital/our-insights/why-senior-leaders-are-the-front-line-against-cyberattacks

7. Visner, C. (2016, November 15). "Cybersecurity is Everyone's Responsibility – And It Starts At The Top." Available at www.csoonline.com

8. Nagele-Piazza, L. (2018). "Create a Cross-Functional Team to Combat Data Security," November 28, 2018, SHRM.org. Accessed on June 15, 2019.

9. Quevedo, A. (2016, September 21). "How Cybersecurity Teams Can Convince the C-Suite of Their Value." *Harvard Business Review*, 2016, pp. 2–5.

10. Dang-Pham, D., Pittayachawan, S., and Bruno, V. (2016). "Impacts of Security Climate on Employees' Sharing of Security Advice and Troubleshooting: Empirical Networks." *Business Horizons*, 59, pp. 571–584.

11. Hooper, V. and McKissack, J. (2016). "The Emerging Role of the CISO." *Business Horizons*, 59, pp. 585–591.

12. Bell, G. (2016, October 25). "Good Cybersecurity Doesn't Try to Prevent Every Attack." *Harvard Business Review*, 2016, pp. 2–4.

Chapter 6. Preparedness

1. Boehm, J., Merrath, P., Poppensieker, T., Riemenschniter, R., and Stahle, T. (2018). "Cyber Risk Measurement and the Holistic Cybersecurity Approach," McKinsey & Company, November, 2018. Available at https://www.mckinsey.com/business-functions/risk/our-insights/cyber-risk-measurement-and-the-holistic-cybersecurity-approach

2. He, W. and Zhang, Z. (2019) "Enterprise Cybersecurity and Awareness Programs: Recommendations for Success," *Journal of Organizational Computing and Electronic Commerce*, July 29, 2019. https://doi.org/10.1080/10919392.2019.1611528

3. Disparte, D. and Furlow, C. (2017, May 16). "The Best Cybersecurity Investment You Can Make Is Better Training." *Harvard Business Review*, 2017, pp. 2–4

Chapter 7. Discipline

1. "What Is an IT Security Audit?" https://www.dnsstuff.com/it-security-audit, March 10, 2020.

2. Schiff, J. L. (2016). "8 Ingredients of an Effective Disaster Recovery Plan," CIO, https://www.cio.com/article/3090892/8-ingredients-of-an-effective-disaster-recovery-plan.html, accessed on August 8, 2019.

II. Books

1. Chapple, M., Stewart, J. M. and Gibson, D. (2018) "Certified Information Systems Security Professional, Official Study Guide, 8th Edition. New York: John Wiley & Sons.

2. Kim, D. and Solomon, M. G. (2018) "Fundamentals of Information Security," 2nd Edition. Burlington, MA: Jones & Bartlett Learning.

III. Other Resources

Chapter 2. The Cyber Attack Epidemic

1. 2019 Official Annual Cybercrime Report, Cybersecurity Ventures, Herjavec Group. https://www.herjavecgroup.com/wp-content/uploads/2018/12/CV-HG-2019-Official-Annual-Cybercrime-Report.pdf, accessed on September 30, 2020.

2. Ninth Annual Cost of Cybercrime Study, Accenture and Ponemon Institute, https://www.accenture.com/us-en/insights/security/cost-cybercrime-study, accessed on April 7, 2020.

3. Cost of a Data Breach Report 2020, IBM, https://www.ibm.com/security/data-breach, accessed on April 7, 2020.

4. Fundera Report on 30 Surprising Small Business Cyber Security Statistics (2020)

5. Human Factor Report (2019), ProofPoint.com, https://www.proofpoint.com/us/resources/threat-reports/human-factor, accessed on March 24, 2020.

6. Data Breach Class Action Lawsuits, https://www.classaction.com/data-breach/lawsuit/, accessed on September 29, 2019.

Chapter 5. Commitment

1. Narrowing the Culture Gap for Better Business Results. ISACA/CMMI Institute Cybersecurity Culture Report. Available at https://cmmiinstitute.com/getattachment/c335c66a-7000-48b4-b953-acbf395c5832/attachment.aspx, accessed on September 30, 2020.

2. 2018 Deloitte-NASCIO Cybersecurity Study. Available at https://www.nascio.org/resource-center/resources/2018-deloitte-nascio-cybersecurity-study-states-at-risk-bold-plays-for-change/

Chapter 6. Preparedness

1. Securing Cyber Assets: Addressing Urgent Cyber Threats to Critical Infrastructure. The President's National Infrastructure Advisory Council, August 2017. Available at https://www.cisa.gov/sites/default/files/publications/niac-securing-cyber-assets-final-report-508.pdf. Accessed October 1, 2020.

2. Okta Identity-And-Access-Management Platform. Available at https://okta.com

3. Fortinet's AI Driven Security Platform. Available at https://www.fortinet.com/

4. paloalto's Intelligent Network Security Suite. Available at https://www.paloaltonetworks.com/

5. Cisco Security Solutions. https://www.cisco.com/c/en/us/products/security/index.html

6. Checkpoint Security Solutions. https://www.checkpoint.com/

7. Virtru's Encryption Key Management Solution. https://www.virtru.com/encryption-key-management/

8. Circadense. https://www.circadence.com/

9. Immersive Labs (https://www.immersivelabs.com/product/benefits/exercises-cyber-training/

10. PhishMe Simulator (https://cofense.com/)

11. SANS Institute for Cybersecurity Training and Certification (https://www.sans.org/about/

12. Center for Internet Security (https://www.cisecurity.org/)

13. Splunk. https://www.splunk.com/en_us/siem-security-information-and-event-manage ment.html

Chapter 7. Discipline

1. "FedRAMP Continuous Monitoring Strategy Guide," April 4, 2018, https://www .fedramp.gov/assets/resources/documents/CSP_Continuous_Monitoring_Strategy_ Guide.pdf, accessed on July 24, 2019.

2. "Key Elements of an Information Security Policy," https://resources.infosecinstitute.com/ key-elements-information-security-policy/#gref, accessed on June 13, 2019.

IV. Certifications

1. CISSP: Certified Information Systems Security Professional. (ISC)².

2. CISA: Certified Information Systems Auditor. ISACA.

3. CEH: Certified Ethical Hacker. Infosec.

4. ISACA. CISM: Certified Information Security Manager. ISACA.

5. CompTIA Security+. CompTIA.

V. Professional Associations

1. (ISC)²

2. ISACA

3. INFOSEC

4. CompTIA

VI. Cybersecurity Frameworks

1. National Institute of Science and Technology Framework for Improving Cybersecurity

2. ISO 27000

VII. Cybersecurity Legislation

1. https://cyberexperts.com/cybersecurity-laws/

2. https://www.itgovernanceusa.com/federal-cybersecurity-and-privacy-laws

3. https://www.blackstratus.com/sox-compliance-requirements/

4. https://digitalguardian.com/blog/what-gdpr-general-data-protection-regulation-under standing-and-complying-gdpr-data-protection

5. https://www.globalpaymentsintegrated.com/en-us/blog/2019/11/12/the-twelve-require ments-of-pci-dss-compliance

6. https://www.americanbar.org/groups/litigation/committees/intellectual-property/prac tice/2018/how-will-california-cybersecurity-laws-affect-us-business/

7. https://www.clarip.com/data-privacy/california-consumer-privacy-act-fines/

8. https://www.blackstratus.com/compliance/iso-27001/

Index

Note: The letter 'n' 't' 'f' following locators refers to notes, tables and figures respectively.

Remote access Trojan (RAT), 13–14, 77
Remote code executions (RCE), 100
Removable media protection, 102
Respond and recover, 125–131, 163
  disaster recovery planning, 128–131
  incident response capability, 126–127
RevvSales, 104
Rickover, Hyman, 52
Risk-based asset identification and
    prioritization, 158–159
  asset identification, 158
  cyber risk assessment, 158
  prioritization, 158
Risk-based protection prioritization
    scheme, 132
Risk impact evaluation rubric, 82t, 158
Risk probability matrix, 83f, 158
RSA Security, 21t, 103. *See also*
    Encryption algorithms

Safeguarding personal information,
    224–225
Sarbanes-Oxley (SOX) Act of 2002,
    1, 110, 148, 220–223
Secure socket layer (SSL) digital
    certificate, 105
Securing e-mail clients and
    browsers, 160
Securing networks, ports, and
    removable media, 160
Securing networks, ports, protocols, and
    services, 100–101
Securing sensitive data and related
    digital assets, 159–163
  access management, 159
  asset maintenance, 162
  awareness and training, 162
  business continuity planning,
    162–163
  configuration management, 160
  data backup and retention, 161–162
  data security, 161
  mobile device usage, 161
  securing e-mail clients and
    browsers, 160
  securing networks, ports, and
    removable media, 160–161

Security audits, 139, 148–149, 165
  disciplined organizations, 149
  drills and, 30, 139, 148–149, 165
  organizations undergo audits, 148
  real-time security audit, 148
  third-party expertise, 148
Security awareness, 170
Security Content Automation Protocol
    (SCAP), 97–98, 145
Security drills, 30, 139, 148–149, 165,
    203–204
Security information and event
    management (SIEM), 69,
    122–123, 163
Security Operations Center (SOC),
    123, 163
"Security through obscurity"
    approach, 150
Separating of production, development,
    and testing environments, 108
Server clustering, 119, 194
Service level agreement (SLA), 30–31,
    42, 71, 111, 130, 141, 162
Shapira, Elad, 71
Shared accountability, 71
Single door serial layered approach, 101
Single point of failure, 94, 117
Small- and medium-sized businesses
    (SMBs), 23
Smith, Richard, 37, 61
Social bond theory, 51
Software-as-a-service (SaaS), 39
SolarWinds Security Events Manager,
    148–149
Sony's PlayStation Network, 22t
SOX (Sarbanes-Oxley Act of 2002),
    1, 110, 148, 220–223
Spear phishing, 13
Splunk, 123–124
Spyware, 10, 13, 15
SQL injection, 13, 17, 18f, 151
Stanford University Hospital, 22t
Steganography, 106, 161
Stored Communications Act (SCA), 210
Strategic alignment and partnership,
    68–69, 156–157
  cybersecurity as a strategic necessity, 69